The French Art Market

Raymonde Moulin

The French Art Market

A Sociological View

translated by
ARTHUR GOLDHAMMER

RUTGERS UNIVERSITY PRESS
New Brunswick and London

Publication of this book was made possible in part by a translation grant from the Ministère de la Culture de France, and a matching grant from the National Endowment for the Humanities.

Library of Congress Cataloging-in-Publication Data

Moulin, Raymonde.
   The French art market.

   Abridged translation of: Le marché de la
peinture en France.
   Bibliography: p.
   Includes index.
   1. Painting—France—Marketing. 2. Painting,
Modern—20th century—Prices. 3. Art and society—
France—History—20th century. 4. Painting—
Collectors and collecting—France. I. Title.
N8600.M6813   1987   706'.8'8   86-27988
ISBN 0-8135-1232-8

This book is an abridged edition of *Le marché de la peinture en France,* first published in 1967 by Editions de Minuit.

Contents

Translator's Note

This translation is an abridgement of *Le marché de la peinture en France,* first published in 1967. Several chapters and other substantial passages selected by the author have been omitted from the translation. No attempt has been made to update the body of the text.

A note on currency denominations: to distinguish between old francs (prior to the 1961 revaluation) and new francs, I have followed the convention used by the author in the French edition: franc (abbreviated f.) means old franc, Franc (with upper case F, abbreviated F.) means new franc. Appendix 1 gives coefficients for converting all currency values to the 1961 basis (using a deflator based on price indices).

Author's Preface to English Edition

The original French edition of this book, published in 1967, was based on my doctoral dissertation and included the extensive notes required by that academic genre. For this translation I have abridged the original version considerably, eliminating most notes and much supporting documentation from the appendices. I have also eliminated two chapters of the text. One dealt with the subject of auction sales, which I believe affect the prices and aesthetic values of contemporary art only indirectly. Public auctions tend to establish prices of "classic" works, already recognized as historically important. Astronomical prices paid for old masters can of course stimulate the art market as a whole, but the prices paid for contemporary art depend more on the dealer market than on auctions. The other deleted chapter concerned the purchase and commissioning of painting by governmental authorities. The situation in this regard has changed considerably since 1967. Government investment in the art market increased sharply in 1981. [A socialist-led government was then elected in France after decades of right-wing rule. Since this new preface was written, that government, too, has been voted out of office.—Trans.]. Art policy was decentralized, with inevitably contradictory consequences. The government has taken steps to encourage art patronage by industry.

Far from ignoring these important changes, I have been studying them, as have other French sociologists. Hence I can say with some assurance that support of artistic creation by government agencies is still heavily influenced by market trends. Although the market is no longer the only distribution channel for artworks, it has more than held its own, and the theoretical analysis given here is, I think, still valid.

Broadly speaking, I see no reason to revise my analysis of the art market as the organizing principle of artistic life. In this work I describe the history of the art market as it developed in France in the late nineteenth century and analyze its structure and function through the mid-twentieth

century. In other western countries the art market has evolved in similar
ways. What is more, the model elaborated here explains further changes
that have occurred since the book was written—changes more of degree
than of kind. The last twenty years have made abundantly clear the connection between the constant quest for new art and what Joseph
Schumpeter calls the "perpetual innovative whirl" of the marketplace.
To bring the documentation up to date I have replaced the original bibliography with a "partial bibliography of works published since 1967."
While neither exhaustive nor inclusive, these books provide a basic list of
material available for more current analysis of the art market.

As one avant-garde quickly succeeds another in the public view, the
market has become increasingly international. The internationalization of
the art business was begun in the late nineteenth century by Paul Durand-
Ruel. By the late 1950s American dealers had achieved dominance. Over
the past few decades, as Howard S. Becker has shown, the importance of
the New York "art world" as both a commercial center and arbiter of aesthetic values has risen steadily.

In this internationalized market, cultural institutions and art dealers mutually support one another. Today I would want to place even greater
stress on this interdependence. The pace of success has quickened. In the
early part of this century a long time generally elapsed between an artist's
first gallery sales and his ultimate acceptance by the museums. Picasso's
works, for example, were not hung in the National Museum of Modern
Art in Paris until afer World War II. In this volume I show that this delay
was shortened considerably in the 1950s. Since then, museums, succumb-
ing to the fever of fashion, have begun to influence the market as much as
they are influenced by it. In the past, the strategy for artistic success was to
play for the long term. Now the emphasis is increasingly on the short
term, adapting to rapid changes in fashion.

Today as in the past, the art market determines, at least in part, which
artists achieve recognition and financial success. From the earliest stages
of my research I have been interested in the relation between aesthetic
evaluation and the economics of the marketplace. The work of art has two
kinds of "value," and success in the art business depends on shrewd judgment of both. An obscure dialectic is at work. Aesthetic judgment under-
lies the work of the art entrepreneur, but the successful entrepreneur can
build on success and do without aesthetic judgment. This is more true now
than ever before, and one wonders whether today's distribution of rewards will stand the test of time.

Modernity, wrote Baudelaire in *The Painter and Modern Life* (1860),
"is the transitory, the fugitive, the contingent half of art, the other half being the immutable eternal." Today, the market and the museums, and
even the artists themselves, have decided to emphasize the first half at the
expense of the second, to the detriment of all.

Introduction

The aim of studying the art market (in the narrow economic sense of the term) is to understand what determines the prices of priceless objects. But the problem of price determination, the oldest problem in economics, requires that we understand not just abstract *homo oeconomicus* but concrete men and women. What significance do works of art have to the individuals and institutions who buy them? How does the system of determining reputations and sales affect the artist's relation to his art? What is the relation between economic value and aesthetic value in a society that accords such priority to the former that it is reasonable to ask whether buyers (or the public) can ever judge a work of art independent of its economic value? The purpose of a sociological study of the art market is to provide at least partial answers to these questions.

I have no illusions about the limitations of such a study. Not all artists are integrated into the market. Not all "consumers" of art are buyers of art works. Painting is accessible to members of many social groups, whereas it is chiefly the wealthy who purchase art. I have chosen to concentrate primarily on the art market in France and to consider the international market only to the extent that it influences the French. This does not mean that I believe that the French market is the most important in the world. Indeed, its position has been challenged since World War II by the ascendancy of the New York School and the growth of the art market in the United States.

Painting became a commodity with the birth of easel painting.[1] The easel painting lent itself to individual ownership and could be easily transferred from one individual to another. The history of the relations between the economy and painting from the inception of easel painting is too broad a subject for a single book, however. I shall therefore concentrate on the period from 1952 to 1962, during which economic and social change combined with the evolution of art itself to produce a flourishing market in painting. A period of exuberant speculation and rising prices, this decade saw the conquest of the French market by nontraditional painting; acceptance by the public (or at any rate by part of the public, which I shall attempt to define as precisely as possible) of the audacity—whether genuine or sham—of modern art; an end of rebellion among artists themselves; and increasingly bitter international disputes, fomented or exacerbated by commercial rivalry. The Wall Street crisis of May 1962 was followed by a depression in the market for contemporary art; this breakdown in the mechanisms of the art market helped to clarify their normal operation. Finally, I have deliberately confined my study to the market for contemporary works of art, produced by living artists, for these tell us something about the condition of painters in our society. Prices paid for older works are used only as a basis for comparison.

As for method, I began by visiting art shows, galleries, and public auctions and by systematically reading the art reviews and journals. My aim was to identify the major trends in artistic production and the individuals responsible for the first stages of distribution. I also tried to understand the relations among artists, critics, and galleries. In short, I sought to familiarize myself with the terrain.

Reputations and prices depend on the opinions of the Paris "art world," which is in fact a set of cliques defined by aesthetic preferences much as religious sects are defined by beliefs. These cliques are mutually exclusive. The situation is rather like that described in Proust's great novel: anyone who accepted an invitation from Mme Verdurin was considered beneath contempt by the Duchess of Guermantes, who kept a rival salon; and vice versa. Each clique becomes the center of a more or less independent network of contacts between buyers and sellers. Members of a clique feel themselves to be set apart from the profane by a shared aesthetic faith; they take themselves to be members of an artistic elite that determines what is good and bad, valuable and worthless, in the art of our time. Signs of belonging are many: personal contacts; knowing gossip about what is happening and who is selling; and implicit knowledge of what takes place behind the scenes, including who is backing whom, what painter is on the outs with what dealer, and what bankers buy from what galleries. No one is formally excluded from such ceremonial rites as show openings, yet the newcomer who is not part of one of the insider groups that congregate on such occasions feels that he or she does not belong.

In order to penetrate these circles I had no choice but to make the right contacts; recommendations are in fact introductions, and without a "sponsor" one is lost. I approached more than a dozen people—dealers, critics, collectors, and artists—who agreed to introduce me to others. As my circle of contacts grew, suspicion of me diminished, and my interviews extended into the kinds of conversations indispensable for developing genuine rapport. Few people talk more smoothly than art dealers, subtle impressarios when it comes to showing off their painters and, in some cases, themselves. Few are more eloquent than collectors when urged to talk about their "passion." No one offers a warmer welcome than an artist convinced that you take an interest in his or her work. My greatest difficulty was to turn the conversation to topics likely to produce the kind of information I sought.

It is difficult to gain access to any closed group, but in this case hostility was heightened by distrust of sociology on the part of many people in the art world, where the discipline is seen as bent on depriving art of its sacred status. The attitudes of the sociologist are incompatible with the prevailing ideology of art, which is based on the notions of uniqueness, irreplaceability, and incomparability. My interviewees were of course not unaware of the differences between the sociology of the art market and the sociology of art. They regarded the former as less offensive than the latter yet believed both to be impossible, though for different reasons.

Society grants high status to works of art, yet those same works are also bought and sold. The art market is the place where, by some secret alchemy, the cultural good becomes a commodity. Deliberate mystery shrouds the way dealers handle the art commodity, for the dealers' stratagems, though they add to the work's economic value, detract from its cultural value. The mechanism of price formation is not transparent. Some deals are made in secret. Unquantifiable or hidden influences affect prices more than obvious, measurable influences. The analyst must contend with the reticence of participants in the market to discuss their activities, reticence due not only to worries about the tax authorities (mentioned by all interviewees) but also to a rule of silence invariably observed by insiders. Even those who urged me to "demystify" the art market were not prepared to divulge what they knew. "You will never find out anything," I was told. And "what you do find out you won't be able to print because you'll have no proof. Your results will be worthless because you are an outsider." In the initial stages of my work I heard such comments frequently, and I often had occasion to recognize how indebted I was to my sponsors: without some inside contacts, it would have been impossible to find out anything.

The first people I approached were dealers in painting. Being businessmen, they were generally easier to reach than artists or collectors. But of all the actors involved in the art market, the dealers were least likely to violate the rule of secrecy: "In this business, silence is the first virtue," I was told. Two sets of questions proved particularly difficult to get answers to: questions pertaining to the social status of the interviewees (class background, education, occupation prior to becoming an art dealer) and questions pertaining to the details of business operations (financing of galleries, annual sales, amounts paid to artists under contract, and so forth). On the other hand, dealers were quite willing to talk aboout their social function, or at any rate about their notion of that function.

With collectors I also had difficulties. The visitor is rarely allowed to see a collector's entire collection, which can be a valuable source of information (revealing not only the collector's status but also his cultural background, his tastes, and his philosophy of collecting). Major collectors often own several homes (sometimes in other countries), so their collections are widely dispersed. Not all the paintings in a collection are hung at any given time, and it is not always possible to visit paintings in storage. An art collection evolves over time, moreover, and its history is no less significant than its content.

Collectors, as members of the upper classes, often find the sociologist's questions offensively indiscreet and reductionist; interpreting their answers requires giving due weight to the justifications they offer on their own behalf. Collectors are not unaware that money can have a distorting effect on cultural activities. They have an elaborate system of defense against charges of this kind. When invited to trace the history of their taste, they are aware that in so doing they may reveal ulterior motives, and they are at pains to paint as prestigious a portrait of themselves as possible. Finally, the sociology of taste is not a well-developed discipline. When sociologist and interviewee share the same tastes in art, the nature of the interview is inevitably affected; the interviewee is more likely to express himself or herself spontaneously, while the interviewer finds it more difficult to achieve the distance necessary for objectivity.

Collectors are perhaps more comfortable with an academic than they would be with a journalist, but the successful painter has little time to waste with sociologists. Between shows in Berlin and Chicago, every minute is precious. Some painters refused to grant me interviews, but it would be unfair on that account to forget those who did see me, generally on the recommendation of a dealer or collector who owned one of their paintings. By contrast, artists as yet untouched by commercial success were ready to show their paintings and express their bitterness toward a system in which they had yet to find their place. Most striking, however, was that in all the interviews with artists, whether obscure or famous, the pattern was the same. First, the work of art was declared autonomous and incomparable; sociology was rejected out of hand: "Sociology is not something that concerns the artist." In the second phase of the interview, the influence of social and economic factors was acknowledged through autobiographical anecdotes, judgments of other artists, and general observations on the state of the art market. In the third and final phase of the interview, we came full circle: external influences on the work were acknowledged to exist, but in the final analysis, the artists insisted, such influences do not affect artistic expression.

For the sociologist, the most obvious danger was to be taken in by the artists' own idea of themselves. A more subtle danger was to reject, because of dogmatic faith in the discipline, the artists' certainty that sociology is wrong and misguided. Is it possible to study in sociological terms a creative act intended to express an artist's free choice? The painter believes that his relation to his work is direct, but it is in fact mediated through his relations to other painters, both predecessors and contemporaries, and to art lovers, critics, dealers, buyers, and the public. It is simplistic to say that the work of art can be understood only in terms of external influences, but it is just as simplisitic to say that it can be understood only from within. The artist, like the scholar, is an individual, both isolated and social. His relation to his work as aesthetic fact influences and is influenced by his relation to his work as social fact.

Most of my information is derived from participant observation. Printed questionnaires would have yielded unsatisfactory results; only marginal participants in the art market—unsuccessful painters and sporadic buyers—would have been willing to take part. It is impossible to identify a representative statistical sample of collectors, dealers, or artists. To correct for any possible distortion, I attempted to check the answers of these three groups against one another. I also compared answers given in interviews with written documents, ranging from memoirs to exhibition catalogues, contracts, and court records. But in the end, the peculiar nature of the art world forced me to approach it as an ethnographer might approach a tribe of savages. I was forced to define my sample—collectors, dealers, and artists—at the outset of my research and without the aid of statistical data: "Some people exemplify common tendencies more clearly than others and, by their example, reinforce those tendencies."[2]

I mention no names in this book; I gave my word to the people I interviewed that they would remain anonymous. Without such a promise many would have refused interviews. I have done my best to make identification impossible.[3] I am not unaware that identification would aid in the interpretation of the interviewees' remarks, particularly in the case of artists. The painter's relation to his work is influenced by the nature of his painting, his personal history, and his standing among his peers and with dealers and clients. The disillusionment of an innovator means something different from the disillusionment of an academic painter; a remark that indicates cynicism in an established painter may suggest anxious pessimism in a painter still out to make a reputation.

Many people were kind enough to grant me interviews, yet for all my precautions the use I make of what they told may in many cases prove irritating. They may feel that a sociologist has unreasonably set herself up as an omniscient authority in the midst of an alien world. Therefore, to all who spoke to me I wish to offer my sincere thanks. Without them this book would never have been written, and I assure them that it was written with their words firmly etched in my mind.

I have traced the progress of my research in order to justify my method. But a major problem remains: the aesthetic judgment of the sociologist. Art is based on values, and even objective investigation of art cannot avoid having some bearing on those values. Value judgments constitute the reality of art, and it would be foolish for the sociologist to abstract from them. Sociology of art must rely on the judgments of experts. "An art historian who did not distinguish between the paintings of Leonardo and those of his imitators would miss the specific significance of the historical object, namely, the quality of the work."[4] The problem for the sociologist of contemporary art is the number of competing artistic schools, each governed by different norms. Artistic conflict is indeed the essence of contemporary art, which by its nature precludes expert consensus. There is no universal agreement on a hierarchy of values. Some forms of modern art reflect none of the values traditionally appreciated in classic art. Rival experts disagree more than they agree. Still, the sociologist must rely on the best judgment of the experts, such as it is. The political sociologist faced with contradictory ideologies deeply embedded in reality itself must resort to philosophy if forced to make a choice. Faced with rival artistic ideologies, I was on occasion similarly forced to make a subjective judgment.

Preliminaries

I

1

Antecedents

In order to understand the present period in the history of art, we must begin with the impressionist revolt. Bourgeois society failed to recognize itself in the works of impressionism, and the official institutions of that society refused to accept those works as art. For impressionist art to win social acceptance and success in the marketplace, new channels of commercial distribution had to be established. Eventually, a market for innovative art was established alongside the existing market for traditional art; in this development both speculation and snobbery played roles. Because I cannot trace in full detail the history of the post–1870 art market, I shall mention only a few milestones.

Historical Outline

In primitive societies the creation and consumption of art correspond to group needs. In more developed societies, art is the property, means of enjoyment, or instrument of power of a minority. In virtually all developed societies speculation on works of art has existed. However, the influence of the art trade on the status of the artist has varied. Between the Middle Ages and the present, artistic life in France was organized, broadly speaking, in three different ways: by the guild, the academy, and the market. In all three systems patronage has existed, but only as a phenomenon of secondary importance.

The creation of a guild of painters and sculptors in Paris in 1391 merely ratified an existing state of affairs, in which no distinction was made between the artist and the artisan. Painters were tradesmen, and if they banded together in a guild, it was to establish a monopoly in defense of their interests and profits. The painters' guild had its juries and its rules governing such matters as apprenticeship, journeyman status, and the masterpiece that every journeyman was required to submit to become a master painter. Each painter was his own dealer; the right to open a shop was legally restricted to members of the guild. This corporate form of organization was already on the decline by the time it was formally institutionalized; in the long run it succumbed to a new conception of the artist, influenced by the ideas of the humanists.

The court painter of the Renaissance enjoyed the protection of powerful princes and the friendship of humanist scholars; socially and intellectually he stood worlds apart from the medieval artisan. The "artist" as human type was a creation of the Renaissance: "In the time of Lorenzo [de' Medici] masters became more sure of themselves intellectually and more concerned about their social position. They liked to think of themselves as standing alongside the poets and humanists, part of a privileged elite with rights and privileges of its own."[1] No longer was the artist a mere workman; now he was a creator, an *alter deus,* exempt from common norms. First elaborated in Florence, this new conception of the artist spread to France, which was linked to Italy by a lively international trade. French kings called Italian artists to their court, while French painters traveled to Rome as part of their training. Circulation of the writings of Vasari and others propagated legends about the masters of the Italian Renaissance, lending credence to the notion of art as a "liberal profession," distinct from the trades and commerce.

In self-defense the painters' guild became increasingly protectionist and xenophobic, tightening already rigid rules to the point where they became unacceptable to "artists" proud of their social position and independence as part of the increasingly sophisticated and cosmopolitan world that surrounded the arts. Unable to make room for the new art and incompatible with the new ideology, the guilds eventually fell victim to the reforming and centralizing tendencies of the monarchy, and in 1648 letters patent were drawn up establishing the Royal Academy of Painting and Sculpture.

The history of the Academy from its inception to the nineteenth century is also beyond the scope of this book. I shall mention only those aspects of the Academy's structure that eventually provoked a reaction and led to the establishment of a rival system. The Academy was founded for two reasons. The first, to ensure free exercise of the right to paint in Paris, quickly paled in significance compared with the second, to defend a particular aesthetic doctrine. As long as the Academy proved capable of absorbing new artistic styles (despite some rather bitter controversies), its prestige survived. In the nineteenth century, under the despotic influence of Ingres (member of the Institute from 1825 to 1867), for whom classicism was the only true religion, the Academy became rigidly wedded to a dying tradition, The election of an ill and aged Delacroix to the Institute in

1857 came too late to produce much in the way of change. After 1830 romanticism, with its own characteristic notions of art and the artist, also helped erode the Academy's authority.

That authority had exerted a highly centralizing influence. As early as 1676 the king had decided to counter this by setting up provincial academies of art (of which there were thirty-three by 1786), but the regional art schools were incapable of resisting the influence of Paris for long. By the nineteenth century they were turning out standardized works compatible with Parisian canons. Artists from the provinces could win official recognition only in Paris. They came to the capital not only to learn the pure doctrine of the great tradition but also to earn the credentials that would qualify them in the eyes of the public and, in particular, of potential buyers.

Its powers strengthened by Napoleon, the Academy controlled the training and recognition of artists. It regulated teaching in the schools of fine arts and dispensed the prestigious Prix de Rome. The jury that decided which works would be accepted for exhibit in the Salons and what prizes they would receive consisted of members of the Academy.[2] Painters had no means to establish themselves other than to submit to the authority of the Academy. What is more, because academicians sat on state art commissions, the Academy controlled official commissions and government patronage. Harrison C. White and Cynthia A. White have shown that by 1860, with the increase in the number of painters, the Academy was no longer able to supervise the training or ensure adequate demand for the work of the younger generation of artists.[3] In 1863 Napoleon III established the Salon des Refusés [for paintings rejected from the official Salon], and in December of that same year reforms were begun at the Ecole des Beaux-Arts in response to an imperial decree. But these were only half-measures, the principal result of which was to replace the academic style of instruction with a defensively eclectic "school" style.

Under the original rules of the Academy its members were forbidden to engage in commerce, in the sense of maintaining businesses for the sale of art. Although artists were allowed to sell their own and even other painters' work to art lovers, it was generally thought better that sales be made through art dealers. In the eighteenth century fortunes changed hands rapidly as a result of social and political upheaval. The art market expanded, and many works of art were sold.[4] Collectors' private agents were supplanted by dealers, large and small, who sold not only old masters but also paintings by contemporaries.[5] Legend has it that Leonardo died in the arms of the king of France, but history tells us that Watteau died in the arms of the art dealer Gersaint.

Underlying the foundation of the Academy was the idea that art is an intellectual activity; in the eighteenth century this same idea gave rise to art criticism. The *Mercure* published the first criticism of a Salon in 1738, and as the press grew in the nineteenth century, art criticism took on new importance.

The Academy, stubborn defender of tradition, may have held a monopoly over the selection and training of artists, but outside it flourished a distribution network dominated by dealers and an information network dominated by critics. As rebel ideologies of art succeeded one another in the nineteenth century, the Academy stood firm. By the time the impressionists arrived on the scene, tension had been building since at least the turn of the century. Unable to destroy the system from within, painters turned to these existing outside networks. The majority of the public still supported the taste of the Academy, but a minority of progressive critics and dealers took the risk of joining the opposition, promoting painters and works of art in new ways.

Changes in the Impressionist Period

Official Artists and Independent Artists

Laureates of the Ecole des Beaux-Arts, official artists were sent to Rome for a stint at the French Academy School there and then returned to Paris to exhibit their paintings at the annual Salon, win medals, and ultimately be accepted as members of the Institute. Their careers were not unlike those of senior government officials, and their paintings enjoyed the favor of the *grande bourgeoisie,* politically, economically, and socially the dominant group in France. This class included the most successful members of the legal and medical professions, top government leaders, and, not least, businessmen, industrialists, bankers, and corporate executives. Their taste in painting was conservative, and they purchased canvases at the Salon or from fashionable galleries such as Boussod, Valadon & Co., where paintings by prize-winning artists were sold.[6] The works of leading painters sold for good prices, and the painters themselves were able to maintain a bourgeois style of living.[7]

The innovative artists rejected by the official institutions were the first to recognize the economic potency of the established system. Some, like Manet, never overcame their desire to be accepted by the establishment. Others attempted to work out some sort of compromise. From Algiers, Renoir wrote to Paul Durand-Ruel in March of 1881:

> "I shall try to explain to you why I send my paintings to the Salon. There are fifteen art lovers in Paris capable of appreciating a painter without the Salon. There are 80,000 who wouldn't buy a thing from a painter not exhibited at the

Salon. That's why I send two portraits every year, little though that may be. . . . My Salon submission is entirely commercial. It's like some medicines: it may not do any good, but at least it does no harm."[8]

Nevertheless, the impressionists and other innovative artists were eventually able to win recognition and sell their works for good prices because a new distribution network was created alongside the official sales channels. Anti-Salon groups, organized by artists who shared common aims and frequented the same cafes, staged private shows[9] and auction sales,[10] established new salons,[11] and encouraged new types of dealers and collectors to join the art market. Figures for a single year cannot give an accurate idea of the income earned by impressionist artists, whose prices were much more sensitive to changing economic conditions than were the prices of more fashionable painters. Still, it is not without interest to note that Durand-Ruel's books for 1880 show that Roybet earned 40,000 francs; Ziem, 29,000 francs; Boudin, 11,000; Pissarro, 12,000; Degas, 16,000; Monet, 21,000; Renoir, 16,000; Sisley, 9,500; and Cassatt, 8,000.[12] At this time the highest-paid civil servant earned no more than 20,000 francs (the chief of staff of a central office in the government bureaucracy earned 18,000 francs in 1871 and 20,000 in 1901).

A New Type of Art Dealer

Paul Durand-Ruel (1831–1922), who succeeded his father in 1865, responded to the new situation by transforming the traditional role of the art dealer.[13] He waged his first battle on behalf of the Barbizon School; then, in 1870, he launched a campaign in favor of the Batignolles group.[14] Charles Daubigny, who introduced Claude Monet to Durand-Ruel in London in 1870, undoubtedly helped arouse his interest in the impressionists, to whose star he hitched his own.

Durand-Ruel waged battle against the public's taste. His faith in the misunderstood impressionists cost him clients faithful to the School of 1830. The economic climate was far from favorable; from 1873 to 1896 prices declined steadily. Among other consequences was the crisis of 1882, which led to the crash of the Union générale, a powerful Catholic bank. Durand-Ruel in particular was hard hit, because Feder, one of the bank's directors, had been his silent partner since 1880. Later, Durand-Ruel confessed that his debts in 1884 amounted to more than a million francs.[15] He was also faced with competition from other dealers who became interested in the impressionists and challenged his monopoly.

Paul Durand-Ruel responded to adversity by redoubling his efforts. In 1869 he founded the *Revue internationale de l'art et de la curiosité,* and between 22 November 1890 and 2 May 1891 he published a weekly newspa-

per, *L'art dans les deux mondes.* Starting in February 1883, he staged a series of one-man shows of artists he supported; such shows, uncommon at
the time, became increasingly popular. In the same year he staged group
shows in London, Rotterdam, and Boston. In 1886 he set out to conquer
the American market by opening a gallery in New York. European dealers had long been attracted to New York; Goupil had had a representative
there, one Michel Knoedlr, since 1846.

Durand-Ruel was one of the first modern art dealers in two senses: he
sought to establish a monopoly, and by championing painting not yet in demand he was able to accumulate a stock that ultimately yielded handsome
returns. In 1866 he bought seventy canvases from Theodore Rousseau.
"This was perhaps the first time that a dealer sought to 'monopolize' a
painter. After him, all dealers conceived the same ambition."[16] In January
1872 Durand-Ruel visited Manet and bought every painting in his studio,
twenty-three canvases for which he paid 35,000 francs.[17] He signed no written contracts with his artists. Accounts were settled periodically, and when
Durand-Ruel found himself in financial difficulties, payment was delayed.
Durand-Ruel was determined to be the exclusive representative of the
painters he championed, but the painters were fearful of allowing a dealer
to control their work. On 6 March 1883 Monet wrote: "I am frightened by
the number of my paintings in your hands."[18] Although Durand-Ruel's
monopoly ended with the commercial success of impressionism, his name
remains forever associated with the new art.

With Durand-Ruel painting ceased to be just another luxury good. Art
dealers could no longer merely satisfy the desires of their clients without
taking a part in the promotion of new aesthetic principles. Ambroise
Vollard (1865–1939) and Daniel-Henry Kahnweiler (1884–1979) can be
viewed as direct descendants of Paul Durand-Ruel.

A New Type of Collector

Among the first allies of the impressionists were critics such as Burty,
Castagnary, Chesneau, and Duranti, and writers such as Alphonse Daudet, d'Hervilly, and Emile Zola. Théodore Duret (1838–1927), a writer
and art critic, offered a wholehearted defense of impressionism in his
Peintres impressionistes, published in 1878.[19] The social and occupational
backgrounds of the first admirers of impressionism vary widely. Among
them were financiers like Hoschedé, chairman of the department store *Au
Gagne Petit;* bankers like Hecht, Achille Arosa, and Charles Ephrussi; the
composer Emmanuel Chabrier and the singer Faure; doctors, such as
Georges de Bellio and Dr. Gachet; customs inspector Victor Choquet;
and a count, Arnaud Doria. There were also wealthy painters, such as
Caillebotte and Henri Rouart; industrialists, such as Jean Dollfuss of

Strasbourg; and small art dealers like Martin and Tanguy. Eugène Murer, a school friend of Guillaumin's, ran a pastry shop and restaurant and offered the painters meals in exchange for paintings. Georges Charpentier, the publisher of Daudet and Zola, helped to launch Renoir in fashionable society through the salon kept by Mme Charpentier.

These men represent a new type of art collector. Their selection of paintings was meant to be progressive, pointing the way forward in the history of art. At very little expense they amassed valuable collections and were looked on after the fact as heroic pioneers, shrewd amateurs, and fortunate speculators.[20]

As each new revolution in painting occurred, the latest innovators followed in the footsteps of the impressionists, exhibiting in new salons and soliciting the support of a few critics, a narrow circle of buyers, and a dealer with an eye for novelty as well as business. Economic success came more and more quickly; it is risky to generalize, however, as individual personalities invariably played a part. Monet, for example, was a better businessman than Pissarro. Gauguin's social maladjustment, Van Gogh's sickness and suicide, and Montparnos's deviant behavior contributed at least as much as financial hardship to the stereotype of the suffering artist.

The experiences of the impressionists and their successors revealed the artists' dependence on their dealers. As Van Gogh wrote to his brother Theo, "the crux of the matter is that my opportunity to work depends on the sale of my paintings. . . . If you don't sell and you have no fortune, you can't make any progress, whereas if you have money, the work takes care of itself."[21] As the experience of the late nineteenth and early twentieth centuries abundantly proves, the market is powerless to predict changes in aesthetic judgment. Bourgeois society failed to recognize itself in modern art; the economic hierarchy established by the market does not coincide with the aesthetic hierarchy established by history. The great art turned out to be not the art for which the bourgeoisie paid dear, but the art that no one, or almost no one, bought.

The moral depends on who is drawing it. For some, the lesson of history is that innovative art is a good investment. Buyers live in fear of getting stuck with today's Meissonier or, worse still, missing today's Cézanne. If yesterday's critics greeted modern art with incomprehension, today's critics often greet it with "overcomprehension."[22] Dealers tend to buy everything in the belief that one lucky purchase can compensate for a host of errors. Artists can work at their canvases, confident that commercial success is no proof of genius. All these factors explain in part why the living art of the 1950s became paying art. But success is no longer a guarantee of aesthetic value. The memory of the late nineteenth century still weighs heavily; history does not so much teach lessons as offer examples. Great artists, it is assumed, create works that only future spectators can appreciate, spectators that their works themselves will help to form. Repentance for the errors of the past does not preclude the commission of new errors, however.

Speculation, Snobbery, and Crisis

La Belle Epoque

The foundations of a new aesthetic were laid in the first two decades of the twentieth century, a period of widespread prosperity. The modern art market had yet to seriously threaten the traditional market, but it did exist. The example of Kahnweiler, who made systematic use of exclusive agreements with his artists, was followed by many other entrepreneurs. A dealer who controls an artist's entire output can afford to bet against the prevalent taste of the moment in the hope of scoring a coup in the long run.

The so-called Bearskin Sale (held 2 March 1914 at the Hôtel Drouot) proved that investment in painting by living artists could be profitable. The winds of speculation had begun to blow. It does not follow that all collectors since 1914 have been "investors," but art was no longer the exclusive province of disinterested amateurs. Today's collectors' clubs are modeled on the Bearskin Club, a group of young men with family connections and common tastes who joined together in 1904 at the behest of André Level for the purpose of amassing a joint art collection. Each partner in the club contributed 250 francs per year for a single share. Purchases were proposed by Level, the club's manager, and approved by a select committee. Ownership of paintings was assigned by lot. Not all the artists represented in the club's catalogue are well known today. Club purchases were eclectic, and there were many "errors." Among the shrewder selections were a Bonnard, ten Matisses, and a dozen Picassos, including *Les Bateleurs,* now on display at the Chicago Art Institute. The sale, attended by Max Jacob wearing a red greatcoat, was an unexpected success. The auction yielded more than 100,000 francs. André Level denied that his original intentions were speculative.

It never occurred to any of those who claimed the right to judge—and judge severely—the members of this association to ask what proportion of the paintings on sale they bought for themselves. The answer is, about one-quarter of the total value, and undoubtedly they would have purchased one-half had they not been surprised and upset by the high and rapidly rising prices, for which neither experts nor appraisers had prepared them, for no one had anticipated the outcome. . . . And anyway, what is the meaning of this foolish refusal to see that selfish interests are a part of any human endeavor?[23]

When war broke out, Franz Jourdain, president of the Salon d'Automne, is supposed to have shouted, 'At last, Cubism is done for!' But Cubism suffered no more than other varieties of painting from the war. It soon became clear that in wartime anything could become an object of speculation. War profiteers who heard of the rapidly rising prices being paid for paintings realized that there was no reason why pictures should be any less profitable than camembert, wine, or steel rails.[24]

Given this climate, it is hardly surprising that the sale of the Degas studio (1918–1919) proved such a success, yielding 8,649,573 francs from the sale of 1,840 paintings, drawings, pastels, and prints.

Postwar Hopes

In the euphoric years that followed the end of the First World War, the attitude of Parisian high society toward avant-garde art changed, beginning with the scandalous debut of *Parade* (with sets and costumes by Picasso) at the Châtelet in 1917. The dazzling success of the *Ballets russes* permanently changed the fortunes of the avant-garde. The social group whose word in such matters was law began to stage parties in settings designed by the boldest of the modern artists. The snobbery began with a small group of restless, enlightened aristocrats and a few Parisian writers amused by the scandal.

Between 1917 and 1930 the values of the rebels became the values of high society. In 1918 Picasso moved in to a house at 23, rue La Boétie. "He looked almost like a wealthy bourgeois. He was never so elegant before or since, with his watch-chain hooked to his buttonhole, well-combed hair, a bow tie, and a white pocket handkerchief in the pocket of his jacket."[25] In the 1930s he drove a Hispano-Suiza.[26] The most bizarre of the Surrealists quickly found a welcome in the salons of Paris high society. Like Thackeray's man of letters, the artist became a "social lion." "He takes the *pas* of dukes and earls; all the nobility crowd to see him: I forget how many baronesses and duchesses fell in love with him."[27]

The confiscation and liquidation of property of German nationals flooded the market with art, however, and made it difficult to maintain prices at a high level. In 1921–1923 the breakup of the collections of Uhde and the dealer Kahnweiler placed some fifteen-hundred paintings and drawings on the market (in five different sales, four for the confiscated

Kahnweiler holdings alone).[28] At the same time these sales stimulated the market for modern art.

> The Hôtel Drouot saw the advent of a new and nontraditional clientele. For these newcomers it was not a question of familiarity with prices and styles but of setting new prices and establishing new styles. This required less practice and experience, perhaps, but more courage, enthusiasm, audacity, and youthful spirit. Imprudence can be a virtue, not to say a shrewd maneuver, in an auction gallery normally mired in routine. And in fact these sales led to further sales, to exchanges, to profits, to revisions, to enthusiasm, controversy, and violence, bringing new life to the market for modern painting. . . . What was particularly important in the sales of confiscated collections was that they established a clear dividing line between the prewar and the postwar periods. They established the reputations of the painters whose works were included in the liquidation sales.[29]

Alphonse Bellier, who became head of the Hôtel Drouot in 1920, sought to take advantage of this new enthusiasm to make his establishment a center for the sale of modern art. Until 1924 modern paintings were sold along with other works (usually canvases from the artists' studios). A sale was held every six weeks. On 22 October 1920 the sale of modern paintings yielded 14,780 francs; around half the paintings were sold, and the others bought back in. On 22 January 1921, sales totaled 20,511 francs; by 19 February sales had increased to 35,000 francs, and by 25 March to 51,000. On 21 May 1924, a sale was held of paintings donated by painters to raise money for a monument to Guillaume Apollinaire, yielding 30,343 francs. On 25 November 1924 a sale was held exclusively of modern paintings (Dufy, Derain, Segonzac, Vlaminck, Camoin, and the cubists), bringing in 354,270 francs. In 1925 the first Carco sale (2 March) yielded 208,150 francs, and a sale of the collection of the fashion designer Poiret (18 November) yielded 530,000 francs. Prices rose even more sharply in 1926. On 22 June of that year paintings owned by Pedron, a coffee importer from Le Havre, went for 888,000 francs, and on 28 October paintings owned by John Quinn (a New York attorney who invested in painting on the advice of Pierre-Henri Roché) yielded 1,640,000 francs, with bids of 520,000 francs for *La Bohémienne endormie* of Douanier Rousseau and 101,000 francs for a Matisse. These sales were violently attacked, accused of being "fabricated" and therefore unhealthy. They should be viewed as part of the larger economic process by which the commercial value of modern art was established. The sale of André Level's collection on 3 March 1927 permits a number of interesting comparisons with the Bearskin Sale and confirms that recent work sold at decent prices: a small Soutine went for 12,500 francs and the most important Chirico went for 5,000.[30] In the sale of paintings from the collection of H. Canonne on

28 May 1930, a Matisse (*The Concert*, 60 × 73 cm) purchased in 1926 for 20,000 francs went for 165,000 francs.[31]

Repercussions of the Great Depression

The Great Depression of the 1930s jeopardized the economic and social success of modern painting. Prices paid in both public and private sales for works by the masters of the twentieth century had risen steadily throughout the twenties, but during the Depression the market for contemporary art was hard hit.

The Depression began with a stock market crash in New York and spread quickly to Austria and Central Europe. The financial panic eventually hit London, and by 1932 France, too, has begun to feel the effects. Artists were badly hurt: more than a third of all art galleries shut their doors; contracts were broken (and even an "established" artist like Marquet saw his contract with the Bernheim and Druet galleries abruptly cancelled); younger painters (and not a few older ones) joined the ranks of the unemployed.

Here is Kanhweiler's account

> The Depression was unbelievable. Nothing was selling. My sister-in-law had joined me as a partner in the gallery in 1920. We were the only employees left. Before, we had had an office boy, but I had been forced to let him go. Whole days went by during which we were the only two people in the gallery. Nobody came in. We were there. It wouldn't have been so bad if I hadn't had to worry about the painters. I didn't want to leave them in the lurch. Not the great ones. Picasso didn't need me. Nobody was buying Picasso, but Picasso could afford to wait. Braque could also afford to wait. So along with some friends we set up an artists' mutual aid society. Everybody contributed so much a month. The gallery distributed the money to the painters, and at the end of the year everybody who contributed was entitled to so many paintings of this artist or that artist, depending on how much he had put in. The gallery took a small percentage in order to keep going but also contributed money so that it, too, could receive paintings. That was how we kept the painters going up to about 1936.[32]

Because of the Depression there were fewer sales of old masters. These safe investments had disappeared from the market entirely.[33] The.Depression also accelerated the fall in the price of older art begun by the change in taste and thus temporarily put an end to the sale of works of the Barbizon School and of late nineteenth-century academic painting. Particularly hard hit were very recent works, whose prices had shot up in the speculative fever of the twenties but fell rapidly once the crisis hit. Many of today's great collections of late nineteenth- and early twentieth-century masterpieces were acquired between 1930 and 1934 at public sales or through brokers.

The bulk of my collection dates from the 1930s. In times of economic crisis the price of paintings drops considerably. You have to be in a position to wait. In a crisis there is no liquidity, so the bottom drops out of the art market. Anyone who has cash at such a time can take advantage of the situation. [C49]

I began making purchases at the Hôtel Drouot during the Depression. You could buy anything for next to nothing. And there seemed to be no risk. Paintings sold for a tenth or a twentieth of the price they had brought the year before. They couldn't have lost that much of their value. I bought this Dufy for 1,000 francs; now it's worth ten million. [C64]

The Second World War: Painting as a Safe Investment

In Times of Inflation

The market had just begun to recover from the Depression when war broke out. The economic function of painting as a hedge against inflation then became clear. Along with gold, foreign currency, stocks, and other scarce goods, painting was not only a good investment in times of inflation but a way of protecting one's fortune from government control. Paintings, easily concealed and readily traded, provide a means of evading the watchful eye of the fiscal authorities. More than a commodity, they could be used as a means of payment in international trade; a deed of sale for a painting could easily compensate a banker for handling an overseas financial transaction.

The nation's economic trials did not affect people in different walks of life in the same way. In hard times producers and merchants often profit as customers bid up the price of scarce goods. As consumption goods disappeared from the market, paintings became increasingly attractive to buyers. Illicit profits could be protected from confiscation by the tax authorities through investment in tapestries, rare books, stamps, or paintings. Black-marketeers looked to painting not only for financial safety but also for social prestige and personal satisfaction. They turned to dealers who offered them decorative paintings of relatively small size, suitable for hanging in relatively modest modern apartments. Still lifes, especially bouquets of flowers, proved particularly popular during the war, no matter when they were painted; this popularity continued even after the war was over. Landscapes were also popular, especially those by eighteenth-century Italian painters and by impressionists. Impressionist paintings and their byproducts became familiar and easy to comprehend; they combined the charm of nature and the outdoors with an air of easy living.[34]

During the war years premonitory signs of painting's future commercial success were easy to spot. On 4 December 1941 Seurat's *Small blue peasant* (46 × 58 cm) sold for 385,000 francs (80,850 F) at the first Fénéon sale. At the first sale of the estate of Dr. Viau (11 December 1942) a painting by Cézanne, *The valley of the Arc and Mt. Sainte-Victoire* (55 × 46 cm), sold for 5 million francs (885,000 F). Two pastels by Degas sold for more than a million apiece, and a third, *Woman drying herself after bathing* (105 × 99 cm) went for 2.23 million francs (394,710 F). On 10 February 1943, in the sale of Paul Jamot's collection, Corot's *View of Mt. Valérien* (42 × 64 cm) sold for 1.1 million francs (162,800 F). In February and March 1944 some modern paintings sold for 50 percent more than was paid for comparable works in 1942; during the same period the retail price index (based on a weighted index of the prices of thirty-four items, 1938 = 100) rose from 175 to 285 and the price of the gold napoleon rose from 2,652 to 3,711, whereas the index of variable income stocks remained unchanged. At the second sale of Dr. Viau's estate, held on 22 June 1948, several records were set: a *Still Life* (80 × 100 cm) by Pissarro sold for 2.8 million francs (61,000 F); Renoir, *Young Girl Reading* (62 × 54 cm) sold for 9,090,000 francs (199,980 F); and Degas, *Woman in Gray* (82 × 73 cm) went for 9.1 million francs (200,200 F).

Although the prices paid for old masters remained higher in general than those paid for the best modern paintings, the gap steadily diminished. Degas, Renoir, Cézanne, and Seurat were already "super values." But prices paid for twentieth-century masters were increasing just fast enough to offset the decrease in the value of the franc. By contrast, innovative modern painting from surrealism on was pacing the market.

Political Circumstances

Apart from the unusual economic conditions, the political situation under the German occupation had direct repercussions on the art market. As part of their anti-Semitic policy the Germans confiscated paintings from private collectors (Rothschild, David-Weil, Veil-Picard, Alphonse Kahn, and others) and dealers (including Seligmann, Wildenstein, Paul Rosenberg, and Bernheim). Old masters were simply confiscated when they belonged to Jews and purchased (sometimes by coercion, sometimes not) in other cases.[35]

Nazi ideology condemned modern art. All art since impressionism was considered "degenerate." Hence "in order to avoid contamination of German taste," confiscated modern works "were assembled, or, rather, isolated, in the most out-of-the-way and inaccessible room of the museum [the Jeu de Paume]. By the end of the occupation, all the great contemporary artists had joined the collection. Paintings by Picasso, Braque, Matisse, Dali, and Soutine outnumbered the rest."[36] Goering appropriated for his museum at Karinhall a large number of canvases disapproved by his party's theoreticians. Other paintings were used in exchanges, and still others were simply sold in Paris or Switzerland. Here is Kahnweiler's cautious commentary on the fate of French collections of modern art: they were not "sent to Germany but stolen in one way or another. Some well-known people were involved in buying and selling those paintings. . . . Many disappeared. Paul Rosenberg lost an enormous number that way."[37] Other paintings were simply destroyed, either slashed or consigned to flames in the Jeu de Paume's inner courtyard.

While the "collaborationist" art market prospered, many Jewish-owned galleries were closed down. Before the war Jewish merchants played a prominent part in the sale of paintings as well as jewelry and furs. Some galleries survived under new names (the Kahnweiler Gallery became the Louise Leiris Gallery, for example) or in different countries (Georges Wildenstein and Paul Rosenberg left for the United States). Others, such as Bernheim-Jeune, Marcel Bernheim, Katia Granoff, Pierre Loeb, and Mouradian-Valloton, ceased operations until the liberation.

Some well-known painters were willing to represent France at the 1942 Berlin exposition, but many artists had already left for America: Marc Chagall, Max Ernst, Yves Tanguy, André Masson, Piet Mondrian, and many others. Through these refugees the School of Paris exerted considerable influence on the development of American painting.

New Forces

In difficult wartime circumstances French painting readied itself for postwar renewal. On 10 May 1941 the Braun Gallery held a show of "Young Painters in the French Tradition," featuring a number of painters who had already achieved some reputation: Bazaine, Estève, Gischia, Lapique, Pignon, Le Moal, Manessier, Robin, and Singier. Fautrier had a show at the Drouin Gallery in 1943, as did Dubuffet in 1944. A number of early abstractionist masters died during the war: Klee in 1940, Delaunay in 1941, Mondrian and Kandinsky in 1944. Yet experiments in abstract art continued in secret during the occupation. In June–July 1945 this underground activity resulted in a show of "Concrete Art" at the Drouin Gallery featuring works by Arp, Robert and Sonia Delaunay, Doméla, Freundlich, Gorin, Herbin, Kandinsky, Magnelli, Mondrian, Pevsner, Taueber-Arp, and Van Doesburg.

Older galleries continued to sell the works most in demand (Degas drawings, small paintings by Courbet and Renoir, landscapes by Lebourg, Lépine, and Guillaumin, and works of Utrillo, Vlaminck, and Derain), but in the meantime new dealers were lending money to avant-garde artists, betting on which side would win both the war and the battle in art. Among these new dealers were Jeanne Bucher (whose gallery opened in 1925), Louis Carré (1938), S. Galanis and M. Villand (who opened the Friedland Gallery in 1940–1943), Paul Martin (whose Gallery of France was founded in 1942), and René Drouin (whose gallery, founded in 1939, was opened to modern art in 1943). Despite the hostile reception given to seventy-four paintings and five bronzes by Picasso shown at the Salon d'Automne of 1944, this show confirmed the reputations of the leading painters of the interwar years: Bonnard, Rouault, Matisse, Braque, Picasso, Léger, and Villon.

Both established and newer dealers were free to choose paintings from a wide variety of styles. Prices of works by impressionists and twentieth-century masters were well established by auctions at the Hôtel Drouot, but the value of surrealist and "traditional French" painting as well as works broadly classified as "abstract art" had yet to be proven in the marketplace. A few dealers possessed large stocks of such works, however, and this fact influenced future sales. More conformist painting also found buyers. The stage was set for aesthetic disputation and business competition.

I have looked to the past in the hope of uncovering the roots of the present, as well as the models on which today's actors base their attitudes and behavior. The innovative artists of the late nineteenth century won the fight that had raged, ever since Courbet, against the absolute authority of the official Salon. Victory came on 11 June 1884 with the creation of the Society of Independents, whose aim was to "make it easier for artists to present their works freely and directly to the public for judgment and sale."[38] But no sooner was independence acquired than it was compromised by the market system, the only outlet available to progressive painters.

As the market became increasingly rationalized and efficient, it also became increasingly oppressive to artists because the profit motive took priority over all other considerations. As early as 1847, Barada, a deputy from the Gers, wrote to Delacroix's assistant Lassalle-Bordes about a "great machine" that Delacroix was proposing to do for the Salon: "M. Cavé [then Director of Fine Arts] said something else that caught my attention. He maintains that before long the government will no longer be commissioning works of art, and then *painters will be forced to turn to the art dealers.*"[39] Supply and demand governed not only the prices to be paid for completed works but also, given the extent to which the fortunes of the artist came to depend on the market, what kind of painting would be done. For the past century aesthetic and commercial values have become ever more closely intertwined.

As the art market developed, moreover, the public was gradually tamed. As everyone knows, the works of genius of the late nineteenth and early twentieth century regularly caused scandals. Since then there has been a great temptation to take anything that causes a scandal for a work of genius. The fact that some art buyers, influenced by historical precedent, made themselves the champions of some rather bold experiments in painting proved to be of great importance in the development of the post-war art market.

2

Multiple Markets

There exists not one but several markets for painting. The most significant difference among them is the type of painting sold. The major artistic controversy of our times, between traditionalists on the one hand and those who believe that the best painting requires constant innovation in technique and subject matter on the other, is reflected in the structure of the market. The speculation that has been so marked a feature of the postwar art market has been encouraged by the avant-garde's predilection for constant challenges to established values and rapid change in artistic fashions.

Degrees of Legitimacy

The physical mode of existence of the work of art is "the existence it possesses qua material object endowed with properties common to all objects of the same class. . . . In this respect the work of any Sunday painter produces the same effects as the work of an artist . . . [and] all paintings exist in practically the same way, as objects composed of certain elements."[1] Hence the use of a single word to denote all "painting" results in total confusion. In order to clarify the structure of the market, I shall therefore introduce my own classification.

First, we have various humble forms of painting, which by general agreement are excluded from the realm of "art." Second, there is "art," which comes in two kinds: past painting, which is consecrated by history, and contemporary painting, which is not. It is possible, of course, to dispute the point at which a painting becomes a "historical" work; I shall explain my criteria.

Non-Art

Excluded from the realm of art are many kinds of genre painting. Virtually interchangeable, these works are painted by anonymous hands or by painters not recognized as such by qualified judges (by "qualified" I mean credentialed by official institutions or accepted by artists working in a recognized school of contemporary art). Common subjects include folk scenes ("Peasant Festival in Brittany" or "Gypsies"), landscapes (heather, brush in spring or fall, deer in the forest, mountain lakes, coastal scenes, marshes or orchards in the snow, sunsets), still lifes with flowers, fruits, fish, or game, nudes, and watercolors of tourist sights (gondolas in Venice or views of Sacré-Coeur in Montmartre). But for minor details such paintings are all of a kind and exist in numerous copies. Products of rigid craft conventions and readily substituted for one another, they are popular with a broad public. All connoisseurs (the professionals, intellectuals, and artists who define the value hierarchy) agree that such works are not art.

Recognized Classics

Similarly, nearly all connoisseurs agree as to which paintings should be recognized as classics. Errors of judgment regarding authenticity and attribution are of course not unknown. There is always controversy over which were the greater and which the lesser masters of the past. Contemporary values applied to works of the past modify our understanding of other eras. Nevertheless, there is a well-defined class of works of historical value enjoying what Pierre Bourdieu has called "legitimacy" as superior cultural goods.[2] Yet the dividing line between recognized classics and controversial modern works is not always clear-cut. My research shows that, while many individuals reject contemporary art as inferior to the "classics," they disagree as to which periods in art history should be regarded as "classic." (Note that the use of the word *classic* in this context has nothing in common with what is sometimes called *classicism* or *neoclassicism* in art history. It has no art-historical referent and is unintelligible except in sociological terms. Understanding and appreciation of art vary with social background, cultural level, and innate individual qualities.)

It turns out that differences over the meaning of the term *classic* are one way of gauging an individual's social and cultural level. For some the impressionists were the last "classic painters"; for others the term can be applied to Cézanne, Picasso, Max Ernst, or Bazaine. The market has adopted a tripartite classification: older painting (prior to impressionism), modern painting (from the impressionists to the twentieth-century masters), and contemporary painting (the work of living artists or those born after 1900). For art historians if not for the general public, the dividing line between established painting and controversial painting falls somewhere between modern and contemporary.[3] The passage of time clarifies historical trends, thereby diminishing both the risk and economic consequences of an error in judgment. As investments, old masters are roughly equivalent to gilt-edged bonds, modern masterpieces to blue-chip stocks, and contemporary paintings to highly speculative securities.

Non-art has no cultural legitimacy, whereas the legitimacy of classic art is assured. But both non-art and classic art share a common trait: they lie outside the realm in which aesthetic judgment is uncertain. By contrast, assertions of value with respect to contemporary painting are open to challenge.

The Burgeoning Contemporary Scene

Never, perhaps, have artists been as concerned about the verdict of history as they are today. They compose their artistic biographies, catalogue their works, and keep archives of all correspondence. Yet the art scene remains diverse, complex, and problematic. The course of history is admittedly never clear to anyone in the midst of it. The common features of any period's art are best perceived in hindsight. Recently, moreover, the pace of historical change has accelerated, affecting art as it has affected everything else. Finally, the clash of different aesthetics is especially vigorous now because there is no authority sufficiently widely recognized to impose its values on everyone. The professionals (here, critics rather than art historians) disagree, and the validity of their judgment is open to question since they, too, are part of the market system; critical disagreement has economic consequences. Much is written about contemporary art, and every critic has his or her own classification to propose. It is not my intention to offer yet another, condemned like the rest to remain incomplete and one-sided. I simply want to notice one fundamental distinction which has important consequences for the structure of the art market. On the one hand there is art that emphasizes technical perfection and respect for tradition, and on the other hand there is a "different" kind of art, whose manifestations are so diverse that no one word can sum them up. This dichotomy is of course simplistic. The two major tendencies can be further subdivided into innumerable schools and sects, each with its own artistic ideology and network of painters, dealers, critics, and buyers. Rivalries within each camp therefore remain, but still the major split in the postwar period has been between what I shall call "conservatives" and "progressives."

Conservative Painting versus Progressive Painting

Problems of Terminology

The people I interviewed often referred to these two great tendencies as "figurative art" versus "abstract art," using the terms *figurative* and *abstract* broadly and imprecisely (to the understandable dismay of scholars). Although abstract art was born in the first two decades of the twentieth century, it did not become widely known until after the Second World War, at which time old studio debates broadened into public controversy over the virtues of one kind of painting as opposed to the other. This artistic debate not only involved competing interests but also pitted two different world views against one another. Because fundamental values were at stake, there was a high degree of commitment on both sides. Blood may not have flowed as it did in eighteenth-century clashes between proponents and opponents of Italian music, but the economic and rhetorical battle was nonetheless fierce. Aesthetic judgments are by their nature subjective, and the cultivated mob is known for its intolerance.

The vehement rhetoric of these controversies might suggest that figurative and abstract art are polar opposites in the spectrum of contemporary artistic production. Yet it is not at all clear what "abstract art" means. The earliest abstract works now hold wide appeal. Yet they belong to a well-defined historical period (cubism). To use the term *abstract* to subsume all the diverse forms of contemporary art is a mistake, not unlike the mistake of uninitiated art lovers who call not only Dubuffet and Giacometti but also Picasso "abstract artists." My interviewees were either referring to a tacit classification of their own or just simply confused. Hence we cannot clarify the terminology by examining how it is used by the parties involved. The words in this case miss the point.

"In all ages where we find bold, original, and revealing new art, we also find an art of imitations and souvenirs designed expressly to please and to reap immediate success."[4] Ever since the age of impressionism, traditionalist art has been opposed by experimental art. Resisting all impediments to its free development, progressive painting has defined itself in opposition to all established values as a creative adventure, a quest for challenge and discovery. It may be, as some would argue, that originality today comes cheap, that innovation upon innovation has devalued painting (however dependent on historical judgment, and hence relative, our values may be), and that art, freed from stifling academicism, is now on its way to extinction. Be that as it may, the distinction between traditionalist, conservative art and progressive, innovative art still seems valid. In using these terms I intend no judgment as to the authenticity or quality of artistic innovation and make no prediction as to the future of painting. The terms chosen may appear reductive because of their political overtones; that is unfortunate, but I saw no other way of avoiding an implicit value judgment.

The Spirit of Contemporary Experimentation in
Art

My purpose in this section is not to describe the art movements of the 1950s and 1960s but simply to identify certain key ideas and tendencies underlying the art of our time, for these have undeniably had an impact on the development of the art market. External factors have often been cited as responsible for the evolution of modern art. Some believe that the history of art is governed by a dialectic of image and object, and argue that the discovery of photography increased the importance of the latter at the expense of the former. The camera also gave artists access to art forms remote in space and time. Psychoanalysis, we are told, liberated the irrational and conferred value on the drawings of children and madmen, encouraging artists to explore "inner space." An ever more rationalized society produced a reaction in the form of a new interest in naive and folk art. To be sure, art is not impervious to influence from other areas of civilization. But painting is still in large measure autonomous. The painter reacts at least as much to the painter of yesterday as to the world of today (as Wölfflin, Lévi-Strauss, and Malraux, among others, have so forcefully pointed out).

Expressive and constructive realism were followed by transformation of the real in nonfigurative art[5] and elimination of the real in abstract art— whether of the "geometrical" or "lyrical," "cold" or "hot," "constructive" or "informal" variety. Not all contemporary experiments can be characterized as nonfigurative (counterexamples include the surrealists, expressionists, and naifs).[6] Yet the absence of figuration has been responsible for much of the public's confusion in the encounter with what has been called the "sovereign will of the painter."[7]

Tradition and academicism were in effect supplanted by a welter of proud and independent individual styles; artists felt a yearning to start with a clean slate and make painting anew. "Training in technique having become virtually a thing of the past, each artist was obliged to retrace the history of art on his own. People gradually became enamoured of the idea of genius and total creation, and even skilled painters such as Picasso renounced their past and put themselves back to school."[8] Artists contrived to unlearn what they knew or simply refused to learn at all. Rejecting academicism as the final avatar of an exhausted tradition, painters began to see themselves as feverish creators, participants in a renaissance of painting.

New experiments in painting paid homage to chance, "the world's oldest deity."[9] Surrealists toyed with "objective chance." Other artists played with electronic painting machines or painted while in a trance. Still others banked on their power to transform any object whatsoever into a work of art merely by signing it: Marcel Duchamp's audacious gesture has often been imitated. For some, the work of art is no longer a work at all but a springboard for the viewer's imagination. The spectator discovers significance in the painting's formal qualities, whose only guarantee of validity is, in Motherwell's phrase, the painter's virtue. We have come to the end of the road. "Whatever the artist spits out is art," Schwitters proclaimed. It is the painter's intention that confers upon the painting its existence qua art.

Still another tendency in contemporary art has been to transform the art work, traditionally a unique and enduring object of value, into a mass-produced object of consumption. One dealer put it this way: "What we have to do at all costs is imitate the American method by establishing the notion that a work of art can age, can deteriorate physically and psychologically. We must teach collectors to discard old paintings as they discard old automobiles and refrigerators, in order to make way for the new" [D170]. Conspicuous consumption of art (necessary in these times of overproduction) thus imitates certain anti-art themes of dadaism.

Viewed more broadly, however, modern art is not lacking nobility. "Tentatively, one might say that modern art, which has apparently done away with works in the traditional sense, has nevertheless been constructing for the past fifty years a vast, splendid cathedral spread out through time."[10] Modern art is history. Artists since the impressionists have been in the business of challenging established values and perpetually renovating the house of art. The history of modern art has been one of new tendencies establishing themselves in opposition to the old, only to be quickly challenged by still newer ones. Since the subject of art is now not nature but history, inventiveness has become a primary aesthethic value, and disputes over dating have become a matter of the first importance. Artists have been known to destroy their own works in order to make good claims to be the originator of some new trend. Modern art is often easily imitated; what distinguishes the creator from his epigones is that the creator comes first. Traditional art encouraged imitation; modern art has opened the way to experimentation with form, color, movement, and matter; to increased scale; and to attempts to create "objects" that defy categorization as painting or sculpture. Painting has deliberately explored both its means and its ends, to the point where art is ultimately nothing more than reflection upon itself. Writers today maintain that writing is impossible; similarly, the work of an exemplary artist like Giacometti is an exploration of its own impossibility.

No one can say with assurance what direction modern painting will take. Many of the most appreciative judgments of modern painting go beyond rational argument; they evince the kind of delight usually reserved for works of philosophy or, even more, for fundamental existential choices. Surveying the uncertain battlefield of living art is a more exciting activity than viewing a selected sample of the masterpieces of defunct societies.

Contemporary art, as I have said, is different from both established art and what I am calling non-art. The potential buyer of a contemporary work invariably feels disoriented and anxious. The work may be careful and deliberate, naive, or polemical; it may glorify speed or the artist at work or pure intentionality. Still, it is more or less suspect. It cannot be otherwise, given the burden of moribund tradition and moralizing aestheticism that it must bear and react against. Modern painting has turned its back on reality, on traditional symbols accessible to all, and, in extreme cases, on painterly skills that can only be learned, not improvised. As such, there is a great deal of room for deceit.

> There is a grimace that puts people off the track. The essence of modern art and modern literature is to facilitate that grimace, to carry it to extravagant lengths. . . . Deception is much less easy to detect than in the figurative art to which our eyes have become accustomed. In figurative art we quickly notice what is academic, imitative, or overrefined. But abstract art abounds with works that are academic, imitative, and overrefined. There are so-called advanced painters who set out to flatter the public and who succeed at it. There will always be society painting. . . . There is even 'naive' society painting.[11]

How can we tell the authentic from the fake, from the witting or unwitting fraud? Without benefit of hindsight how can we tell creative innovation from idle experimentation? How can we distinguish between necessity and frivolity? The new painting challenges our culturally conditioned habits of perception and claims legitimacy as art, yet the authorities—the critics, art writers, poets, and philosophers who champion this or that school—have been unable to achieve consensus. Paradoxically, the uncertainty of aesthetic judgment of contemporary art, coupled with the accelerated pace of change in artistic fashion, has encouraged speculation in the contemporary art market, where genius and fashion coexist and where somehow, notwithstanding the errors, mystifications, and manipulations inevitable in the marketplace, the aesthetic values that posterity will recognize are forged.

The Paris Market and the Provincial Markets

Paintings not regarded as "high art" sell for modest prices. There is a broad market for such works, produced by a large number of painters and bought by an even larger number of buyers throughout France. By contrast, works by old and modern masters are sold by a small number of major dealers concentrated in Paris. The market is quite small, and prices are very high. Buyers come from all over the world. These are the two extremes. In between, the nature of the market depends on the type of painting sold.

Decentralization of the Market for Traditionalist Art

Some contemporary painting does not challenge habits of perception or accepted ideas about art. Painting of this kind, whatever its quality, sells briskly in the provinces of France. The provincial art market is sustained by local painters. Buyers purchase works of painters they know or who are regarded in their hometowns as artistic personalities. Sales are made by artists in their studios or through shows organized by a town or local art school. In small- and medium-sized cities furniture and antique dealers and interior decorators provide space for artists to display their works; there are few art dealers as such. Paintings (and deluxe art books) are also sold in the provinces by salesmen, who call on local political leaders, professional men, industrialists, and important merchants. The following excerpt from an advertising brochure is typical: "R.G. stands ready to personally visit your home anytime, anywhere in France and to show you the latest and most sought-after works of the best contemporary artists, including some of the most famous names in the art world."

In larger cities and tourist centers galleries rent space to amateur and professional artists from the area. They also sell paintings first displayed at Paris shows such as the Salon d'Automne or the Salon des Peintres témoins de leurs temps. Works are supplied by Paris dealers, who offer a 30 percent discount to provincial galleries, as well as by painters who have not signed exclusive contracts with Parisian galleries. Quite eclectic, the larger provincial galleries will sell any painting rated highly on the Paris market, regardless of school or style: the works of Brianchon, Buffet, Carzou, Michel Ciry, Fontanarosa, and Legueult can be found alongside those of Atlan, Klee, and Manessier.

Sales of the Avant-Garde Concentrated in Paris

Collectors whose collections include at least some avant-garde works are found in most regional capitals of France (e.g., Lille-Roubaix, Lyons, Marseilles, Nantes), but they prefer to make their purchases in Paris. In part this is, of course, a matter of discretion. But it also reflects the fact that Paris offers a broader range of choice and internationally known dealers, thus diminishing the probability of error. Those who do go to local dealers are generally modest collectors more likely to purchase a print, drawing, or watercolor than a major painting by an important artist.

Few provincial dealers are willing to engage in the risky business of challenging the public's taste by selling paintings for which there is no preexisting demand. They do not enjoy the luxury of selling to foreign buyers, who account for a considerable proportion of the sales of avant-garde dealers in Paris. Only major regional capitals and cities on the Riviera can boast of galleries offering "advanced" works. Most local galleries are either modest establishments that take the work of young local artists on consignment or associates of major Paris dealers. The former are often sustained by another line of business (a photo studio or bookstore, for example), while the latter serve as outposts of the Paris market, selling works by painters who have established reputations in Paris. Avant-garde painters therefore have no choice but to brave the Paris market.

> I opened for business in 1947. I have never shown regional artists. I have no contract with any artist. I know the scene, I visit painters in their studios, and when I see something I like, I buy it. I don't count points,[12] I buy what I like. And I buy directly from the artists. If they have a dealer, or if I have a special relationship with the painter, I work things out with the dealer. I have very few shows, two or three a year, with no more than fifteen paintings each, because they all have to be good. I have had shows of Fernand Léger, Vieira da Silva, Estève, Poliakoff, Lanskoy, Bellegarde, and Germain. Invitations? People always send too many. Catalogues? Never, especially not for abstract painting. Clients? I have a few big collectors from here and from Belgium and small collectors who buy a few paintings each. The big collectors do most of their buying in Paris. The clients are always in Paris. We're too close. [G.E., a dealer in a large city in northern France.]

The primacy of Paris has been accentuated by the internationalization of the market for innovative contemporary painting. Whereas most artistic production, if not consumption, was until recently mainly European, contemporary art has become a worldwide phenomenon. Wherever new aesthetic trends originate, they quickly spread their influence throughout the world. Artists, critics, buyers, and sellers are no longer restricted by national frontiers. They meet at international shows, and painters of all nationalities compete in lucrative international competitions. Traveling shows tour the world. The leading painters are known everywhere, or at any rate in all the capitalist countries. Similar paintings are sold the world over; buyers and dealers are cosmopolitan, and sales are international. In France, only the Paris dealers are equipped to take part in this global trade.

Regional Markets

The picture of the provincial market as drawn thus far is somewhat oversimplified. There are important regional markets centered in such cities as Lyons and Marseilles. In Lyons, for example, the leading collectors (who own works by impressionists and twentieth-century masters) have a special interest in the painting of the nineteenth-century Lyons School, which included Auguste Ravier (1814–1896), Louis Carrand (1821–1899), and François Miel, known as Vernay (1821–1896). The works of Jean Couty (born 1907) and Etienne Morillon have been bought mainly by fellow Lyonnais. Although the pride of a typical Lyons collection might well be relegated to a major collector's back room or country home, this tendency of Lyons buyers to systematically purchase works by regional painters has continued in the present generation. (Lyons buyers seem to prefer figurative to nonfigurative art, however.)

In Marseilles, works by Monticeli (1824–1886), Emile Loubon (1809–1863), Auguste Aiguier (1819–1865), Paul Guigou (1834–1871), and Gustave Ricard (1823–1873) are much in demand. Speculation has been rampant in regard to the work of René Seyssaud (1867–1952), Mathieu Verdilhan (1875–1928), and Auguste Chabaud (1882–1955). Individual collectors and groups of collectors in Marseilles have managed to acquire most of the output of certain contemporary painters from the region. Some more fanatical collectors own virtually no paintings other than the thirty or forty or fifty signed by their "protégé."

It matters greatly, however, whether or not a regional reputation is confirmed in Paris. Paris critics and dealers are regularly called upon to "do justice" to artists "neglected" during their lifetime or to "launch" the careers of artists still unknown. Thus, increasingly, the sale of paintings has been concentrated in Paris. Provincial markets are important mainly to provincial "investors," who must subsequently turn to the Paris market if their investment's potential is to be fully realized. It is not farfetched to see a parallel to this situation in the relation between the Paris Stock Exchange and the regional exchanges. This book is concerned mainly with the Paris market, where the commercial as well as the artistic worth of an artist is established, or at any rate confirmed.

The Actors

II

Art Dealers

There are some who refer to dealers as "slave traders" and others who call them "patrons of the arts." This divergence of opinion reflects the fact that the term *dealer* masks considerable variety. Art dealers differ in many ways. Some sell the work of dead artists, others that of the living. Some specialize in the paintings of creative innovators, others in the work of epigones. Dealers themselves have different ideas about the nature of their work and their place in the market hierarchy, seeing themselves as antiquarians or pioneers, dynamic entrepreneurs or simple brokers, aristocrats of international trade or modest speculators. The art market is complex, diverse, and changeable; so is the art dealer. I have attempted not to establish a rigorous classification of art dealers but only to identify significant types.

Most of my information comes from survey research conducted in 1958–1959 and repeated on a broader scale in 1962–1963. I asked myself the following question: Are there fundamental differences between, on the one hand, dealers who sell the work of established painters for which there is already a public demand and, on the other hand, those who support the creation of new kinds of painting? I believe that this question can be answered in the affirmative. Art dealers exist in two ideal types: the traditional and the new entrepreneurial. Besides these two major types, other actors also play significant market roles: brokers, collector-dealers, and consignment dealers.

In practice, however, it is not always easy to decide whether a particular dealer is a traditional trader or an entrepreneur. Many dealers champion living artists and speculate on their work while continuing to sell "safe" works to their customers.

> Our gallery shows few painters who are not under contract to us. We launch unknown painters aged thirty to forty, but we require that they sell all their work

through us. If a painter under contract participates in a group show somewhere else, sale of the works still has to be handled by us. The gallery takes care of everything, setting up one show a year for each painter.

We also handle paintings by masters, but in such cases rapid turnover is essential. We buy new paintings when we sell the old ones. The gallery isn't well enough endowed to put paintings in storage and wait for prices to go up. [D135]

Other dealers handle contemporary art but act essentially as brokers (that is, they have no direct contact with the artists and sell paintings purchased from other dealers). Some galleries sell paintings on consignment or for commission. Many painters have or have had more than one dealer. Once a painting is sold, it has a life of its own and may turn up in another gallery or in the hands of a broker.

The number of art galleries in France cannot be ascertained. (Published sources are inconsistent.) The Comité professionel des galeries d'art, a select group established in 1947 to represent mainly Paris art galleries, claimed 81 members in early 1958 and 115 members in October of 1962. The total number of art dealers in Paris, without distinguishing quality of merchandise sold, is about four-hundred.[1] Because my interest was primarily in the market for new art, I interviewed seventy-five dealers chosen at random from among the 115 members of the Comité professionel. These interviews form the basis of the following discussion.

From Art Brokerage to International Commerce

Brokers and Collector-Dealers

Many art brokers pay no licensing fee. Having no legal existence, they are little known except to insiders in one sector or another of the art market. Many are wealthy individuals who began as collectors; they are joined by painters' widows, wives of painters whose work is not yet selling or is selling badly, the young painters who occasionally deal in painting as a sideline. Other brokers are people who move on the fringes of high society; for them, selling painting is a means of access. Salesmen who learned the art of selling in other branches of commerce rub elbows with both scholars who deal in painting to finance their passion for art or research and former gallery employees interested in becoming dealers but lacking financial resources to operate alone. Art brokerage is ennobled by the occasional participation of some of the most illustrious names in the art world. Likewise, it is discredited by insincere status-seekers and the occasional crook, who thrive in a bustling but disorganized market. Of course, the vast majority of art brokers fall somewhere between these extremes.

Some art brokers are interested mainly in the work of painters no longer living. They trade at public auctions or privately with collectors and dealers. A collector will sometimes engage a broker to represent him at an auction. "That kind of work is the private preserve of dealers and brokers. I had three brokers representing me at one auction, where a painting I wanted was to be sold. It sold very low, for 500 Francs. I gave each broker 50 Francs. So the painting cost me 650 Francs—practically nothing." [C39] Brokers act not only as buyers but also as artistic advisers. Those who specialize in established painting are sometimes given charge of major collections, while others make the rounds of the auction houses. The major houses dealing in old art maintain agents worldwide.

Other brokers prefer to deal in current painting. Almost all are forced to sell older works, however, if only to help collectors whose tastes are evolving to get rid of earlier acquisitions. By contrast, many brokers specializing in older art will not deal in modern art at all, either because they have no appreciation of it or because their dealers and clients have no interest in it.

With so many galleries selling modern art, why are modern art brokers necessary at all? Brokers themselves answered this question in a variety of ways.

Why do collectors buy from me rather than from a gallery? For a number of reasons. There is a psychological aspect: they come to me looking for bargains as they might go to a flea market. Mr. X, a collector, frequently calls to see if I have anything "interesting." Some collectors don't like buying from galleries; they don't like "gallery goods." They're afraid of being had, of buying one of those "roving canvases" that go from gallery to gallery. Last but not least, a lot of brokers buy paintings from one gallery and sell them to another. Galleries can't visit one another, so to speak. . . . I never buy from painters and almost never at auctions. I buy from collectors and galleries. And I sell to a lot of foreign dealers and to foreign as well as French collectors, even small collectors with only three to four paintings. I have never lost a single client. I work mainly with a few galleries, just four or five. . . . A lot of people go hungry in this business. Yet I just don't see how anyone can fail. It's a very good business. The biggest years were 1958–1961. Overall the market was down in 1962, but it didn't affect me personally. My only regret is that I never committed myself fully to the business. People frequently offered to put up money to finance me, but it's a different business when you're spending other people's money. [N.H.]

I was a painter but I couldn't live on my painting. . . . I considered my work as a broker a sideline. It was work. You have to stay in touch. Prices change from week to week. You have to keep an eye on the public auctions, the careers of painters, who's just signed with whom and who's just broken with whom. . . . I work on commission. I buy from a few dealers, from other brokers, from collectors, and occasionally from painters. I sell to dealers, brokers, and collectors who are actually dealers in disguise. This is how it works. Take a painting that sells for 1,000 Francs a point. The gallery gives me at least twenty percent off because I'm a dealer. So it costs me 800 Francs a point. If I'm hard up for cash, I can sell it for 850. Profits are very uneven. Commissions have to be divided among so many people! When things are going well, I can average 1,000 Francs a month. [H.M.]

Brokers thus create a sort of "parallel market" that keeps prices flexible despite dealers' attempts to fix them. Brokers will sometimes go directly to the artist, cutting dealers out. "A broker came to see me. He offered to buy four of my paintings for 2 million francs, which is half what they'd bring in a gallery. It's a kind of black market. I refused, but the offer was tempting because for me in the short run it came to the same thing." [P249]

Speculators work closely with brokers to ensure that the parallel market stays hot. "When you want to trade canvas for canvas, you go to a dealer. When all you want is cash, you go to a broker." [C63] Brokers know their collectors and their holdings, and they know the gaps in each collection. Through brokers paintings change hands discreetly without outsiders' knowing who is buying or selling. Brokers have no reserves of capital or paintings. In some cases a number of brokers will cooperate on a deal, each taking a share of the painting.

Even more elusive than the brokers are the collectors who speculate in art. A few have dealings so extensive that they should really be considered brokers in disguise or camouflaged dealers. Some collectors offer regular monthly stipends to painters in return for all or part of their output. Some of these paintings are then resold. Collectors who engage in this activity are not unlike dealers who hold works by certain painters (waiting for prices to rise) and thus become, in a sense, collectors.

Dealers in Established Works

In this section I consider dealers specializing in painting whose cultural value is established; what they sell is essentially safe investments. In this they are not unlike antique dealers, "sellers of all and makers of nothing."[2] Their artistic judgment is determined by the judgment of history. Error is possible only in the identification and authentication of works. Yet nothing requires these dealers to deal only in the tried and true. As Daniel-Henry Kahnweiler remarked: "Many dealers buy and sell commodities

that are in demand. But someone could have set out to do in older painting what I did in modern painting. For example, someone could have
bought El Grecos or Vermeers or La Tours in 1900."[3] In other words,
dealers in older painting can seize the initiative by buying works from periods for which there is no current demand.

In setting prices on old masters, dealers have relatively little latitude.
Prices of paintings by a particular painter are determined by the amount
paid at auction for works of similar quality. If two collectors of international stature bid up the price of a painter's work at auction, gallery prices
will also rise. Dealers must decide whether to hold a work in inventory or
sell it immediately. Among the factors influencing the decision are the size
of the gallery's holdings and cash reserves and the quality of the work.

Dealers compete fiercely for famous works. Duveen is said to have
bribed servants in aristocratic households so that he might know the minute a Roman prince or English duke found himself in difficult financial
straits. Dealers compete for important clients. Lawsuits between rival galleries are common. Competition among art dealers is as fierce as that
among robber barons in the heyday of American capitalism.

Successful dealers owe their good fortune not to theoretical knowledge
(which few possess) but to taste and practical knowledge acquired through
experience. "The dealer knows his trade as the peasant knows his land."[4]
The entrepreneur relies on his artistic adviser; similarly, the dealer in established painting relies on the art historian whenever his practical knowledge
falls short. Nevertheless, success depends primarily on business sense, including bold purchases and shrew manipulation. Joseph Duveen, for example, maneuvered his clients the way Napoleon manipulated enemy armies
at Austerlitz without their being aware of what was happening.

Leading international dealerships have been held in families for many
years, and the bigger houses are not unlike dynasties. Consider Wildenstein, whose position in the traditional art market is rather like that of
Rothschild in banking. In 1870 Nathan Wildenstein (1851–1934) opted for
French citizenship. After moving to Vitry-le-François he established himself in the textile business. One day, by chance, he was commissioned to
sell a portrait from the School of Van Dyck. This kindled his interest in
the sale of painting. In 1875 he opened an art gallery in rue Laffitte; in
1890 the gallery moved to more prestigious quarters at 46, rue faubourg
Saint-Honoré. He established contacts with New York dealers and
through them obtained a number of leading American collectors as customers. Although he never crossed the Atlantic himself, a branch of the
gallery was established on Fifth Avenue in New York City in 1902. Three
years later Wildenstein crowned his achievements by moving to distinguished eighteenth-century quarters in rue La Boétie. The business was
built on the sale of older paintings, particularly the eighteenth-century

works in fashion in the latter part of the last and the early part of this century. His knowledge of art, though acquired without the aid of schools, was nevertheless considerable. He was aided by a sure eye and a prodigious memory. His commercial genius is summed up in a maxim that many other dealers have adopted for their own: "Boldness in buying, patience in selling. Never hurry. Time does not count."[5]

Upon Nathan's death in 1934, his son Georges Wildenstein (1892–1963) became head of the gallery, now with branches in Paris, New York, London, and Buenos Aires. While Nathan had confined himself to the eighteenth century, Georges had been buying Degas, Renoirs, Cézannes, and Monets, which enabled him to emerge triumphantly from the Depression. "From then on his power grew steadily."[6] "Learn to wait" remained the golden rule, made easier to follow by having a vast stock of paintings upon which to trade. The strongrooms of the New York branch held "2,000 paintings worthy of the best museums:"

> 400 primitives; a Fra Angelico; two Botticellis; eight Rembrandts; an equal number of Rubens; three Velazquez—a very rare painter; nine El Grecos; five Tintorettos, one more than thirteen feet high; four Titians; and twelve Poussins. Last summer there were seventy-nine Fragonards alongside seven Watteaus. . . . The moderns turn over more quickly. Wildenstein never has fewer than twenty Renoirs on hand, along with fifteen Pissarros, ten Cézannes, ten Van Goghs, ten Gauguins, ten Corots, and twenty-five Courbets. Of the three hundred paintings done by Seurat, coveted by all the museums, no fewer than ten can be found in Wildenstein's New York basement. At one time there were 250 Picassos. Wildenstein sold them all; he doesn't like Picasso. Imagine the buyer's stupefaction before such opulence. One buyer comes in, interested in the Spanish School. An order is given, and the delighted and dazzled client sees ten of the best known Goyas displayed before his eyes. The few people who have been privileged to visit the basement storerooms at Wildenstein's all agree: this is Ali Baba's cave.[7]

Wildenstein's capital reserves give the gallery unlimited buying power, and it has often bought entire collections outright—the Kahn in 1907, the Fould in 1927, the Schmitz in 1936, the Weil in 1938, and the Goldmann in 1940.[8] An international network of agents and brokers keeps Wildenstein informed when single works are available for sale or when a gap in some major collection needs filling.

The gallery also maintains a substantial, well-organized library of information on art. The library holds 100,000 photographs, 300,000 books, and 100,000 sale catalogues.[9] This vast accumulation no doubt reflects Georges Wildenstein's scholarly tastes, but it is also essential if one wishes to do a rational business in old painting. Help is often sought from specialists, art historians, and other experts. A long collaboration with Bernard Berenson continued until Berenson's death.

Georges Wildenstein bought the *Gazette des beaux-arts,* found in 1859 by Charles Blanc, and in 1924 established a weekly magazine called *Arts.* His son Daniel worked with Jean-Gabriel Domergue (1889–1962), curator of the Musée Jacquemart-André in Paris, to organize a series of exhibitions.

Wildenstein's influence has been so powerful that renewed current interest in various periods in the history of art is due in part to him. There is a corollary to the dictum "learn to wait," namely, buy what is not in fashion. "For fifty years his personal folly was to buy Poussins that nobody could get rid of. He has never regretted it."[10] It is hardly surprising, therefore, that appraisers, dealers, brokers, and collectors paid close attention to what Wildenstein bought, especially when those purchases seemed to reveal some pattern. Conversely, his outspoken hostility to abstract art made him suspect to proponents of abstraction, who saw his hand in all the campaigns and "plots" against nonfigurative art. His ways with competitors were sometimes rough, as evidenced by a 1955 New York wiretapping case, which ended in the conviction of Wildenstein's United States vice-president, E.H. Roussek. Wildenstein's relations with certain government officials have been analyzed in an article by André Chastel, who attacks the influence of powerful businessmen on what is supposed to be a disinterested activity.[11] A writer who can hardly be called an enemy of the Wildensteins offers little by way of defense: "A few years ago, he [Georges Wildenstein] amused himself by proposing a budget for the ministry of culture to a friend of his who happened to be secretary of the National Assembly's committee on the arts. Truthfulness compels me to say that the budget was approved by unanimous vote."[12]

Wildenstein's supporters and detractors have jointly fostered a "Wildenstein myth," elements of which include his fabulous wealth, his international power, his behind-the-scenes influence, his racing stables, and of course his art collections. Some considered his election to the Académie des Beaux-Arts on 27 March 1963 an unfortunate ratification of the worst capitalist methods, others a just reward for a distinguished career. But Wildenstein is just one example—more spectacular than others but not fundamentally different—of the art dealer's ambiguous function. Profiting from what is in essence a "free" good, the dealer feels guilty and frustrated and seeks to justify his activities to himself and others by engaging in noble and unselfish pursuits. Inevitably, however, the fabulous profits earned from sales of painting cast doubt—rightly or wrongly—on his good faith.

Some dealers, like Wildenstein, are big businessmen with extensive worldwide interests; they use scientific management techniques and enjoy

contacts with influential political leaders. Others run relatively small operations. Smaller galleries are often begun by successful brokers or people
who inherit a collection. Through contacts in high society they quickly
learn when a death, divorce, or business reverse is likely to result in the
sale of all or part of a collection. The prices of old masters are so high,
however, that such small dealers cannot afford to maintain an inventory.
Working on commission, they act simply as intermediaries between two
collectors or between a collector and a museum. Painters refer sarcasti-
cally to the shops of such small dealers as *maisons de passe.*

Art dealers, I have suggested, are either traditional or entrepreneurial.
The distinction, though useful analytically, it not always clear in practice.
Even Wildenstein, the archetype of the traditional dealer, championed
some contemporary painters. Knoedler & Co., which sells large numbers
of old masters in the United States, also handles Poliakoff, Vieira da
Silva, and Olivier Debré. Major impressionist dealers also show works by
living painters (sometimes on consignment). Avant-garde galleries, on the
other hand, often hedge their bets by keeping an impressionist painting or
cubist paper-and-glue construction in the back room, if only to tide them
over in difficult months. The pure ideal types are not the galleries most
commonly encountered in practice. Yet the pure types do exist; there are
dealers in old masters who have no commercial contact whatsoever with
current art, and there are entrepreneurs who handle no paintings other
than those done by artists they have under contract.

Resellers of Contemporary Painting

Some dealers handle works by contemporary artists not under contract to
them. They act as intermediaries between an auction gallery, dealer, or
collector and a client (possibly another dealer, collector, or broker). They
do not buy directly from the artist. Dealers with substantial financing and
an international clientele can drive up the price of an artist's work. For example, a big Left Bank dealer will buy, at dealer's prices, the work of an
artist under contract to a major gallery and then turn around and sell that
work at a higher price to a wealthy foreign client or another dealer. Picasso drawings are generally less expensive at the Louise Leiris Gallery
than anywhere else, but not just anyone can buy them. Regular clients, resellers, and collectors have priority. Demand exceeds supply, so the price
increases with each transaction.

Resellers can also drive prices down. A gallery with an exclusive contract tries to maintain a certain level of prices for a given painter's work,
but resellers are not obliged to ask the official price. Having acquired
paintings from a painter's dealer or early speculators, they are free to reduce prices to stimulate interest in the work. Along with brokers, resellers

are key players in the "parallel market," where monopolist dealers cannot control prices.

Resellers are not prophets. They are interested in paintings of proven commercial value and follow rather than anticipate the desires of their customers. These buyers and sellers of works of art have no personal commitment to the artists. Since they deal in paintings that have already been sold, their risks are minimal, and their actions have limited influence on the fortunes of the artist. Resellers are the most common type of dealer in contemporary art but not the most typical.

Entrepreneurs

Paul Durand-Ruel (1831–1922), Ambroise Vollard (1865–1939), and Daniel-Henry Kahnweiler (1884–1979) typify the new breed of art dealer. Like the publisher, this new type of dealer enters into contracts with producers of works which he then turns into commercial properties. He thus helps gain social acceptance for new art. Such art dealers are entrepreneurs of a unique kind.

An Exemplary Career: Daniel-Henry Kahnweiler

In an engaging memoir of his life, D.-H. Kahnweiler deliberately paints his activities in a simple light.[13] "I don't have any secrets. I know only one way to sell paintings, which is to get hold of some and wait for people to come buy them. No mystery about it. . . . It's all so simple. There's no secret, you see."[14] Entertaining as it is, this book does little to demystify the work of the art dealer. Similarly, Vollard's *Souvenirs* affect a naiveté that fails to carry conviction.[15]

Kahnweiler is best known for his dealings in cubist art. He was the cubist dealer when cubist painting was not selling, and he has remained the cubist dealer ever since. In 1907, around the time when the center of the art business moved from the rue Laffitte to the vicinity of the Madeleine, Kahnweiler opened his first large gallery at 28, rue Vignon. From 1914 to 1919 this gallery was forced to suspend operations. After the war, in 1920, Kahnweiler opened another gallery in partnership with André Simon at 29 bis, rue d'Astorg. In 1943, anti-Jewish policies made it expedient to change the gallery's name, so the Simon Gallery became the Louise Leiris Gallery, a name which was kept when it moved in 1957 to 47, rue Monceau in a neighborhood that became the center of the postwar art trade.

Born 25 June 1884 at Mannheim, Kahnweiler moved with his parents to Stuttgart five years later.

"My parents were of good bourgeois stock. My father was in finance. He was as we would now say a commission agent, representing one of my uncles in London, who was a stockbroker, what we call in France an outside broker. At that time a lot of people were interested in gold mines, and he handled some large transactions. That was what my father did for a living. . . . We were comfortable but not especially wealthy.[16]

Kahnweiler's family wanted him to be a banker, while he dreamed as an adolescent of becoming an orchestra conductor. In 1902 he came to Paris and worked for two and a half years for an exchange agent; he continued his training in finance in London until 1907. At that point his family agreed to let him try his luck at selling art; they gave him 1,000 pounds (25,000 francs in gold) and one year to prove that he could succeed.

Today he compares his calling with his youthful desire to become an orchestra conductor; he sees his work as an art dealer as a displacement of his need to create.

Fundamentally, I think, it was the same desire, the same need, that drove me to become an art dealer. I knew that I was not a creator but, how shall I put it? an intermediary in a relatively noble sense of the word, if you like, since I wasn't capable of composing. I later found in painting a way of helping those whom I considered to be great painters by serving as intermediary between them and the public, clearing a path for them and helping to free them from material worries. If the profession of art dealer has any moral justification, that has to be it. When I was young, my greatest pleasure was to applaud music that I liked while other people hissed and booed. It was the same with painting: it gives me pleasure to stand up for what I like.[17]

How did he decide which artists to support? He had no contacts in the art business. "I knew nobody. In Paris I knew only stock exchange people, people with whom I had worked when I was at the Bourse. I knew one or two dealers from whom I bought prints. That was it. I knew no dealers, collectors, painters, or critics."[18] He knew, however, that painting played a vital part in his life. At the Stuttgart Museum he had acquainted himself with sixteenth-century German painting. He completed his artistic education at the Louvre, the Luxembourg Museum, the National Gallery, and the salons (Salon des Artistes français, Salon de la Société nationale des beaux-arts, Salon des Indépendants, and Salon d'Automne). He started by collecting reproductions, then prints.

I had two Cézanne lithographs, quite a few Lautrecs, a very beautiful Manet, *The Barricade*—things like that. . . . I tried to collect engravings and prints by painters whose paintings I liked. I also owned a Renoir print, for instance. You can see it from here. And I owned a Sisley lithograph as well as prints by artists who have since come to be called neo-Impressionists or Pointillists. Seurat made no prints, but I had works by Signac and Cross. That should give you some idea of the kind of small collection I had put together.[19]

Kahnweiler quickly made up his mind to back the painters of his own generation: "I loved Cézanne. I loved Gauguin even more than I do today. But it never occurred to me that I might get to know them; that wasn't what I wanted. When I decided to become a dealer, it never occurred to me to buy Cézannes. Those painters belonged to the past, or so I thought, and my role was to fight for painters of my own age."[20] In choosing painters he trusted to instinct: "I had read plenty of weighty tomes about older painting. But my reading was of no help in making aesthetic choices. It served me as a historical and intellectual guide, if you like, but as far as aesthetics were concerned I had to find my own way, and I don't think I've changed very much since those days."[21] Of cubism he says "the painting affected me physically right from the start."[22] In an interview he claimed that "I was convinced I was right, convinced that I knew what I was doing."[23]

Kahnweiler's first contracts were with Vlaminck, Derain, and Braque; a little later he signed Van Dongen. "Matisse was already with Fénéon (at Bernheim-Jeune). I came on the scene too late for him. Otherwise I would have signed him because I liked his work a great deal."[24] Although he first met Picasso in 1907, no contract was signed until 1912. "Picasso was and has remained far too suspicious a man to sign immediately with a young man from God knows where whose foolhardy business venture might easily have gone under."[25] Agreements with Gris, Léger, and Manolo followed soon after.

Business was interrupted by the war, during which Léonce Rosenberg made sure that Kahnweiler's artists continued to eat. Kahnweiler's confiscated holdings were sold in four sales held in 1921–1923. He himself bought back a number of paintings through agents. Few dealers were interested. Even the American museums ignored the painters whose works were up for sale. "The people who bought them were mainly young writers and poets such as André Breton, Tristan Tzara, Paul Eluard, and Armand Salacrou,"[26] joined by a few American buyers.

In 1920 Kahnweiler reestablished contact with his gallery's painters. Other artists joined the prewar group: the sculptor Laurens, the Lascaux painters, and André Masson. "Other names were gradually added to the list: Suzanne Roger, Kermadec, Beaudin, and later Rouvre. I hope I'm not leaving anybody out. I also bought paintings from a few others, such as Borès, but that didn't last."[27] Some of the early recruits left: Vlaminck and Derain in 1923, partly for financial reasons and partly because of their hostility to cubism; and Braque and Léger because Paul Rosenberg outbid

Kahnweiler. Picasso followed them. "He never had a contract with Paul Rosenberg, but Rosenberg was a wealthy man and bought a lot of paintings. By 1923 Picasso was selling to me again, and we did a growing volume of business until finally, much later, we reached an entirely new understanding."[28] The only one of the four great cubists who remained loyal despite more attractive offers was Juan Gris.

The basic idea underlying Kahnweiler's business activities is simple and clear: "I had but one idea about how to make money in art: buy the works of the great painters of your day while they are still young and you ought to turn a profit."[29] His aim was not to sell paintings for which a demand already existed but to promote a new kind of painting: "I wanted, if I can put it this way, to be a dealer who held up for the public to admire the works of painters about whom they knew nothing and who needed a start."[30]

Although Kahnweiler describes his sales methods as "silly," they produced results. Early in his career he had the idea of buying everything a painter painted; he was the first to employ the monopoly contract.

> In those days I made written contracts, which I no longer do. Today, when I make a deal with a painter, what matters is that there is perfect good faith on both sides (and truly, I've never been disappointed), but there is nothing in writing. In those days, though, I used contracts. The painter agreed to sell me all his works. I agreed to buy them, and the price was set by the 'number,' that is, the dimensions of the painting, as was customary. . . . For my part, in any case, it's been years now, dozens of years, since I signed a contract with a painter. Now the deal is sealed with our word of honor only, just a friendly agreement with no contract, nothing in writing, not one word.[31]

Kahnweiler likes to emphasize not the contract but the personal relationship between artist and dealer, which he thinks should be trusting and friendly. "I must tell you how friendly our relations were, how we trusted each other. It was not at all the way people imagine, war between painter and dealer. On the contrary, we worked together in complete trust."[32] For Kahnweiler, the basis of this trust is the mutual interest of painter and dealer. "The dealer is the painter's representative. His aim is to free those whom he considers great painters from material worries. . . . Our understanding was based on mutual esteem and interest."[33]

Thus Kahnweiler's two leading principles were these: sell the work of innovative painters and secure a monopoly of their production. His third principle was to buy and sell young painters' paintings at low prices. An art dealer should enable his painters to earn enough to live and work, but it is a mistake, according to Kahnweiler, to set prices for contemporary painting too high (as they were in the late nineteenth century and are again today). On this question he invokes the authority of Picasso, who argues that if an artist's work is eventually to be worth a lot, it should be sold cheaply when the artist is young.[34]

Kahnweiler seems to have regarded his understandings with artists as commitments to the future. As long as he deemed an artist's work aesthetically interesting, he paid a monthly stipend regardless of sales. Large number of paintings in inventory did not frighten him. "They will sell two years hence, twenty years hence, thirty years hence, but in any case they are there to be sold. My method has been never to hide anything. I don't see the point of it."[35] Convinced that demand for a painter's work is what makes prices rise, he never "overprices" a painting for publicity purposes. He sells each painting at the price he would be prepared to pay to buy it back, with due allowance for his costs; this, he says, is the only guarantee of a healthy market, but it of course requires strong confidence that one has made the right aesthetic choices. "My young colleagues' prices are too high. If there is an economic downturn of any kind, I'm afraid that prices of the work of younger painters will drop precipitously."[36]

Kahnweiler shuns advertising of any kind.

> People usually think that an art dealer "launches" painters with a lot of fanfare and publicity. Well, I've never spent a penny on so much as a newspaper announcement. . . . The last show I did before 1914 was the Braque show in November of 1908, which was when Vauxcelles introduced the word "cube." What's more, the painters I bought from didn't show in any Salon; we were agreed on that. We held no more shows at rue Vignon . . . which proves that we held not only the critics but the majority of the public in absolute contempt. Nowadays such things are unimaginable, because with this pseudo-painting flourishing in the Salons these days and with those pretentious styles of appliqué known as abstraction and tachism, there's nothing left to get angry or laugh about."[37]

Kahnweiler is fond of collectors as well as painters. Not that he has many illusions about the average man's perceptiveness: "People think that, had they lived in Cézanne's day, they would have bought dozens of Cézannes. The truth is, they wouldn't have bought any."[38] But he speaks warmly of prominent collectors, including his friends from the early days: Roger Dutilleul, Hermann Rupf, Shchukin, Morosov, Gertrude Stein, and W. Uhde. And he refuses to accuse collectors of speculating on art. Experience has been his teacher. He knew collectors who bought cubist painting when it was still cheap. Now most of his clients are foreigners. "In this business export sales far outweigh local sales."[39]

What about the dealer's relation to the works he sells? Kahnweiler is widely recognized as a connoisseur. Those who accuse him of selling less good paintings and keeping better ones for himself only pay homage to his taste. He has his own art collection: "It consists of paintings I like a great deal, but I feel no jealousy when a collector buys a painting that I also like. I wouldn't want to own them all. I take as many as my walls can hold, no more."[40]

Georges Wildenstein said: "Paintings interest me more than painters. Had I known my favorite painters, perhaps I would have liked their painting less."[41] Compare this with Kahnweiler's attitude: "I am not a collector but, like Saint Paul, more a fisher of men than of paintings."[42] The contrast between these two statements points up the difference in attitude between dealers who handle old painting and those who promote contemporary art.

The Economic Function of the Dealer-Entrepreneur

"To act with confidence beyond the range of familiar beacons and to overcome [resistance to change] requires aptitudes that are present in only a small fraction of the population and that define the entrepreneurial type as well as the entrepreneurial function."[43] The entrepreneurial type of art dealer is an innovator, a dynamic market agent. He does not sell established art works for which a demand already exists but aims to discover and promote new kinds of painting. Some entrepreneurs are forced by circumstances to innovate. Others like to speculate. Still others are drawn to novelty. In any case the entrepreneurial dealer plays a creative role.

> Around 1935 I went into the art business in a rather bohemian way, without any capital. My problem was to find a way of earning a living so I could remain in Paris. I took an interest in progressive art because no capital was necessary. I made very little money, incidentally. I bought works at low prices from painters who were not highly rated. In 1935 I bought certain surrealist paintings for 1,000 francs and resold them for 2,000. [D155]

> I'm always interested in what hasn't yet made it. It's a matter of taste, and anyway I can't afford to buy anything else. [D121]

> I love discovering painters, and I didn't have enough money to do it as a collector. I like to be the first buyer and then have other people clamoring for the work. [D138]

> I try to understand how this work relates to other contemporary works. Any important work throws a fresh light on subject and technique. The byproducts wander off into mannerism. [D166]

To discover and champion new forms of art: that is the heart of the matter.
[D142]

The innovative dealer is betting on an unknown quantity. His goal is to bring new work to the attention of the public and to attract buyers. Convinced that new forms of art will sooner or later find admirers, he tries to anticipate how the tastes and wants of his customers will evolve.

The artist, of course, is the true innovator. The dealer's innovation is of a different kind: the painter's work is primary, the dealer's secondary. The successful dealers are the ones who sign the great painters. Since we cannot rank living painters on purely aesthetic grounds, we also cannot predict what current art dealers will be remembered by history.

Even if the dealer's innovation is only secondary, its effects are decisive in a system where the artist's livelihood depends on the market. "Innovativeness" is my basis for classifying entrepreneurial dealers. We may assume that all dealers are capable of rational economic calculation; some are unwilling to support innovative painters, while others make such support the cornerstone of their business. Some avoid risk and stick to proven practices, while others venture out upon risky waters. What separates the dynamic from the conservative entrepreneur is the type of painting sold: traditional or new. Aesthetically, however, it is hard to say where authentic innovation lies. Without hindsight how can we tell the truly innovative from the merely fashionable painting of the moment? Galleries have been constantly adventurous since the turn of the century, but the market's capacity to absorb novelty has also increased greatly, driving some painters and many dealers to seek novelty at all costs, even at the risk of mistaking what is really new. This dangerous trend threatens the very essence of painting. The market is increasingly governed by a mystique of the new, of which some dealers are cynical beneficiaries and others victims. The meaning of an artistic revolution, like that of a political revolution, is a question that only the future can answer. Each new wave of innovation vanishes more quickly than the last, and some dealers and collectors are invariably left stranded when the wave they were riding suddenly collapses.

The dealer finances the artist; the money he provides enables the painter to live and work. The sources of this money depend on the generation to which the dealer belongs. Dealers old enough to have lived at a time when avant-garde art was still inexpensive were able to speculate on new art without large reserves of capital. Having built up large inventories of works that have since become famous, these dealers can afford to support unknown and unheralded artists. Other dealers made money selling relatively undemanding works of modern art during or just after the war;

they are now able to support painters condemned for years to a wretched existence by Nazi hostility to modernism, to say nothing of widespread public incomprehension of their work.

By contrast, dealers who began doing business in the 1950s without vast inventories faced a very different problem of financing. Living art became remunerative after the war, and young artists sought high prices for their work. Opening a gallery or sponsoring a group of painters required a substantial investment. "To get back to the question of the young dealer today, I don't think you can start a gallery nowadays and buy only younger painters. At some point I think you'd get into trouble. Even if you could sell the work at low prices, you wouldn't make enough money to support the painters. And if you tried selling at high prices, I just don't think you'd do very well."[44]

Young dealers have solved this problem in various ways. Some have turned to their families for support, at least temporarily. Others act as brokers, keeping a few good paintings in the back room for buyers who can afford them. Still others take paintings on consignment, without paying the artist any advance. And some go into business with silent partners.

> A lot of financing comes from outside the art world, generally from private French financiers. [D158]

> It is well known that certain Swiss galleries are supported by the banks. And it is likely that some large French galleries are financed by loans from foreign banks. [D170]

Dealers carefully calculate their business strategy. The profession requires good business sense combined with keen aesthetic judgment. The first decision a dealer must face is how many artists to support. Most claim to rely on intuition. Vollard explained: "How did I become acquainted with Cézanne's work? The first painting of his I saw, of a river bank, was in the window of a paint shop in rue Clauzel, old Tanguy's place. It was as if somebody hit me in the stomach."[45] And Kahnweiler described his reaction: "My temperature goes up when it's hot and down when it's cold. In other words, I make my choice on the basis of what I feel while looking at the painting."[46] Several other dealers concurred: "It's purely a matter of instinct" [D167]; "You can smell greatness." [D113]

But intuition, I think, is only part of the story:

> How do I, as a soldier in the wars of the marketplace, make up my mind? Well, first of all, my attention is called to a painter's work by other painters or critics. As I look at the first few paintings, something happens that I can't analyze. I feel excited or dizzy or faint. I become the painting as I look at it. And I also feel a sense of pride.

Then I try to add depth to my judgment, building on my initial intuition. I try to find out all I can about the painter and his work. I look for a style that is new and still developing. I have to see a number of paintings before I can tell whether the first one was an aberration or part of the mainstream of the painter's work. I try to understand how this work relates to other contemporary works.

I seek out the painter. The only objective guide is the painter's personality. Real painters are interested in technical problems. Technique enables a painter to capitalize on luck. It's not purely a question of getting a mental image down on canvas. The process is more dialectical; the true artist never simply projects a ready-made image. What counts is the number of simple, limited problems to which a man is able to find ingenious solutions. F.'s problem, for example, was the following: how to regain a lost spontaneity. The problem was simple and clear, and he knew what he was doing.

I take the painting home to see if my feelings survive familiarity. But I do not make comparisons. Comparison is possible when you're dealing dispassionately with works of the past. Mummies don't mind being compared. But it's an illusion of hindsight to think that works of art cohabit the way paintings in a museum do. Those [painters'] talents were seen differently in their time. [D166]

Looking back, dealers always attach too much importance to their own intuition. A close look at who actually contributes to the discovery of an artist shows that the dealer is practically never the first; painters and critics preselect the works that come to the attention of dealers. Vollard, by listening to what was said around Tanguy's shop and talking to Pissarro, quickly discovered that Cézanne was the impressionist most likely to achieve greatness and the only one without a real dealer of his own; in hindsight this knowledge was translated into the statement, "It was as if somebody hit me in the stomach." In reality, Vollard's great strength was his ability to ask questions and listen to the answers. Even the most perceptive dealers are cautious enough to make choices only at second hand— which does not reduce the weight of the final decision. The greatest danger a dealer faces is that, as he grows older, his tastes will become more rigid.

Once the basic choice is made, the dealer must examine the state of the market, his own (or his partners') finances, and the demand that exists (or can be created) for the work of the painters he intends to support. Then he can make his selection: a minimum of four or five artists, a maximum of thirty. The soundest decision from a financial standpoint is to choose a group consisting of both "established" painters and younger unknowns. The most dynamic group is one composed of younger artists engaged in similar avenues of artistic exploration.

After choosing "his" artists, the dealer arranges to "promote" them.

The goal is to take a painter in whom he believes (but thus far known only to a small number of artists, critics, and connoisseurs) and create a "name" able to command a good price in the marketplace. To that end the dealer will organize one-man and group shows, enter the work in international exhibitions, and, if he is so inclined and has the resources, bid on the painter's work at public auction in order to drive up the price.[47] He will also try to publicize the work through catalogues, private editions, and international competitions (by pressuring jury members to award prizes to his protégé). He will contact important people in the art world and use his influence with experts and collectors. In short, the dealer helps the artist overcome the obstacles to fame and fortune. Commercial success requires substantial investment; the strategy of that investment is the dealer's province.

All the dealers interviewed maintain that the art market is governed by supply and demand and that the painter alone controls supply. True, the dealer has no legal power to compel the artist to do anything. His contract gives him the right to buy whatever the artist produces, but the painter is subject to no discipline and his output is unpredictable. "Painters are suppliers of a special kind. There is no automatic delivery schedule." [D118]

Do dealers really refrain from influencing their artists' output, even by indirect means such as the lure of money? Or do they try to persuade the artist to produce more "commercial" painting? The answer is all too clear. Some dealers succumb to temptation: to help business they push the artist to produce a certain kind of painting.

Dealers can also influence supply in another way: by manipulating their inventories. These policies vary from generation to generation. Dealers who started in business in the late nineteenth and early twentieth century were able to buy young artists' works at low prices. Over the long run they reaped huge profits by selling paintings from inventory as demand developed for them (without resorting to advertising). While Vollard sold Cézannes, his Rouaults remained in the cellar. Prices for Rouault did not begin to rise until a show was organized by Louis Carré in 1942, after Vollard's death.

For dealers with the requisite patience, waiting was still the royal road to success. As long as they remained confident of having made the right choices, it made sense to keep paintings in inventory: art doesn't wear out. Even if they made errors, their effect over the long run was negligible; the artist who did become famous made up for all the bad investments and more. "You can be wrong eighty percent of the time." [D113] Understandably, however, painters view dealers' attempts to regulate supply as a form of exploitation, regardless of whether the motive is speculative manipulation of the market or simple lack of buyers. One painter explained:

"They sell just enough of your paintings so you can live and keep all the rest. They buy six [paintings by a well-known painter] and sell one; the other five they hold on to, and they wait." [D113]

The economic climate after the Second World War forced a change in the way business was done. New dealers who opened galleries in the ebullient 1950s and 1960s were driven to engage in short-term speculation by artists clamoring for money, collectors bent on quick profits, and their own greed. It was a time for hasty decisions rather than long-term calculation, for a strategy of wheeling and dealing rather than waiting. "Dealers in the past frequently put works in storage when they couldn't sell them. Nowadays, in order to keep an inventory, you need a lot of capital, and if you store too many, the painter doesn't become known. In order to make a reputation you've got to let the paintings go." [D131]

The dealer's role as organizer is correctly summed up, I think, in the following interview:

A painter who seeks out a dealer is rarely if ever chosen. Artists become known in certain circles by word of mouth. That's what counts.

Once the artist obtains the gallery label, the long, hard job of organizing his career begins. You've got to set your sights on the long term.

The dealer's role is very important. I'm like a lawyer, but I choose my own cases, obscure cases that I happen to believe in. I wouldn't defend just anybody. And I have to make my judgment before other people make theirs.

The next step is to win over important collectors as allies. You've got to keep your eye on the long term and not sell to just anybody, to people who will turn right around and sell again. Who are they? There are perhaps fifty collectors who count, but they're widely scattered. Through the collectors you start the propaganda machine rolling. We make concessions in order to make sure that paintings go where we want them to go.

The critics also count. G. F. came tonight to see the current show. He was quite favorable. Another citadel fallen. The painter is worth more now than he was before. A lucky break: the critic liked the paintings. We didn't do anything to make it happen.

International prizes have some importance, but not as much as you might think. They don't boost prices right away. . . .

On prices, you understand, there's no turning back. So you have to be circumspect and move cautiously. You wait for a show to revise your price list, and you don't do it every year.

A book proves that a painter has arrived; it's good for his ego, but that's about it.

A gallery always has to be conscious of economic necessity. You've got to be a realist, even if reality is not necessarily fair.

As for T [a painter], frankly I didn't think things would move so quickly. But I've got to keep pace. There are collectors who have been waiting two years for one of his paintings. And don't get any ideas about this scarcity having been created deliberately.

B [another painter] is very much in demand right now, a regular fad. But we've got to slow things down. If we let go, he would collapse quickly.

In regulating supply you've got to be aware of two things. The work has to become known; you need propaganda. But then you've also got to think like a capitalist. The ideal is to strike a balance between the two.

Propaganda means letting the paintings go. Maintaining an inventory takes a lot of capital. Our only capital was the painters and our own work in the gallery. We had some private financing, but no banks as silent partners.

Some of my painters were formerly with another gallery, which put their works in storage and did nothing to publicize them. They came to me. I agreed to publicize them, to make propaganda. As a result their prices went up. I did M. B.'s job for him.

You don't buy a painting, you sell it.

Fénéon once said something like this: This is a profession in which you don't make money but you can make a fortune. Excuse me, I'm quoting from memory.

Our painters have won many international prizes. That simply means that our choices have been good ones.[D131]

Exploitation of painters is a product of the system more than of any individual. Painters combat it by capitalizing on competition between dealers. Well-endowed dealers lure painters away from rival galleries. In fact, the competition among galleries for painters is rather like the competition among sports teams for talented athletes. Painters allow themselves to be enticed, not because they are disloyal or ungrateful (despite dealers' laments of artists' "feminine infidelity," "prostitution," and "ingratitude") but because they feel compelled to protect themselves and their careers. From the Left Bank to the Right Bank and from there to Milan, London, New York, and other international art capitals, artists feel that they must climb the ladder of fame rung by rung. In a world of unbridled competition where security is unknown, is it surprising that painters will sell to the highest bidder? All things considered, the painter-dealer relationship is a struggle for power: when the painter is little known and not highly rated, the dealer is omnipotent, but an established painter is in a position to dictate terms to his dealer.

Innovator, financier, and organizer, the art dealer is also a risk-taker. The public's lack of understanding of new art is one source of risk. René Drouin organized two shows for Fautrier (1943 and 1945), two for Dubuffet (1945 and 1947), two for Wols (1945 and 1947), and three for Kandinsky (1946, 1948, and 1949). These nine shows resulted in very few sales, and paintings that did sell went for ridiculously low prices. (It is not always possible to "wait.") Durand-Ruel faced similar difficulties until he found a new market for his painters in the United States. So did Léonce Rosenberg, who went bankrupt before the war.

Another source of risk for dealers lies in their aesthetic commitment: they may bet on the wrong painter or school. When a dealer backs an artist, he knows he is staking his all. In the end he will be judged on the quality of his choices. Which painters did he champion and which did he reject? In the short term publicity may be able to create a passing fad and commercial success. A dealer who turns his paintings over quickly may, by shrewd calculation, compensate for dubious aesthetic choices. In the long run, however, the aesthetic value of the work is the only thing that counts. Even when the dealer doesn't risk his fortune, he always risks his reputation.

Unpredictable economic conditions are yet third source of risk. Art is a luxury good, and galleries, particularly those specializing in recent painting, are vulnerable to recession.

Dealers have responded to these problems in various ways, transforming the art market in the process. Yet the justification of dealer profits remains the same. Organizing a painter's career is hard work, for which a reasonable profit is just recompense. More important, the risk taken justifies the reward. Risk was cited by the Church in the Middle Ages as reason for permitting loans at interest; the economic value of this argument may have diminished, but its psychological force remains.

Ambiguous Motives

Some dealers are motivated primarily by the desire for profit.

> I was a painter, but I wanted to make money quickly. [D109]

> What I like is to buy a painting for 500 F and sell it for 5,000. I'm the one who lives in style, not the painter. [D177]

Hasn't love of money always been the merchant's most basic passion? To be fair, it must be conceded that profit has an economic function in a capitalist society: it is the basis of new investment. A portion of the profits earned on one artist's work can be reinvested in the work of other artists. Only the greediest dealers put accumulation ahead of economic duty. And the painters complain:

> He is a greedy man who likes painting and money. He doesn't give a fig about artists. [D227]

He is so stingy that he does nothing to enhance our reputations. He wants us to remain in obscurity so that we're beholden to him. It's slavery. [P213]

Speculation, in the form of gambling on the new, excites the younger avant-garde dealers.

A dozen of us are playing an extraordinary poker game on the younger painters. [D109]

I was at first scandalized by this wheeling and dealing, but then I got used to it. I speculate myself and find it quite exciting. It's a virus, and there's no escaping it. In any case, it's a more complicated business than people think. [D170]

People can speculate on anything, of course, but some things seem to lend themselves to speculation better than others: items not traded in a normal, routine manner and whose prices vary widely. Contemporary painting is an excellent case in point. Investing in newly discovered artists is a bold and often profitable form of investment. Nearly all dealers have a keen gambler's instinct and like to make discoveries:

A living painting is such a miracle that you never tire of searching for it. [D154]

I would be very uncomfortable with older painters. I definitely want to be with youth. What interests me is discovering and launching unknowns—putting artists on the map. [D156]

What interests me is discovering painters and staging their first shows. I take on one or two new painters a year. In the beginning I take paintings on consignment or buy a few. I'm not interested in established painters. [D169]

I buy the painters I like when nobody else likes them. What interests me is discovering painters throughout the world. I live in an airplane. Once a painter has begun to establish a reputation, I hand him over to a dealer with a good head for business. [D138]

Some dealers who describe themselves in these terms like to think of themselves as adventurous pioneers. Others resemble speculators in real estate. Having discovered virgin land in some likely tourist spot, they advertise the charms of the place, entice a few well-known customers through special deals, and sell vacant lots to all comers; then they use the profits generated to begin the same operation all over again in a new location.

Last but not least, dealers like to see themselves as men in heroic roles. "I am a soldier of art" and "I am an activist" are frequently heard. One dealer admitted: "I have a taste for noisy controversy. I love a fight. I like to fight for a cause. When the battle is won, I lose interest. But I can still take up cudgels in behalf of some of my artists who are not yet known *urbi et orbi.*" [D142] Compare this confession by a leading Paris dealer with Schumpeter's description of the entrepreneur's motives, which include "the dream and desire of founding a personal empire and usually, though not always, a dynasty as well. . . . Then comes the will to win. On the one hand a desire to fight, on the other to be successful for the sake of success itself. . . . Last but not least, there is the pleasure of creating a new kind of business."[48]

In their work some dealers may also find compensation for unsatisfied desires to create. By surrounding themselves with artists of a particular school, they create the illusion that they are somehow leading an orchestra. They do not make art history, but, in Lucien Febvre's phrase, they have a "right to history." "Becoming a dealer was a response to my failure as a painter, a way of escaping from myself, a kind of transference. From that moment I gave my all to my new line of work, twenty-four hours a day." [D166]

Unsatisfied creative urges, as well as the desire to emulate others and acquire prestige, make dealers like patrons of the arts, except that the disinterest of the patron is in contradiction with the logic of the dealer's profession.

When a dealer chooses to back a group of painters, his pride is at stake. [D166]

If he is merciless, it's not for money so much as for glory. [P227]

These motives are not mutually exclusive; usually they coexist. All art dealers are devoted to art in one way or another. When asked why they chose this line of work, all begin by saying that they cared about art. There is no obvious reason to question their sincerity, even if what they do is invariably influenced by economic necessities. Here we touch upon a fundamental ambiguity. The art dealer is a merchant, but the "merchandise" he sells is a work of art. The quest for the absolute and the pusuit of profit are inextricably intertwined in what Jacques Berque has called a "remarkable pastry," much as religion and economics were intertwined in the past in "divine accounting" and the "sacred marketplace."[49] Dealers try to conceal the mercantile aspects of their profession. In this they are merely playing the role expected of them by society, which, though ruled by profit, wants to protect the purity of its cultural values. They maintain that they "do their work as artists," that they "sell only what they like," that "art counts more than money," and that "every show is a statement of faith." Few dealers are fully aware of the ambivalent nature of their activity:

What's selling and what's not selling are things I pay no attention to. [D149]

I do this work as a priest. I am not an involved party. [D144]

[Painter X] has done well because he is good. He has done well because of my efforts. As a commodity I manufactured him. I take an aesthetic good and turn it into a commercial one. [D166]

Dealers, Artists, Collectors, and the Work of Art

Painters and dealers relate to one another both as human beings and as business partners: sometimes allies, sometimes enemies. In any case such relations are so complex and changeable that they are always to some extent mysterious. It is impossible to assign specific roles (in contrast to the relation between employer and employees or impresario and star). Between artist and dealer there is a personal tie not unlike that which existed between artist and patron in the past. Here, I want to make just two remarks, based on the remarkably consistent answers given by my interviewees. First, the relationship between artist and dealer evolves as their respective careers evolve. If both advance together (the artist becomes more famous as the dealer becomes wealthier), loyalty is possible; otherwise, not.

This relationship always involves a struggle for power. The unknown artist goes hat in hand from gallery to gallery and is more often than not shown the door. The most cynical comment I heard was the following: "Ten artists a day come in to show their work. It seems that a dealer once said, The only artists I want to see in my office are dead artists. I'm not far from sharing that thought." [D145] On the other hand, the unknown dealer without substantial financial backing goes to artists looking for paintings and is often rebuffed—even by younger artists without contracts—because he cannot offer the prestige and financial guarantees they seek.

The atmosphere in the studio when a dealer visits is determined by the balance of power.

You have to climb seven or eight flights of stairs. Beginning artists always live on the top floors. The painter's wife has put out cheap wine and cookies. She says that she is particularly fond of such and such a painting which her husband has not shown and asks him to pull it out. It's horribly painful, absolutely my worst fear. [D120]

He came in wearing a camel's-hair coat, looking like a banker. He had heard of me because I'd been included in some foreign show. He asked if I had any paintings anywhere else. When I answered no, he responded, "So, then, you're free?" He asked me to show him some paintings. "In what order?" I asked. "Chronological." He was interested in my paintings starting in such and such a year. He passed them in review the way a general inspects an army. His comments were brief: "That one hangs together, that's interesting." And then, pointing majestically with his finger at each painting, he said, "I'll take that one and that one and that one." Since no price was ever discussed, I finally got up the courage to ask as he was leaving. "See my secretary," he said. [P123]

The dealer is in command at the beginning, but later it's the painter who's in charge. I used to have to go to them to show my paintings, but now the dealers come to me, and they're polite about it. [P222]

The economic, social, and artistic climate of the 1950s and 1960s altered the nature of the painter-dealer relationship. Prices rose steeply, and painters demanded a more equitable distribution of the profits. This made some dealers bitter, even though they profited handsomely in these boom years. Dealers commonly accuse artists of pride, greed, and ingratitude.

They're not always easy to deal with. They're jealous of one another. I would like to establish a sort of community, but they all want to be number one. [D127]

There's no sympathy among painters. The only thing they have in common is me. [D165]

They're sensitive and awfully jealous of one another in every way, even in regard to me. I sometimes feel as though I'm keeping a harem. [D131]

Artists are bores. They're as sensitive as open wounds. They'll make a scene over a comma in a catalogue. The problem is to maintain a good relationship in spite of it all. [D109]

With few exceptions painters are very tough businessmen. [D111]

They come in looking disconsolate and saying they're willing to sell at any price. And then as soon as they've sold three paintings, they want to raise their prices. . . . For them the problem is making money. In the past artists worked for love, but not today. [D127]

Young painters are spoiled. They're rotten and greedy. [D158]

If the painter is exploited today, it's a temporary situation and the roles will soon be reversed. And everything seems natural. The minute a painter "comes out," he's no longer willing to settle for moral satisfaction; he wants money. The painters all compete for status. As proof of their talent they want to drive the best cars and to buy mink coats for their wives. [D157]

My relations with painters are very bad. I hate them, I detest them. They're all eccentrics. Some are downright deranged. E. used to be a factory worker. He's twenty-six years old. I show him in Paris and abroad. I pay him 200,000 francs a month. Well, for him that's not enough! They wear me down. [D166]

Painters don't interest me. Only their work interests me. You lose all emotional sympathy in this line of work. . . . I don't sign contracts, but I forbid my paint-ers to show their work anywhere else. As soon as their prices go up, they want a contract. Money is all they think about. [D177]

As for collectors, dealers sometimes treat them as collaborators in the discovery and promotion of an artist's work. When buyers known for dis-cerning taste purchase a work, the dealer's judgment is confirmed. It is an important step for an artist to have his work included in a collection of in-ternational importance, and every dealer is aware of this. Dealers, more-over, are well aware that collectors champion "their" painters in society circles, lending snobbish appeal to the work. Thus, the collector is an indis-pensable part of the campaign to establish an artist's reputation. When painter, dealer, and collector all "debut" at the same time, they some-times become friends.

The gallery's business is based on friendship. We're all fighting the same battle. [D165]

The collectors who take an interest in the gallery are friends. Friends become clients; clients become friends. [D128]

We worked hard to create an atmosphere, an ambiance. We invite collectors down here. They receive us in their homes. [D156]

Yet dealers in different types of galleries exhibit somewhat different atti-tudes toward collectors. Most critical were those who sell the most expen-sive paintings. Their clients lacked taste, they said, and knew nothing about art; they were vain, ostentatious, and, worst of all, interested mainly in speculative profits (unjustified by either work or risk). Vollard's *Souvenirs* are full of anecdotes, whether true or false, about the stupidity of parvenu collectors. My interviewees were no less harsh. "They buy whatever the dealer sells," was the leitmotif. "They buy with their ears and not their eyes."

When you first go into business, the problem is to find thirty imbeciles who will buy thirty paintings a year. . . . I keep a tight rein on my collectors. [D177]

A dealer with taste trains his clients, of course. But there is a huge gulf between those who love and understand painting and those who simply buy it. The ones who buy do not love. Why did so-and-so buy 400 drawings by F? The collectors we've been talking about haven't discovered anything. Or what they've discovered is garbage. They've been able to find paintings only through the galleries. . . . I don't see them often. My contacts with high society have not drawn me to it. [D166]

Ninety percent of buyers are speculators. Clients always ask the same question: Do you think the price will go up? They'll buy a painting at auction today and turn it over to a broker or an auction house two months from now. . . . Collectors buy on speculation in ninety percent of all cases. They're far more dishonest than we are. [D161]

Although dealers rarely admit to contempt for their clients except in private conversation, the important ones are generally reserved or condescending toward buyers. They want even the wealthiest and most self-confident customers to feel intimidated when they walk into a gallery, the sanctuary of art.

Paul Guillaume was a man who could make you uncomfortable. . . . When you went into his gallery, you were received by a fashionably dressed secretary who always said, "Mr. Guillaume is in conference" before resuming her chilly smile. Then you were kept waiting for a length of time appropriate to your importance before being led into the office, where Guillaume, blowing smoke rings from his armchair, invited you with a regal wave of the hand to have a seat.[50]

The behavior of dealers toward clients depends not so much on the personality of the dealer as on the type of work sold and hence on the type of client. The best strategy for establishing a new market is different from the best strategy for exploiting an old one. Galleries that sell traditional painting take the attitude that the customer chooses the appropriate dealer. On the other hand, dealers in more modern painting take the attitude that the dealer makes the customer. To put it in negative and possibly misleading terms, traditional dealers sell to snobs willing to suffer humiliation as part of their intiation into the world of art, while contemporary dealers flatter a clientele of philistines. No doubt this is too strong. And in any case the dealer's behavior is affected by his own status and position.

Finally, we come to the relation between the dealer and the work of art itself. Is there something special about it, or does the art dealer sell paintings as any merchant would sell any kind of merchandise? The four most important dealers in nontraditional painting (most important in terms of both prestige of painters handled and total sales) have varied backgrounds. One was a banker. Another was a brilliant law student. The third, a merchant, took as his partner a graduate of the Ecole des sciences politiques. And the fourth, an ex-journalist, is now in partnership with another lawyer. Most younger dealers have attended business or law school. There is no program of instruction for art dealers as there is for museum conservators.

Ideally, entrepreneurial dealers should be connoisseurs and art lovers as well as champions of a cause and good businessmen. The current state of the market requires a combination of these rather contradictory qualities. In any case, a painting looks different to "buyer and seller, because the seller prefers the painting to the money that the sale will generate, whereas the buyer prefers the painting to the money that the purchase will cost him."[51] The work of art exists as both a possession and a commodity; the incompatibility between the two is a source of conflict. Dealers are able to live with this conflict because they have chosen to let economic objectives guide their behavior.

The function of the dealer-entrepreneur is to discover new artists, establish their reputations, and make their work pay. It is to choose one artist out of a hundred and allow him to work in peace. Not surprisingly, dealer-entrepreneurs have attracted no end of flattery. The poet E. Tériade spoke about Kahnweiler in 1927:

> His glory was to have been the first to defend the revolutionary Cubist movement while he was still a young man.
> He defended Cubism by selling Cubist art. *Defense* is a pleasant word to apply to those who have used and sometimes risked their fortunes in the art business, the most intelligent business there is.
> The word *defense* has a deeply paternal meaning. It means taking a painter in the flower of his youth, when he is weak and vulnerable, and guaranteeing him a life free of all worries, at least in the short term. It means guiding and encouraging his passions and leading him, like a good father, to success and, beyond success, to glory.
> *Defense* also has a heroic meaning: fighting external and often internal enemies, preaching the faith like an apostle to people benighted by habit, and being the first to intuit, understand, and love things that the herd will learn to love only later, possibly through our efforts. Finally, *defense* suggests a sporting attitude toward business. And that, perhaps, has had a lot to do with the decision of so many young people to go into the art business.[52]

"Soldiers of art," dealers are also soldiers of capitalism, ready to fight, to compete, and to face risk and even adventure, if, as Georges Lefebvre thinks, capitalism is the "bourgeois form of martial behavior." Yet the fact of the matter is that the artist shares the dealer's risk. The artist receives only a small fraction of what his work brings in. If prices decline, the dealer will break his contract with the artist before he will go bankrupt.

The present system ensures that the artist's life will be one of insecurity. And the point is not that the dealer is somehow "inhuman," even if generosity sometimes falls by the wayside in the race for power and profit.

The dealer-entrepreneur, historically associated with the conversion of the work of art into a commodity, has adapted to a competitive system in which the physical and moral well-being of the artist depends on the sale of his works. He is the catalyst who brings new painting to the attention of the public (or, at any rate, of a select clientele) and wins it a place in the market. To be sure, there are far more art brokers, consignment galleries, and traditional dealers than there are entrepreneurs. Yet I feel that the disproportionate amount of attention devoted here to the latter is justifiable. Like Durkheim, I believe that the most common is not necessarily the most typical. The art market is anarchic for dealers as well as artists. I cannot claim to have plumbed the depths of its complexity, nor can I overemphasize the fact that most dealers combine entrepreneurial with more traditional roles.

In his review of Vollard's *Souvenirs* Gabriel Brunet criticizes Vollard for neglecting the dealer's role in the economy of art. For the dealer, according to Brunet, is a "regent of painting, whose sovereign fancy and commercial stratagems create reputations and ensure the victory of one school over another."[53] Vollard responded with a diatribe that concludes:

> But, Monsieur Brunet may further protest, explain to me how a dealer can sell for 200,000 francs a painting for which he paid 100? The answer is simple: the dealer picked the lucky number. I'm reminded of what someone said one day to Odilon Redon: "Do you understand how a Delacroix can possibly sell for less than a Muckaczy?" To which Redon replied: "The reason is that no one has the power to make the price of a painting go up. An occult force controls these things, against which we are all powerless."[54]

In my opinion art dealers are one component of this "occult force." If dealers honestly fail to see this, they know not what they do.

Art Critics

Until the mid-eighteenth century there was little distinction between art criticism and general aesthetics. During the second half of the century, however, it became increasingly common for reviews to be published in newspapers and periodicals: this was the beginning of art criticism as we know it today. Diderot, who reviewed exhibitions of art from 1759 to 1781, was the first great art critic: he commented on artistic activities as current events. As one who chose not to meditate upon the past but to wager on the future, Diderot was a critic who "innovated in daily judgment"[1] and took the risk of being judged on the validity of his prophecies.

In the nineteenth century, a great period for both French painting and criticism, art criticism flourished as both a journalistic form and a literary genre. Numerous art exhibitions competed with or combatted the official Salon. Mass-circulation periodicals and specialized art reviews published growing numbers of articles and columns devoted to art. Throughout the century writers, painters, engravers, and musicians met in small groups, literary salons, and society gatherings or collaborated in the publication of innumerable journals. Endless discussion and controversy gave rise to a series of artistic ideologies. Finally, Baudelaire bestowed upon art criticism its letters of nobility.

The nineteenth century bequeathed us two contradictory opinions: criticism is necessary, and criticism is contemptible. The art critic was seen as an indispensable intermediary between the artists and a public disoriented by constant change in the form and technique of painting. Yet the romantics and their successors held that those who imagine and create are superior to those who examine and judge; for them there was a profound difference between the criticism of creators and the criticism of critics.[2] Since 1870 most art critics have failed to recognize the great innovative artists; their errors have tended to discredit the critical profession.

Contemporary art has plunged the critics into disarray, for it can neither

be attacked nor defended on traditional grounds. The influence of art dealers has further exacerbated the malaise. The people whose opinions set
aesthetic values maintain close relations with those who set the prices of
works of art; rightly or wrongly, this situation has cast doubt on the independence of the critics' judgments.

Professional Art Critics

The works themselves are silent, but around them there is a growing
clamor fostered by the widespread belief that everyone is qualified to offer
an opinion about art. The contemporary art world is so eclectic in its tastes
that neophytes are unafraid to discuss pre-Columbian art as connoisseurs
or write about Chinese painting or the latest in abstraction; the humility
that accompanies specialization is increasingly a thing of the past. As one
painter remarked: "This is the golden age not so much of the painter as of
the art review and art journal." [P203]

Philosophers, poets, novelists, art historians, and museum curators are
specialists in language or art, possibly both. For them, criticism is a sideline, a task performed only occasionally. Few comment regularly on art.
They may from time to time contribute a preface to a show catalog or
write an article, lending some of the prestige earned in their regular activity to painting. By contrast, professional art critics write or appear regularly in the newspapers or on radio and television. Some also serve as
artistic advisors to galleries or as artists' agents. Their status is therefore
ambiguous.

The Syndicat de la presse artistique française (Union of French Art
Writers) was founded in 1899. Its membership includes not only journalists but also conservators, art experts, historians, collectors, artists who
write or have written about art, and others who occasionally engage in art
criticism. The 1961 membership directory contains 344 names. The Syndicat professional des critiques d'art (Professional Art Critics' Union) was
founded by Raymond Cogniat in 1936 and has since become the French or-
gan of the International Association of Art Critics (founded in 1948). It is
more selective: in May 1959 it comprised sixty-five active members and
seventeen associate members. All but eight active members write regularly for daily or weekly periodicals, art reviews, and literary magazines.
The group has refused membership to applicants who "misbehaved politically during the war" as well as those deemed "corrupt" or "mediocre."
All but three live in the Paris area; two are from Lyons, one from Geneva.
Most associate members are museum curators. All but twenty-eight of the
eighty-two active and associate members also belong to the Syndicat de la
presse artistique.

Only those critics who are also professors or curators have special training in art. About one tenth of the professional critics are former painters. Others became critics after pursuing academic careers, most often in philosophy, during which they learned to manipulate an esoteric vocabulary but not, it seems, to be wary of it. Still others trained as journalists and began writing about art because either they liked it or things just worked out that way. None trained specifically as a critic: "This is a difficult business, something that can't be learned," the union's president confided. "Critics teach themselves. They do not graduate from the Louvre School of Criticism." Another critic observed that "since there is no degree in criticism, you have to prove what you can do, that you have good taste and know how to write. The two don't necessarily go together." [F.C.]

The critic who is not a journalist has no clearly defined status; there is no code of ethics or fixed scale of remuneration covering critical work. "In order to live as a critic, you have to have a column in a major publication or a number of different columns in lesser publications (for example, as correspondent for various foreign magazines). Most important of all, you've got to have other sources of income." [D.S.] Besides writing for periodicals, critics can earn money by lecturing, organizing foreign shows, and publishing monographs and essays on art. Some critics do other work apart from writing, serving as secretaries to established painters, artistic advisors to dealers and collectors, and agents to groups of artists; others act as informal art brokers.

Critics are the "poor relations" of the family of art. They are also scapegoats: those who cannot rely on personal wealth or income from another occupation are frequently suspected of base motives. "They have no money, so you can't trust them. They acquire a taste for high living, society, fashionable dinner parties, and scotch." [P270]

Critics today help dealers promote new painting. They uncover new trends and make the reputations of painters, reputations that ultimately translate into higher prices. Critics play many different roles: they spot new talent, introduce promising artists to galleries and collectors, advise dealers (at times as salaried employees of galleries, organizing shows and preparing catalog copy), and keep museum curators and exhibition jury members informed of the latest developments on the art scene. Critics accept the ambiguity of their situation and willingly see themselves as playing an economic as well as an aesthetic role. "The critic should play the same role for the gallery as the reader plays for the publishing house. Every critic has a major influence on certain galleries. I worked first with Gallery X and later with Gallery Y. Now I'm with a third gallery. The critic has a part to play in the launching of new painters." [L.S.] Despite the diversity of critics' roles and objectives, the method is always the same: critics "talk painting."

The Defense of Traditional Painting

This section is based on a content analysis of eighty show catalogues and invitations. In criticism of traditionalist painting, moral judgment outweighs aesthetic judgment. Praise for the traditional artist's sincerity, modesty, honesty, and earnestness is explicitly or implicitly linked to charges that the avant-garde artist is somehow morally defective: a schemer, social climber, fraud, or shirker.

Roger Montané shows that he puts nothing above honesty in art.[3]

Nothing is more laudable in 1964 then to reject the facile solutions offered by "masters" of dubious and counterfeit originality. It takes courage to stand up against fraud.[4]

He can look back with some pride on a long career as an honest and conscientious painter who has never taken any short-cuts.[5]

Implicit in such criticism is the notion that a work of art represents earnest effort. A painter's quality is determined by training, mastery of technique, and knowledge of tradition. The artist is praised for being "professional," for having a "solid technique," and for "conscientiousness" and "responsibility." The painting is not defended as such, abstracting from the artist's intention and from the effort required to produce it. The implicit assumption is that good painting can never be the result of an accident or "objective chance." The human intention must be judged. A painting is good if it is painted by a well-trained artist who has taken pains to see that it is good: it is the reward of virtue. Like action for Kant, painting has no value apart from the intention behind it; for the painting to be good, the intention must be good, that is, explicit, conscious, and capable of mobilizing means adequate to the task.

They remain true to their innate need to express themselves through painting and to the discipline acquired in training.[6]

Opinions to the contrary notwithstanding, no one can paint reality without preparation. Draftsmanship is still fundamental, no matter how talented the artist, and Lemeunier is a master draftsman.[7]

He still believes in slow maturation, quiet work, reserved sensibility, and modesty. . . . He learned this respect for genuine values in art as well as in life from good teachers such as Gili and Thibaudet. To them he owes more than his technique; he also owes his scruples and his aversion to dishonesty of all kinds.[8]

This is his first one-man show in Paris, summing up his work for the past two years. It is the result of quiet, steady effort, of diligent, unflagging labor, and of tranquil meditation far from our distressing "art bazaar"—unmistakable sign of the times. Come discover this painter's work. It is *serious, sincere, and carefully pondered.* Such qualities have become so rare that the artist who has them can claim to be original.[9]

More subtle critics argue that an artist chooses to paint in a traditional style of his own free will, not because he is incapable of modernist innovation. The critics who defend the avant-garde reverse the argument.

Roger Bertin is one of the freest men I know. . . . Though sufficiently imaginative and technically gifted to attempt the sort of calculated audacity that so titillates today's adolescents and greengrocers, he preferred his natural originality to prefabricated sensationalism. His love of freedom may well have preserved his sensibility as a painter, which is discreetly in evidence in every painting in this show.[10]

The writer's moralistic tone is calculated to suit the reader's expectations. By vouching for the painter's honesty and qualifications, the writer gives the person looking at the painting the facts he needs to judge its quality.

The Reference to Reality

Traditionalist criticism is of necessity "referential" criticism. Unlike abstract painting, which avoids reference to the external world, figurative painting allows the spectator to compare what is on the canvas to a reality that exists objectively outside it. Aesthetic judgment that depends on the relation between the painting and reality, whether scrupulously represented or intentionally deformed, is more applicable to painting as image than to painting as object. Yet the objective quality of the painting is rarely ignored; commentaries generally include a more or less elaborate analysis of the plastic techniques used to "transpose" or "recreate" reality. This leads to a divergence of views between those who defend painting for simply reproducing the beauty of the world and those who advocate an "aesthetic of ugliness."

Aesthetic discourse is at times a plea on behalf of the pleasure to be had from painting, a homage to beauty and pleasant feelings.

What do they represent?
A frank, serious, and solid talent, equally notable for draftsmanship, handling of color, and composition.
And images.

Flowers so real you can smell them. Fruits you'd like to take a bite of. Beautiful, healthy male and female bodies. The gods in their abode, like us, making the same gestures we make every day. Mothers nursing and caring for their babies. Triumphant fathers carrying kids on their shoulders. Undisguised faces. Children watched by a tender youth, fond not only of his own kids but of kids in general. Blazing city signs and dark crowds. Meadows, forests, skies, fields reaped by mechanical harvesters.
Anecdotes?
No.
Eternal themes.[11]

Aesthetic discourse sometimes encourages and supports expressionist tendencies in art. Today's expressionists have their own salon, the so-called Peintres témoins de leur temps (Painters, Witnesses of their Times), and are the preponderant influence in the Salon des Indépendants. They enjoy a much wider audience than Rouault, Gromaire, Goerg, Soutine, and Gruber enjoyed in their day. Much has been written about their distress and anger, their hallucinatory, tragic view of the world, their metaphysical anguish. This new expressionism, which distorts reality in the hope of touching on inner mystery, contains enough vestiges of realism, enough tokens of nature filtered through temperament, to have won the support of modern-minded exponents of realist painting.

He gives a creative strength to anxiety. . . . Slowly this gives shape to the extraordinary, stupefying world that he shows us head on.

If you like your art facile and pretty, if you are attracted by the purely decorative experiments of the pseudo-abstractionists, then you will probably be repelled by the intense creations of this visionary, Gachet. But if you feel that Art is above all an emotional transformation of reality, you will slowly find your way into his kingdom. Truth to tell, death is often represented there as it is in Ligier-Richier, Goya, or Ensor. Is that to upset us?

He likes Rembrandt, Van Gogh, and Rouault. They, too, savagely tore matter apart by breathing into it a bit of the "sovereign spirit."[12]

The Invocation of Genius

The excerpts cited above exhibit a technique common to both conservative and progressive critics—to link the painter under review to recognized geniuses. But they make clear that the new artist, while belonging to the same family as illustrious predecessors, is no mere imitator.

Speaking as one who has neither the knowledge nor experience of an art critic, I feel that it is not out of place here to mention the name Cézanne.[13]

This is a full-blooded work, the first of its kind we have been given to admire since Van Gogh.[14]

We are in the presence of a contemplative painter, who sought advice from Rembrandt, Velazquez, Goya, and Jongkind but without imitating them.[15]

I find here something of Tintoretto the colorist and the rigorous Manet, but these remote kinships in no way impinge on the artist's individuality.[16]

Painters can be praised by associating their names not only with other painters but also with writers and musicians. These cultural references purport to give stature to the artist under review. This kind of writing assumes that its audience is cultivated or at any rate passingly familiar with the names invoked.

The Invocation of Modernity

The critics associated with figurative tendencies in art see themselves as humanists, imbued with aesthetic values whose history can be traced back to the Renaissance. Yet they have no desire to be called conservatives. Hence they have adopted the concept of innovation and linked it to that of tradition. "Innovation takes place within the great tradition," according to J. Darle, who cites Albert Camus: "Originality varies with time. Today it is perhaps original to say that an artist can be a rebel without breaking windows. To be original means simply to say things well."[17] Epithets favored by progressive critics are also commonly used by traditionalists: painters always have "powerful," "marked," "original," or "singular" personalities; they create forms that are "uncommon," "novel," "surprising," "unusual," "strange," and "bizarre." So far from despising modernity, traditionalists claim it for artists to their liking. But for them modernity involves no sharp break with the past; it is part of a moral as well as an artistic tradition. "This is a courtly art, refined, patient, subtle, heir to the work of the illuminators who did books of hours for Gaston Phébus, say, yet as modern and contemporary as Paul Klee."[18]

To sum up, traditionalist criticism is cast in terms of a moralistic aesthetic. The quality of a painting depends on the qualification and training of the artist and the effort involved in making it. Good painting combines good technique with genius and associates tradition with "contemporary style." Painting as image is more important than painting as object.[19] Images are judged by their fidelity to the real, by "likeness." In some cases infidelity to or distortion of reality is tolerated, but only to the extent that the image has become a sign; it is then judged on the basis of legibility, intelligibility, and meaning. The intention behind the work is never ignored.

The relation between the image and natural beauty is also significant, and here we must distinguish between "ancients" and "moderns" among the figurative critics. The ancients believe that beauty is eternal; hence their aesthetic is invariable (a sort of neoacademicism). The moderns, on the other hand, are willing to tolerate the unusual, the peculiar, the surprising, and the ugly, provided that some clearly communicated intention is responsible for these qualities of the image. Traditionalist criticism rejects the idea of painting as object. Judgment is based on values external to painting, and objective guarantees of validity are essential.

The Champions of Progressive Painting

"Pataphysics" and Mystical Effusion

In progressive criticism painting is but a pretext for a display of critical rhetoric borrowed from other disciplines. Much confusion is engendered by the use of terms from philosophy and the "human sciences." To make matters worse, the writing is often confused and fraught with comparisons of dubious validity. The following words occur with great frequency.

METAPHYSICAL: "metaphysical painting" and "metaphysics of painting," "new metaphysics of the pictorial substance," "metaphysical action," "reflexes derived from the metaphysical Unconscious"

ONTOLOGICAL: "ontological painting," "the ontological nature of painterly motion," "the essential dual manifestation of its ontological autonomy," "an ontological, structural approach"

IMMANENT AND TRANSCENDENTAL: "immanent color," "transcendental action"

PHENOMENOLOGICAL: "the physical, phenomenological existence of the work," "this extreme quality which marks the starting point of an artistic phenomenology"

DIALECTICAL: "dialectically constructive approach," "dialectical approach of abstraction," "distrust dialectics"

SIGN, SIGNIFIER, SIGNIFICANCE, SIGNIFIED, SIGNIFIABLE, SIGNIFICATION: "more ordered, signified abstraction," "significant gestures," "universal significance," "a modern, signification-making intelligence for overcoming the rigidity of concepts and rhetoric"

STRUCTURE, STRUCTURED, STRUCTURAL, STRUCTURING, STRUCTURATION: "structured lyricism," "structural approaches," "textured material which is the structuring fact of painting"

SPACE (GENERALLY ASSOCIATED WITH "STRUCTURE"): "gradual conquest of structuration of space," "in order to animate pictural space throughout the surface and in all planes, to punctuate or modify the overall structure"

Coupled with the philosophical and scientific vocabulary are words indicating initiation into powerful mysteries: there is talk of a "different" art, which comes from "somewhere else," from "within," and looks "beyond," carrying with it a modern "world view," a "cosmic" vision, not to say an "architectonic and cosmic" vision. The artist's task is to "unveil" the world's mystery by attaining "a higher Reality, a Reality more profound and more essential," "beyond the real," "surreal," and "hyperconscious." The artist's work is "initiatory," "magical," "demiurgic," "Promethean," or "prophetic." His ecstasies are "telluric," his dramas "mystico-erotic," his approach "sacral."

Although aesthetic discourse borrows readily from philosphy, it is rarely willing to submit to the philosophical requirement of logical rigor. We find Sartrean overtones in talk of nothingness—"the negating gesture" and the "reduction of being to nothingness"—along with allusions to Heidegger in discussion of "vacuity," "availability," and "unveiling." Also common are references to the mystics and to oriental philosophy, especially Zen, and of course to psychoanalysis.

Homage is paid to the artist in terms borrowed from both scholar and prophet: "He is attempting to extend his organic domain into the realm of modern physics; [his] structures [are] laden with the mystery of the inner world now being explored by so many pioneers of scientific philosophy." Or consider the following passage:

> The miracle of our century is the advent of abstract art. This same miracle has occurred in physics, with the discovery of the principle of uncertainty and even the individualization of energy. Thus Fontana shows us a world view arising before our very eyes. He does not invoke mathematics or minute philosophical argument. No: he shows us a prophetic vision.[19]

In hyperbolic language set to incantatory rhythms the artist is cast as a new prophet, a modern magician:

> There you have the most heretical of miracles: this egocentric excess keeps Yves in a constant state of pantheistic exaltation which accepts no (theoretical) limit to its appropriation of the cosmos. . . . The Promethean temptation becomes clear: rather than brave the gods, Yves Klein rivals Moses, he offers us a cosmogony for modern times.[20]

Bizarre couplings occasionally result in teratological offspring, to use a rather pedantic adjective that might well be added to the list above. For instance: "His phantom-ridden morphological universe derives its inner necessity from the very adventure of the quest for self-expression."

Of course not all commentary on art suffers from esoteric vocabulary and mystical effusion. Nor does obscure prose preclude a flair for discovering new painters. If I dwell here on the obscurity of some art criticism, it is because "esoteritis" would appear to be a characteristic feature of the present day and age. The pretentious terms in which progressive art is often discussed may limit consumption to an elite of initiates. The content of art criticism suggests that art writers think of their readers as snobs. The most clearsighted artists are aware of this: "For a while I was hostile to criticism. Critics lack the necessary humility. They create a sort of fog around art, a lyrical effusion, a mythification of creation. Critics ought to show people reality rather than shroud it in smoke. They should come back down to earth, to the creation of forms." [P228] In the absence of a tradition of modern art criticism, some critics evidently cannot resist the temptation to engage in a kind of "criticism of the absurd." For less demanding painters, as well as dealers and collectors, this may be enough. But the great critics of our time are those who seek and find a language, both original and intelligible.

The Functions of Art Criticism

The critic who discovers and judges new art and informs and educates the public engages in a disinterested activity. But the present market system allows the critic's economic function to interfere with his cultural function, threatening his moral integrity and undermining his authority.

Some critics judge according to traditional criteria and reject progressive painting outright; others, afflicted by the "waning of indignation" and "overcomprehension," allow discovery to take the place of judgment. "Advanced" critics feel a duty to make up for injustices committed by their predecessors; they are afraid of missing the messiah. If artists have become obsessed with discovering new styles in painting, critics have become obsessed with discovering artists in the process of discovery: "The critic will not let go. Whatever the cost, he will *discover*. That is his mission. *This era is unlike all others.* Every week he needs to toss something new into the arena, to flourishes of trumpets."[21]

The critic is not always the first to discover an artist's work—other artists often precede him. He is rarely the only discoverer; rather, his role is to bestow cultural legitimacy upon the work by writing about it. New schools of painters develop aesthetic doctrines and find critics champion their work. The various schools vie for cultural legitimacy (a prelude to competition in the marketplace). Each has its own hierarchy of values, which it attempts to enforce. A critic becomes "authoritative" when he is widely enough respected to transcend these rival value systems and impose one of his own (at least within a particular area of contemporary artistic production). Are even the most influential critics authoritative in this sense? In the final analysis, authority rests on consensus, or at any rate near consensus, among the dominant market actors: painters, critics, dealers, collectors, and museum curators.

When authoritative critics lay down the law, they help to form public taste. Their conversation sets the tone. The larger the critic's audience as a writer, the more influence he wields as a critic; Marcel Proust made Vermeer familiar not to connoisseurs, who already knew of the artist from Thoré-Bürger, but to his large readership.[22] As a purveyor of information, however, the critic (and even the novelist who ponders questions of art) has little influence beyond a select group of intellectuals and snobs. Society at large does not recognize critics as professionals possessing specialized knowledge which they are charged to promulgate. Education is officially the responsibility of educators, who adhere to widely accepted values and only rarely teach the new art, about which authoritative judgment is impossible.

History has taught that art critics are not infallible. The economic functions performed by critics today, willingly or not, have cast doubt on the authenticity of their judgment. A critic's authority can contribute to the decision to purchase an artist's work for a major collection or secure him a contract with a gallery—circumstances not without influence on the prices paid for that artist's future work. The critic who serves on an international jury awards more than just a symbolic prize; he takes a decision that sanctions an artist's reputation and therefore has economic consequences.

> Under such conditions, what is the duty of the disinterested critic? Should he shun the whole system of competitions and prizes and follow the lonely path of integrity? It would be too easy, and falsely heroic, to wash one's hands in public and withdraw into an ivory tower. The critic would then cease to be a critic. No matter how he uses his talent, even for reproach, he inevitably influences opinion and therefore prices. Under the circumstances he may conclude that the logical thing to do is to take part in the cultural battle and attempt to abide by his own standards of honesty while persuading others to do the same. But he may also conclude that part of his task is to put an end to a system so fundamentally unjust.[23]

Criticism is a necessary part of the current market system. The critical functions of judgment and education are perverted for purposes of publicity. Dealers know that ordinary advertising is of no avail with cultivated buyers (or buyers who think they are cultivated). They prefer to have intellectuals and critics take up cudgels on behalf of their fledglings. The ostensible independence and competence of the critic are used covertly to sell paintings.

By compromising the critic, however, the market has devalued criticism and robbed it of part of its usefulness as a sales tool. Not only the public but also the critics themselves are uncomfortable with the present situation.

> Compromised by our involvement in the marketplace and worn down by the number of shows that many of us are obliged to see, some critics have become blasé and skeptical; because they no longer believe in much of anything, they are ready to defend anything anyone is willing to pay them to defend. With us, 500 F. is enough to buy a prostitute. [O.S.]

> Criticism has been enfeebled by its deep involvement in the marketplace for the past twenty years. [Z.N.]

> Who knows if the critics are honest or not? If a critic believes in a painter, why not? The painter will try to pressure the critic in a more or less naive way: he will invite him out to lunch before a show or give him a print or painting that the critic particularly liked. It's hard to turn down an offer like that. Editors also exert pressure. Negative reviews cause galleries to withdraw their advertising, and that can create problems. Pressure from dealers is something else entirely, but not all critics are beholden to dealers. [F.C.]

There are many different kinds of art critics, ranging from writers who criticize art on the side to full-time professionals. Some are conservative, others progressive, still others eclectic, willing to give all new art a chance. Some are poets, others publicists. Some are journalists, others art brokers. Some are charlatans, others prophets. But the critic stands in a special relation to the artist: he is the intermediary between the artist's work and the public. What he says influences how the public will view the work and what kind of reception it will receive. The critic bestows legitimacy upon new art. Nevertheless, criticism today is in crisis. Developments in art itself are partly to blame, but so is the encroachment of economic concerns upon what is supposed to be a disinterested activity. That said, it is only right to point out that critics earn far less than the more successful dealers and artists.

5

Collectors

The painting market is concerned not with the public at large but with the limited public of art buyers. Of course buyers' decisions are determined in part by their knowledge and appreciation of painting, their attitude as spectators. But not all spectators are buyers. Once the painting is viewed not simply as a work of art but also as a commodity, the question of its economic value arises. Aesthetic preference has no economic meaning until it is translated into a concrete offer. This chapter is concerned primarily with the relation between the desire for art, governed by norms that implicity or explicitly determine aesthetic preference and behavior, and economic means.

Major collectors may not be in the majority among art buyers, but it is their tastes, financial resources, and rate of acquisition that set the tone for the art market as a whole. I have therefore chosen to concentrate my research on them and to ignore occasional buyers and small collectors (study of whom would require statistical surveys). Small collectors (of whom there are a large number) have considerable influence on the market for relatively inexpensive paintings that reflect mass taste. They have little influence on either the market for "high art," which is too costly for them, or the market for avant-garde art, in which they take little or no interest.

This chapter is based largely on interviews with 90 collectors chosen at random from a list of 850 French collectors. The list included the names of collectors who loaned paintings for major shows (in particular, shows at the National Museum of Modern Art, the Modern Art Museum of the City of Paris, the Museum of Decorative Arts, and the Charpentier Gallery), along with other names provided by collectors' groups, art galleries, and artists. Dealers, artists, and critics with art collections of their own were interviewed along with other members of those groups. Priority was given to collectors of modern and contemporary painting, in accordance with the overall orientation of this book.

Not For Profit: The Stated Ideology

I shall begin by analyzing what collectors say about their activities. Only after having done that will I examine what their collections and behavior objectively reveal. How do they analyze their own conduct? What values do they invoke to justify their activity?

Uniqueness

All the collectors interviewed resisted any attempt to pin them down with rigid questionnaires, but they were quite willing to engage in extensive conversations. Clearly they wish to see themselves, and to appear to the observer, as unique human beings, not as members of a class. "Every case is a special case," I was told. Every collector is deeply convinced that he is "unclassifiable." Many refer in conversation to facts about their lives, to emotional and intellectual failures, to "frustrations" and "compensations." They are generally quite receptive to psychoanalytic explanations of their behavior. This, I think, reflects their eagerness to associate attitudes as collectors with deep and abiding personal traits. Yet their introspection is selective. Apart from aesthetic motives, which they know are never pure, they cite mainly the passion for ownership, the taste for gambling, the wish to acquire culture, and metaphysical anxiety as reasons for their interest in art.

Art Lovers

Collectors assert their sensibility by defining themselves as lovers of art. Those with relatively small collections like to be called collectors; those recognized by the art world as major collectors dislike the term. Because collecting is often considered an ostentatious or lucrative activity, major collectors therefore prefer to emphasize their love of painting rather than the fact of ownership.

> Collectors? They are enthusiasts, snobs, or speculators. I am simply a lover of art. [C81]

> I dislike publicity. . . . . I loved painting at a time when having an art collection was not the status symbol it is today, along with the yacht, the racing stables, and the sable coat. [C67]

> I am not a collector. The term carries with it an irritating suggestion of speculation for profit. I am an art lover. [C27]

Collector, a word with rather commercial connotations, should not be confused with *art lover.* To acquire a collection you have to have a sensitive nature, so that you tremble whenever you stand in front of a beautiful work of art. I am a humanist. [C49]

In French, the word for art lover is *amateur,* taken in its root sense [from the Latin *amator,* lover]. The same word is pejorative when applied to the painter (the amateur painter is one with neither vocation nor profession, the "Sunday painter"). But *amateur* in the sense of art lover is not at all pejorative; the art lover is one who buys paintings for love, not money. The emphasis is on disinterested acquisition of art—*amateur* as opposed to speculator. But *amateur* does not necessarily mean connoisseur. Often, though, the term art lover carries the connotation "enlightened." The true art lover is distinguished by the selective nature of his collection and the quality of his "finds." Thus the collectors who style themselves "art lovers" imply that they are disinterested and possess good taste.

Love

Collectors express themselves in the vocabulary of love. Plausible or not, the passion for art is characteristically effusive. Collectors themselves are quick to draw an analogy between the love of art and love in general—a comparison long made by astute observers of the art scene, such as Balzac. They are fond of describing their behavior as irrational and invoking psychoanalytic explanations.

I buy whenever lightning strikes. [C49]

I buy when a painting has an effect on me, when it's irresistible. [C44]

It was a newly born passion. [C80]

Painting is my passion; it's my life. [C61]

The collector's desire, like Don Juan's, is stimulated by resistance. Possession causes it to flag. Its aim is to be perpetually unsatisfied.

Finding the right painting is by far the most exciting part. [C60]

All forms of art interest me, with the exception of what was a youthful passion, the eighteenth century. . . . My purpose is not to make money. It's a diversion, a passion, a revived passion, an obsession. I think about owning a painting for two or three months before buying it. I thought about buying a painting of T.'s, but it was put up for auction and I missed it. . . . I've just bought this painting. I stayed up late last night staring at it. I'll leave you to stare at it. . . . Sometimes I tire of painting. I have enough of it. I take my paintings down from the walls and put them in storage. That way I can forget them. Then, several months later, when my interest revives, I discover them a second time. Or else it turns out that it's all over. Nothing can be done about it. . . . The painting I like best is the one I've purchased most recently, or the one I do not yet own. [C34]

The collector feels jealousy and anxiety akin to that of the lover. He aspires to sole and total possession.

When I own a work, I can look at it whenever I want. I can touch it. It's totally different from looking at a painting in a museum. I almost hate museums. They're places you go to learn about a subject. [C78]

Having painting in your home is quite different from looking at it elsewhere. It's the same with women. Marriage is one thing, having a woman on Saturday night is another. The problem is always one of sole possession. [C60]

I was twenty-four years old when I discovered the silent world of painting. That encounter turned my life into an adventure. With paintings I experienced the lasting pleasure of absolute possession that so long eluded me with people.[1]

Collecting as Amusement

Some collectors view collecting as a hobby, "an unremunerative secondary activity undertaken for pleasure"[2] during nonworking hours.

[Collecting] is not a need but a pleasant occupation, like going to the theater. It's an amusement. We work during the week. On Saturday afternoons we go to galleries. [C79]

I suppose I would have nothing to do if I didn't occupy myself with painting. I spend all my leisure time at it. It diverts me. [C36]

Part of the pleasure of collecting lies in risk and competition. Collectors gamble on paintings and artists the way racing enthusiasts gamble on horses or market enthusiasts on stocks. They are frank about this aspect of their activity, arguing that collecting is justified because it is done purely for pleasure, even if profit sometimes results. But collecting is usually held to be different from ordinary amusement becaue of its cultural implications. It is an elite recreation, a game in which the losers are presumably those without culture or artistic flair.

Culture

Collectors feel a need to explain their aesthetic choices in cultural or pseudocultural terms. Some speak the language of scholars, others of the studio (picked up in visits to artists), still others of fashionable art openings. Their remarks range from learned commentary on art and artists to vague formulas: "the work is amusing"; "it's interesting"; "it's important"; "it's a turning point"; "it exists"; "it's great"; "it's strong"; "it's powerful"; "it's structured"; "it's highly refined"; or "it's mature." Many collectors acknowledge that collecting led them to learn more about art, and as their knowledge increased their tastes changed.

One collector who kindly agreed to be interviewed subjected me to an examination before allowing the interview to proceed: he asked me to identify the painters of various works that he showed me and to state which I liked best. This case was fortunately exceptional. Yet it reveals an attitude common to all the collectors: they see themselves and others in terms of taste. Ultimately they identify with what they own, with the collection they have "created," which gives them a sense of accomplishment. According to Sartre, the attitude of the bourgeois is, "I am what I have." But for collectors the attitude is, "I am my paintings." Identification with the painting gives them a positive sense of themselves, a feeling of cultural superiority.

Collecting is lazy. It is a way of appropriating other men's work, of embellishing oneself as with the feathers of a peacock. It is a way of sharing in the artist's creative genius, his demiurgic power. You feel that somehow you've taken possession of the imaginary world of Picasso or Braque or their younger colleagues. It is a way of feeling superior, of growing, of absorbing the world elaborated by the artist. Unable to create himself, the collector creates at one remove, using works created by others with which he has identified himself. You can write about Picasso, but it's easier to buy him. [C41]

It was as if I myself had won the Biennale prize. [C29]

The Sacred

The ultimate justification of the activity of collecting is metaphysical. Art is supposed to transcend the human condition. Collectors accordingly claim that, in buying works of art, they are pursuing the timeless and eternal. Art is a form of, or substitute for, sacred things, and collectors use it to slake their thirst for the absolute.

Here one escapes from the human condition. It is passion without drama, a love story without tears. You can shed tears even for a pet cat, which can always die. [C32]

Art is an intermediate state between heaven and earth. Absolute Beauty is God. Through art we glimpse a portion of that beauty. There is something ecstatic in it. [C29]

Painting does not replace religion, but almost. [C46]

Money

Economic calculation does not figure in collectors' descriptions of what they are about. When I introduced the subject of money in our conversations, their reactions ranged from outrage to cynicism.

The fact that painting is expensive makes no difference to me. It is indecent to translate a painter's work into banknotes. To do so is to treat artists in a materialistic fashion. You can't set a price to a work of art. It's insulting to the painter. I have no idea what my collection cost me. And I don't want to know what it's worth today. [C32]

I use brokers as little as possible. It makes my heart bleed to do it. Brokers are for stocks, not works of art. I do not sell my children. I do not sell love for money. [C29]

But consider the alternative response:

What interests me is to buy a painting for 50,000 francs and sell it for 500,000. [C35]

In between these two extremes one encounters a subtle casuistry: the irrational passion of art collecting is justified because it is a good investment, while the profits to be made from investing in art are justified because they require sound judgment.

The financial aspect is relatively unimportant. I do not buy painting with the idea of making a good investment; I buy it because I like it. But I am not sorry to see prices go up, because I have children. [C59]

Making a sound investment is comforting, no doubt about it. For one thing, it's good for the ego. I would be upset if my daughter thought I had made a bad choice. Your children think more of you when you leave them paintings. You leave them a living memory. You don't feel that you've squandered their fortune. [C50]

When prices go up, I'm doubly satisfied: I feel that I was clever, and I have proof that I haven't squandered my children's capital.

When prices rise steadily, I naturally feel something. I've never figured out how much my collection cost me. It's a matter of mental health. I remember quite clearly how much I paid for each painting, but I've never added it all up. I fall somewhere between the type who buys art out of passion and the type who invests as if in a stock—closer to the former than to the latter. But prices matter to me, probably for two reasons. If they go up, I feel that I've won a bet. And my artistic sense is confirmed. Any anxieties I may feel on that score are alleviated. It's reassuring. But I would make a host of sacrifices before parting with some of my paintings. [C60]

Owning a beautiful painting, a masterpiece, is a very great pleasure. But often what interests me is the course of the painter's development, a certain stage of his research. In such cases you feel not only aesthetic pleasure but pleasure of another kind: that of having been right. . . . Money? No, it's of no interest at all—except from the standpoint of gambling, of having picked the lucky number. [C46]

Clearly, rationalizations of the financial aspects of collecting come in many forms.

Particularly striking was the desire of each collector to differentiate himself from other collectors. Each sought to explain his activity in terms of a unique combination of psychological factors. But none would admit to collecting because it is lucrative. Sensibility, metaphysics, passion, recreation, culture—all these are acceptable motives; profit is not. What collectors say about themselves is always to some extent, wittingly or unwittingly, apologetic.

A Typology of Collectors

Avowed or unavowed, conscious or unconscious, the motives of collectors are complex and ambiguous. By contrast, their behavior can be classified objectively according to a fairly simple pattern.

Prestige Purchasers and Ostentatious Consumption

Those members of any society who cannot afford prestigious possessions are excluded from the top rungs of the social hierarchy; conversely, possession of prestige goods is an objective sign of high social status. In our society, painting is a prestigious commodity. It not only has cultural value but is also a luxury good traditionally associated with an aristocratic way of life. Many status symbols—houses, clothes, yachts, and airplanes—have use value, but painting is purely a pleasure good. Owning paintings is a status symbol evident even to those not in a position to observe the daily activities of the wealthy. Collectors who buy painting to buy prestige are ranked by wealth.

Magnificent Millionaires

In recent years prestigious art collections have been amassed by individuals wealthy enough to spend upwards of a million dollars on a single painting. Their collections include works that have stood the test of time and whose value is attested by major cultural institutions: older paintings by celebrated painters and more recent paintings already judged to be modern classics. These are works known to be priceless—meaning literally, in this case, that their prices put them out of reach of all but a select few.

A typical prestige collection now includes not only old masters but also large numbers of works by impressionists, postimpressionists, and early-twentieth-century masters; since the end of World War II these have been granted access to the pantheon of painting and accordingly bring high prices on the international market. If post-1870 art has replaced old masters in the prestige trade, the reason is that few old masters come on the market nowadays. Many are in museums. And progress in art scholarship has made buyers wary of false attributions, common with older paintings. The now-familiar painting of the impressionists is particularly congenial to the bourgeois sensibility: it is painted out of doors; nature, light, and women are its preferred subjects; and it expresses a bourgeois vision of the good life, much as Watteau's *fêtes galantes* expressed a corresponding aristocratic vision.

Thus the content of the typical prestige collection has changed since the late nineteenth century; it could hardly have done otherwise, given the scarcity of old masters. But those who collect painting as a status symbol are much as they have always been, interested in painting as a sign of their social ascension: from the robber barons of the nineteenth century to the American tycoons of the twenties and thirties to today's patrons of the arts, not much has changed. Wealthy collectors still rely on the advice of professional counselors, including dealers, brokers, and auctioneers as well as art historians and curators. Big collectors will buy entire collections if the opportunity arises. They make spectacular bids at public auctions either directly or through agents. They are neither reluctant to pay high prices nor to let it be known that they are paying high prices. Eager to show what they own, they do not hide their holdings and lend to major traveling exhibitions when the opportunity arises. Some donate all or part of their holdings to museums (even without the encouragement of tax write-offs) in the hope that their posterity will remember their generosity and good taste. From beginning to end, their interest in art is ostentatious.

The triumphant capitalist bourgeoisie remains fascinated by the symbols of defunct aristocratic society. Nostalgic for the impressive if unproductive expenditure of the aristocrat of old, the great tycoon is reluctant to behave as a purely rational *homo oeconomicus*. As Ernest Labrousse has said, wealth is "socially repressed." The wealthy therefore look upon the acquisition of expensive, recognized art as a noble way of spending their fortunes and winning respect. Yet the great capitalists changed the aristocratic models even as they adopted them. For the bourgeois mentality was forged in opposition to the aristocratic mentality. The capitalist entrepreneur is to the feudal lord as hoarding is to squandering. The one is closed, the other open; the one calculates, the other dreams; the one has an economic temperament, the other an erotic temperament.[3] But in bourgeois society expenditures on luxury goods, though modeled on aristocratic munificence, are not wasteful; they are an investment in prestige. And since the paintings purchased are of well-established value, such investment is not always pure of ulterior economic motives.

Owning celebrated and costly paintings makes people feel powerful and enhances their social status. It is risky to compare social phenomena in different cultures, but the competitive mentality of many contemporary collectors is reminiscent of the attitudes promoted by the custom of potlatch in primitive cultures.[4] (Potlatch is a form of ceremonial exchange of gifts during certain festivals; the items exchanged are not useful objects but luxury goods that confer prestige or have magical powers.) Marcel Mauss, in his analysis of potlatch, has emphasized the way in which rivalry destroys wealth.

> What is remarkable in these practices is that the principle of rivalry and antagonism is paramount. . . . Accumulated wealth is destroyed solely to outdo the other chieftain, who is a rival but at the same time a partner in the affair. . . . There is a marked competitive aspect to the chief's offering. It is in essence excessive and sumptuous. What we see above all is a struggle for superiority within the nobility from which the clan of the victor derives a benefit.[5]

Collectors compete in many ways: for example, who can spend the most, or who was the first to discover a new trend in art? Competition among major buyers may apear at first sight incompatible with economic rationality, yet the motives involved are not altogether unselfish. Ostentatious expenditure may not win a leadership role in today's society, but it is nevertheless a visible symbol of social rank.

Furthermore, the purchase of enormously expensive works of art is not as economically irrational as one might think. The man who owns a number of works by a particular painter is shrewd to drive up the price for that painter's work in public auction sales; the value of his holdings increases as a result. Under the American tax system, this can prove beneficial later on, when the collection is donated to museums. The most prestigious paintings are least susceptible to changes in the economic climate. Lord Duveen, for one, was clear about the need to modify aristocratic traditions so as to bring them into line with bourgeois values. To be sure, he sold prestige to his newly wealthy clients (of the first or second generation). For one thing, he offered them a past. For another, when he judged that their collections were important enough, he offered them the supreme distinction of a catalog of their holdings in which the names of all those who had owned their paintings before them were recorded; the most recent buyers were thus associated with the princes and dukes of old, all under the aegis of art. Thus Duveen sold not only a past but also a future.

Renaissance patrons had achieved immortality by commissioning the artists of their day to do works expressly for them. Similarly, the gift of a collection to a museum, carefully worked out by Duveen, was a way of associating the donor's name with that of the artist. Duveen understood that his wealthy clients were buyers hopeful of rivaling the great aristocrats but that they were also puritans—businessmen in the habit of calculating their investments, hence hostile to waste. Sound business reasoning reassured clients not convinced that prestige alone was enough: when Frick felt uneasy about having paid $400,000 for Velazquez's *Philip IV*, Duveen pointed out that Philip IV had paid the artist the equivalent of $600 for the work; if that $600 had been invested at interest in 1645, by 1910 it would have been worth so much that the price of the painting would have seemed ridiculously small by comparison. In Duveen's sales psychology, the value of art as show was never separated from the value of art as investment. He sold not only prestige but also sound investment value (neglecting occasional errors of attribution).[6]

The most expensive paintings are bought by a small number of millionaires, for the most part newly wealthy individuals of the first or second generation. Foremost among them are American press barons, Texas and Middle Eastern oilmen, Greek shipowners, Australian sheep ranchers, Canadian and South American mineowners, businessmen, bankers, industrialists of all nationalities, and a few movie stars.

Some know him as the "conqueror of the oceans." Others know that he is also a conqueror of the arts. Ship owner and art lover are one and the same: one makes the money, the other spends it. . . . The art lover's watchword is his freedom to choose. . . . His princely nature is evident not only in his proud contempt for chronology but also in his acquisition of art works of royal origin. . . . The conqueror can be seen in his triumphal bearing.[7]

Such is Pierre Verlet's portrait of Stavros Niarchos, whose several residences (including the Hôtel de Chanaleilles[8]) house one of the most noted collections of modern times. Making full use of his "freedom to choose" as well as his ample cash reserves, Niarchos has managed to amass, in less than ten years' time, a collection that includes El Greco, Goya, Corot, Delacroix, Degas, Renoir, Cézanne, Gauguin, Toulouse-Lautrec, Matisse, Rouault, and Van Gogh. Niarchos's paintings have been shown in Zurich, Vienna, London, and New York. He has bought several whole collections, including Edward G. Robinson's collection of paintings, the Ricardo do Esperito collection of furniture, mainly Louis XVI (at public auction), the Chester Beatty collection (bought privately), and the collection of the goldsmith Puiforcat. The last was given to the Louvre. Clearly, the aristocratic model, evident in the combination of magnificence and munificence in Niarchos's behavior, has lost none of its attraction.

Prestige comes not only from the ability to spend vast sums but also from the way in which that money is spent. Recently amassed collections exhibit a sophisticated form of ostentatious consumption. The collector who can afford prestige no matter what the cost has no need of a shrewd acquisition strategy. He can buy only works of unquestioned value. Of course nothing says that the great collector cannot also be an enlightened art lover with a well-developed personal taste and a deep knowledge of art. But my purpose here is simply to explore possible social interpretations of collectors' behavior. It would only confuse matters were I to cross this self-imposed boundary to examine a welter of individual cases.

The "Proper" Bourgeois Collection

Only the wealthiest collectors can rival the museums in their purchases. Less wealthy buyers must make sacrifices: "If I could afford Picassos (from the Blue, Pink, or Cubist periods) and Braques, or Uccellos and Piero della Francescas and Memlings and Van Eycks, I would prefer them, but they're out of the question. They're for Greek shipowners and Texas oilmen." [C29] Thus, the less wealthy buyer is left to choose between the two main tendencies in modern art, and the one to which he is drawn most directly is figurative painting. This is not to say that collections of avant-garde art cannot be fashionable; nonconformity has its uses, not least as a way of manifesting cultural pretensions. But the proper bourgeois buys nothing that is not "as it should be" [C25]. The choice of avant-garde painting is seen as a sign of deviance; it may be a good investment, but ideologically it stands for something unacceptable. Such has been the experience of those who have attempted to champion avant-garde art in bourgeois circles.

Among my peers I am waging a battle for a lost cause. [C23]

At first [my choice] attracted much ridicule. My father talked about disinheriting me. My brothers, my children—everybody was against me. Now they think I did well. [C59]

When I was younger, my husband used to tell me that people took me for an eccentric.[C73]

I was inhibited when it came to buying modern art because the man I was married to preferred older painting, the art of the eighteenth century. I was not always able to do what I wanted to do. Whenever I hung a painting in my bedroom, my husband used to say, "Another one of your follies." [C46]

My wife didn't like [modern art]. She thought it deluded. [C34]

You mustn't frighten your clients. [C60: a physician, who had hanging in his waiting room a large painting by Commère, the only figurative painting I saw on his walls]

Hostility to avant-garde art reflects an aesthetic-moralistic attitude defined by negative as well as positive norms. Avant-garde art is dismissed as insignificant: "It doesn't represent anything, it doesn't mean anything." Art should not be a pretext for the artist to indulge his fantasy and imagination. The rejection of avant-garde art is less categorical with some people than with others. Fashionable art collecting is not a throwback to nineteenth-century academicism, eclecticism, and anecdotalism but a compromise between tradition and imitation on the one hand and novelty on the other.

Fashion is a form of domination of the individual by the collectivity. Bourgeois snobbery, nostalgic for aristocratic distinction, requires uniqueness and seeks to create distance through difference; fashion, on the other hand, tends to promote uniformity. Art can become fashionable only if it conforms to buyers' implicit expectations and habits of perception and does not disrupt their intellectual and moral complacency—when it attenuates originality and absorbs innovation after a suitable period has elapsed. Fashionable art offers the illusion of modernity without the scandal.

Today's bourgeois art collections are filled with this art of compromise, whose main showcases are the Salon d'Automne and the Salon des Peintres témoins de leur temps. Bourgeois epicureans buy what they like, but not without concern for its quality as art (this is what distinguishes them from petit-bourgeois and working-class buyers of art). The works they buy must be painted by qualified painters, certified by diplomas, honored by awards, and approved by the critics in which this segment of the population places its confidence. The bourgeoisie seeks the "pleasures of figurative art" with a more or less discerning eye.[9] "I would have nothing to do if I didn't take an interest in art. . . . I buy what I like: genre painting, landscapes with human figures." [C36][10]

It is natural enough to expect painting to convey the beauty of the world, but that fact alone cannot account for what traditionalist collectors collect. The "aesthetic of the ugly" has become remarkably popular in bourgeois circles since World War II. "Miserablism" is in the forefront: what has become fashionable is more a morbid than a tragic vision of the world, a representation of banality, of common, mass-produced objects— a figurative version of the "garbage aesthetic" adopted by some avant-garde circles.

It is simplistic to divide prestige collections into just two classes: one contains consecrated works whose value is attested by their inclusion in the academic syllabus, and the other contains recent painting whose value depends on fashion. Many prestige collections are eclectic; old masters hang alongside paintings by today's artists, and minor artists commingle with the great. Each collection reflects a moment in the history of taste. The collection of Margaret Thompson Biddle was auctioned at the Charpentier Gallery on 14 June 1957 under the direction of Maurice Rheims.[11] The sale included works by Bauchant, Boudin, Buffet, Carzou, Corot, Constable, Benjamin Constant, Van Dongen, Jean Eve, Gauguin, Lorjou, Monet, Matisse, Yvonne Mottet, Otto Friesz, Renoir, Trouillebert, Vlaminck, Vuillard, and Ziem.

Prestige Buyers

As we discussed, ostentatious expenditure confers prestige by demonstrating wealth, but the purchase of innovative painting can confer prestige in the absence of wealth. Discoverers and promoters take the place of conservatives and conformists. While scholars shed new light on past epochs in art, men of sensibility identify which current works are destined to endure. In the nineteenth century Thoré-Bürger revived Vermeer, while Victor Chocquet anticipated the future of impressionism. Without the aid of hindsight it is difficult to judge which of our contemporaries may be prophets.

Scholars and Their Collections

With a large fortune a collector can afford to be without knowledge of art. Conversely, with knowledge, a collector can do without a large fortune. Not all past art is in favor at any given time. Each new generation of scholars alters our vision of history. Museum curators and art historians can rediscover and popularize previously neglected periods and schools. By writing, lecturing, and organizing exhibitions they alert nonprofessionals eager to be on the cutting edge and perhaps also to turn a handsome profit.

Consider, for example, the collection of art historian Denis Mahon, a specialist in Guercino. It features paintings of the seventeenth century: Mahon's "collection followed his intellectual interests. . . . A collection based on scholarly considerations alone would be sterile. But he allows his choices to be influenced by other than subjective considerations: a painting's glorious history, for instance, or its importance for subsequent artists, or its significance as the point of departure for a new style."[12] Guido Reni, Domenichino, the Carracci brothers, and Guercino are represented.

> Thirty years ago the early Guercinos could claim only a handful of admirers. Most people felt that they were too melodramatic. Perhaps thirty years from now new intellectual fashions will lead us to prefer his later works. By refusing to pay undue heed to ephemeral tastes and by acquiring as many as he could of the paintings that obsessed the imaginations of men at a particular time in history, Mahon has managed to amass a group of paintings that any museum with a sense of history would envy.[13]

Scholarly research logically leads to "professorial" collections: learned and didactic. The following is an excerpt from an interview with a collector of neoimpressionist art.

> When I was in my twenties I was interested in the Pont-Aven School. The show at the Gallery of France in 1942 converted me to neo-impressionism. At that time it was still possible to purchase neo-impressionist works. . . . I became interested in this painting for scientific reasons. I felt that this was where modern painting was born. I saw it as the birthplace of cubism and abstract painting. . . . The basis of my collection was scientific. I wanted to explain and give proof of the way in which painting style had evolved. When I sold paintings and bought others, it was to fill in gaps in my argument. My collection has a didactic aspect. That is its professorial side. I have worked assiduously to complete it, to eliminate the historical gaps and improve the quality. . . . I have many documents, letters, and notebooks. I have read all the criticism of the time. I go from the works to the men who made them and from one artist to another. I have followed the trail of H., who served as liaison among the neo-impression-

ists. I am working on a biography of S. I am consulted as an expert on the subject. [C39]

Discoverers and Avant-Garde Collections

Collectors of contemporary art also look for innovation, but their risks are far greater. Scholar-collectors can rely on their knowledge of art history, but modern art buyers have no beacons to guide them. To the question whether it is possible to amass an art collection without vast wealth Kenneth Clark answers:

> The only alternative is to buy works of contemporary artists before they become famous. That is undoubtedly the riskiest sort of collecting. It offers a maximum of excitement, because it is a game of chance and because the art of our era touches us more deeply than that of the past. The element of chance has increased over the past fifty years in the sense that modern art depends on its immediate shock effect, and the collector can no longer rely on his knowledge to "read" a canvas as Cassiano del Pozzo "read" a Poussin.[14]

Contemporary judgment is based on a logic of priority. For the progressive spectator the "great" painter is the one who marks a turning point or stage in the development of art. Change is valued in itself: it points the way toward the future. Eclectic collectors combine paintings of all the various postwar schools, like so many strata deposited by the ever-changing history of art. When the paintings in a collection are united only by the collector's desire to affirm forward-looking values, the result is incoherence. Collectors of this generation, like artists, define themselves in opposition to the preceding generation.[15] Everything depends on precisely when the collector chooses to memorialize his own past rather than continue the adventures of his youth.

While some modern collections embrace all that is "new," allowing nothing to escape, some more personal collections reflect a coherent set of preferences: the Apollonian as opposed to the Dionysiac, if you will. Neither excludes eclecticism, but in the more personal collection eclecticism expresses a temperament. Some dream, like Matisse, of a balanced art of purity and calm; others aspire, like Dubuffet, to an art that is disorienting and traumatizing. Some emphasize meditation, serenity, harmony, and repose, while others accentuate anxiety, pain, and distress. These different desires were met in various ways by cubism and geometric abstraction on the one hand and expressionism, surrealism, and abstract expressionism on the other.

Collectors with taste define themselves more by what they reject than by what they accept. The catalogue of the Sonja Henie-Niels Onstad collection, for example, emphasizes the collection's refusal of despair, violence, lament, and confusion. "Max Ernst is the only true surrealist, but he is represented by two works that are more cubist-decorative in nature than they are surrealist."[16] The introduction to *Itinéraire d'un jeune collectionneur 1948–1958* illustrates the other tendency.[17] Polynesian idols sit alongside Odilon Redon's fantasies, Picasso's distorted figures, surrealist dream-painting, unbridled Pollocks, Dubuffet's thick paint, and Bettencourt's erotic reliefs.

If the scholarly collection serves to teach, the modern collection acts as polemic. The goal is not merely to become familiar with an artist but also to make him familiar to others and to win him recognition. The stronger the resistance to a painter's work, the more ardent the desire to convince others of its worth.

> Ever since I was fourteen or fifteen I've wanted to write about painting. But I chose the same line of work as my father.[18] My colleagues have little interest in the art of their time. I did my military service in one of the few cities in France whose museum has made room for modern art. When I saw the Picassos, I realized that this was a powerful new force in art. Since my youth I have written in defense of modern painters, attacking the provincial fortresses that remained closed to modern art. . . . I started buying art later on, after I was established in my career. . . . Because I'm rather remote from the noisy Paris scene, my collection lacks homogeneity. It reflects my avidity for life, my desire to know everything and to try everything. Everything interests me. I know a little about everything. I do not like eclecticism, but I recognize that my collection is eclectic. . . . I am a member of the Council of Museums. I became an art critic so that I could defend the painting I liked. I give introductory lectures. I organize shows. [C23]

Snobs

The art lover who champions works he does not own acts out of unquestioned sincerity. The case of the collector is not so clear, however. He is liable to two charges: snobbery and speculation. Speculators are easy to identify, but it is much more difficult to distinguish between collectors who discover or rediscover works of art and mere snobs. Their relation to artwork is the same in both cases: aesthetic choices are used as a means of differentiation. The buyer buys what other people do not. "I am a person who wants to participate in my era and not fall behind the times. It's the same in music. I try my best to appreciate atonal music." [C50]

Avant-garde art, more difficult to grasp than realistic forms of art and in many ways esoteric, is limited by its very nature to a minority of the elect. Thus it fulfills a major requirement of snobbery: it demands initiation.

The quasiphilosophical language of modern art criticism creates a "deliberate jargon"[19] known only to a select coterie. This art jargon is a sign of belonging, which designates initiates as belonging to the "happy few." "Every leap forward in art is met with incomprehension, except for a small elite of initiates." [C55]

Even the most deliberately provocative experiments of American pop artists and European neorealists failed to discourage their enthusiasts. There is no lack of cultivated people ready to explain and justify their efforts. Snobs have been quick to hail the bizarre as novel and the garbage as bizarre, availing themselves of the noble's traditional privilege to amuse himself, even to debase himself, without tarnishing his image. "Living amid such tiresome comfort, you eventually feel the need to display your garbage in the center of the living room." [C30] As the pace of innovation in art increased, art lovers and snobs alike were forced constantly to revise their taste. For the avant-garde, the danger is that quick assimilation will reduce the advanced to the merely fashionable. The snob and the *amateur* determined to remain ahead of the pack must support whatever group occupies the current cutting edge. Posterity may overrule their judgment, of course, but this is of little concern to the snob, who is out not to recognize innovative genius but simply to assuage his "unhealthy need for novelty of every kind."[20]

The collector commits the sin of snobbery not by favoring progressive art but by unwittingly allowing nonaesthetic considerations to influence his aesthetic judgment.[21] It is snobbery when a person derives greater pleasure from being up to date or belonging to a sect of initiates than from the work itself. Given the nature of today's art scene, it is therefore quite difficult to distinguish between the snob and the enlightened art lover. We must look not only at which works are purchased but also at how they are purchased.

> Outwardly conformist behavior is nothing unless its manner, betrayed by a thousand imponderable signs, is legitimate. And the only definitions of this legitimate manner are circular: the accomplished man is one whose manner is correct, but to have the correct manner one must be an accomplished man. . . . The culture offers not only models of behavior but also models of behavioral modalities.[22]

It is easier to become the owner of an avant-garde art collection than to enjoy avant-garde art as an aesthete, although the former can of course easily simulate the latter.

To be recognized as authentic, one must belong to an elite, which imposes new values rather than recognizing old ones. This elite is both cultural—new values are created by intellectuals and artists—and social—

high-status individuals capable of welcoming innovation in the arts influence others of lower status to do the same. Thus, members of the cultural professions can embrace the new without being suspected of snobbery; so can established members of the social elite. Both groups can claim cultivated status regardless of their attitudes toward modern art.

On the other hand, people who have neither cultural nor social privilege will be suspected of snobbery if they embrace modern art, since the only apparent motive for their behavior is its social significance. This motive is avowed in the following interview with a collector who owns a retail business and whose collection contains a sampling of recent work of various tendencies:

> I have always been interested in art. I used to be a bibliophile and owned only a few small paintings, to decorate my walls, paintings by [various well known twentieth-century masters]. But then I bought a larger, more modern apartment. I sold my library. I sold the paintings, which were too small, and turned my attention to modern paintings. . . . I had no guide. I cannot be influenced. I'm a very instinctive person. I never read the critics, or else I read them only after I have made my selections. . . . My choices have been eclectic and international, but all avant-garde. I tend to buy what will soon be happening rather than what has already happened. I buy young painters or painters who, though no longer young, are still unknown. When I bought F. in 1950, he was not yet well known. I was the second to buy E. and among the first to buy V., U., and D. I also bought many paintings by Americans. . . . I'm always looking. I want to be up to date. It makes sense to help today's artists and craftsmen to live and work. We have to do today what the kings and popes used to do and what the bankers and industrialists of the United States are also doing. . . . I don't really like Pop Art, but its role is pivotal. . . . I've contributed to the success of certain artists. When I buy a painting, ten or fifteen other people will do the same. . . . Painting gives pleasure to the eye, and of course it's part of the culture of a civilized person. . . . I lead a relatively isolated life. I am not one of those—very chauvinistic people, by the way—who sell paintings back and forth among themselves. [C79]

Wealth is the mark of prestige among collectors who buy paintings of generally recognized value, whereas discernment is the mark of prestige among collectors who buy paintings the value of which is not yet generally recognized. "Discoverers" can make up for inferior wealth with superior culture. Snobs like to pass for discoverers and pretend to lead the way. No matter how wealthy they may be, they distrust wealth as a measure of social distinction. Since ostentation is associated with the parvenu, the snob prefers to buy "what costs nothing" but requires keen judgment. But speculators take advantage of both economic and cultural prestige.

Speculators

Speculators wager on both the aesthetic and the economic value of the works they buy. Some market sectors lend themselves to speculation more than others. Speculative opportunities are not as good with older painting as with contemporary painting, but it is possible to speculate profitably on historical works; prices do fluctuate, partly in response to changes in taste brought about by scholarly research and changes in the overall economic climate. But buying Poussin when the demand for eighteenth-century art is high, or buying minor impressionists when impressionist masterworks are no longer to be had, are fairly predictable strategies. To make huge profits as a speculator requires taking major risks, and this usually means investing in contemporary art.

Speculators have shown some interest in contemporary painting that to one degree or another embodies traditional values and techniques. When a "proper bourgeois" decides to take a flyer in the art market, he will generally bet on epigones of established trends, buying minor impressionist, cubist, or fauve paintings or the work of "younger" painters whom he hopes will turn out to be new Bernard Buffets.

> My taste? It runs toward modern painting, but I'm quite eclectic. I have some paintings from the late nineteenth century and some from the early twentieth. Abstract art doesn't interest me much, but every now and then— . . . I had some paintings by D., quite a few actually, but when I saw all the publicity he was getting I sold everything, and I think I made the right move. Nothing has gone up more than modern painting. There's no other investment that can match it. I've given advice to friends, who made good profits, to say nothing of their pleasure. [C65]

Nevertheless, speculators have naturally been more attracted to progressive than to traditionalist tendencies in contemporary art. The experience of the late nineteenth century showed that there was money to be made investing in revolutionary art. Today's rapid pace of innovation encourages short-term speculation, and speculation, in turn, enables the market to absorb new directions in art. Artistic innovation feeds speculation and vice versa.

Speculators are imbued with the very spirit of capitalism. Their judgments are quantitative. For them, money is "a remarkably convenient way of quantifying those values which by nature are difficult to weigh or measure, thus bringing them within the sphere of comparative judgment. . . . It becomes possible to say that this painting or this jewel is worth twice as much as this other painting or jewel."[23]

Innovativeness is thus the speculator's primary criterion. The collector who looks for innovation risks being wrong, risks confusing the authentic discovery with the fake. Furthermore, the speculative attitude is by no means incompatible with a sort of snobbery of the new.

> Speculating means buying an artist's painting just as it is taking off, buying new art just as it begins to register on the chart. . . . I sold all my D's. I would like to sell my two F's. I took them to a dealer who told me that for the time being he had no buyer. I'm waiting. I'm selling these paintings because I feel that the painters have been turning out too many of the same kind of thing. I don't believe in them any more. [C71]

> You have to choose painters who don't imitate anyone else. Speculating on epigones is possible, but it doesn't get you very far. [C77]

Speculators are adventurous souls who like to gamble; they play roulette, and they buy painting. "Passion, luck, and risk are as much a part of economic activity as of gambling. Pure greed does not act, nor does it gamble. Risk, chance, uncertainty, and tension are the essence of ludic behavior."[24]

Finally, spectators are drawn by the lure of profit. While few collectors deny that collecting can be lucrative, money must never be avowed as the aim of their activity. For obvious reasons, most collectors rationalize their behavior in this regard. Speculation is gambling, and any reward is simply compensation for risks taken—the spoils of victory. Collectors pride themselves on their good investments. A collection that costs nothing cannot be criticized as wasteful; it is the opposite of spendthrift folly. The enlightened art lover is commended for his knowledge and taste; the market ratifies his choices and rewards his virtue.

One collector, who owns several different kinds of art, gave answers that typify the effusive enthusiasm of the speculator.

> I don't collect just modern painting. . . . I refuse to pay high prices. I dislike spending millions on what my father bought for pennies. I buy young painters. I enjoy discovering them. By the same token, it's more interesting to buy small oil companies than to buy Royal Dutch Shell. Gambling plays a large part in what people refer to as speculation. Obviously I buy only those works that please me, but I often buy more than one work by a painter. If I'm right, I sell the ones I like least. . . . Deals? I make them all the time, but I buy only what I like. I keep accounts. My purpose is to bequeath to my children a collection of modern paintings that will not have cost me a cent. H. needed money. I bought 3 million francs worth—eighteen or twenty paintings—in one fell swoop. I sold three little ones that I didn't like, and I've already made back 2 of the 3 million. It's a mind game. Speculation is meditation, it's prediction. It's also fun. [C44]

Of course there is coyness in this confession. Collectors who know that no one would ever doubt their wealth like to say that they "can't afford" this or that. Those who have lived on intimate terms with art from birth can indulge themselves by treating painting as an object of speculation. Others are not so comfortable.

I paid between 30,000 and 200,000 francs per painting. Lately I've been making trades so that I can buy more expensive paintings without putting out too much cash. Still, it's impressive to know that a painting for which you paid 2 million is now worth 100 million. The present value of my collection is far beyond my means. That pleases me, but it also worries me. I wonder, as I do with the stock market, when it will go down. You can't help wondering, even if profit isn't your motive. . . . I hope I haven't shocked you. There are also speculators, but even if they start out speculating, they end by being caught up in the game. [C65]

We bought the paintings because we liked them. We didn't want apples and pears. Anyway, 500,000 francs was too much for a Soutine in 1949. . . . In the beginning, it wasn't for investment but to find some stuff to put on the walls. Who could have predicted that the investment would turn out so well? Like the painting by D. that we bought for 60,000 francs and sold three years later for 700,000. But it's still pleasant to feel that you made the right choice. [C71]

To speculators, paintings are much like shares of stock. They pride themselves on having built their collections with very little outlay of cash. Many are bankers and businessmen whose rational calculation enters into their appreciation of art. Art collecting also lends dignity to other business activities. Speculation, whatever its object, is amusing. Because good taste and good investment go hand in hand, the speculator qualifies as a connoisseur by the profits he earns.

Speculators in avant-garde art are quite eclectic, ready to embrace whatever is new. They are likely to own or to have owned almost any artist who became well known after 1948. Because the collection is treated as an investment portfolio, its contents are constantly changing. The behavior of speculators is largely governed by a simple market strategy: buy low and sell high; and buy enough paintings to be able to influence the market. There is a clear difference between collectors who systematically adopt such a strategy, regularly turning a profit on the sale of paintings from their collection, and those who from time to time part with a painting for reasons unrelated to speculative advantage.

Spectacular profits have been earned from speculation on the works of painters who died prematurely, such as Nicolas de Staël, Wols, and Pollock. Another opportunity for speculation is to buy the work of older artists who have not yet "made it" commercially, provided that there are not already too many canvases in circulation; otherwise the existing paintings have to be bought back at the new, higher prices. The most common approach is to monopolize the output of a fairly young painter (unknown to all but a handful of specialists) by paying him a regular stipend in exchange for the right to buy everything that he paints. In some cases one or more collectors will sign a contract with an artist. After the collectors have stocked up on the artist's work, they persuade a gallery to take him on. The support of experts is sought. Once excitement is aroused, a chain reaction begins, as buyer after buyer seeks the work of the newly discovered artist. Finally the price reaches that magic level where prestige buyers want to own the man's work. At that stage the speculator sells all his holdings of the artist's work, if he is a pure speculator; if his motives are more complex, he may sell only part of his holdings.

In the short term the risk is minimal. What matters is not what will actually happen but what other speculators think will happen. In the long run everything depends on the quality of the works selected. Hence speculators anxious about the validity of their aesthetic judgments, or purely rational in their economic behavior, will not wait. Since successful speculation requires selling at the right moment, they calculate profits in the manner of stockbrokers and adjust their portfolios constantly to changing market conditions.

> Painting didn't interest me as such. . . . People who came to see me and who didn't care much about abstract painting told me that there were good deals to be had. . . . A color drawing by F. that was worth 15,000 francs two years ago is now worth 250,000, but that won't last long. There's an F. fad right now as well as an R. fad. I was offered 1.2 million francs for a painting by F. I wanted 1.5 million, so I didn't sell. I'm sorry now. When you hit the peak, you have to sell, because it doesn't last long. Once you've sold you can buy something of more solid value. [C77]

Over the decade 1952–1962 the spectacular increase in prices paid for painting fostered confusion between two systems of values. The art market increasingly resembled the stock market. Since 1962 the market has cooled off, and collectors have begun to reexamine their behavior. Falling prices raised doubts about the wisdom of investing in contemporary art in the minds of those who lacked confidence in its aesthetic value. Collectors tried to sell their holdings. One influential art broker told me: "There are twenty-five or so collectors who buy to influence prices. They store the works for a time and then resell to foreign brokers. They're the scourge of the market. When panic sets in, they sell. When the crisis hit Wall Street, the bottom dropped out of the art market, too, because those buyers lost their heads and were willing to sell at any price." Or they simply stopped buying. Some switched from speculative to more solid investments, from painting of dubious aesthetic value to established works. Others, unrepentant speculators, looked for new corners of the market in which to carry on their speculation, turning to modern sculpture and primitive art.

It is naive to think that falling prices punish speculators for their excesses. The calculators who played by the rules of the economic game were not hurt, any more than those who purchased paintings solely for aesthetic pleasure. The crisis of the early 1960s showed the two worlds poles apart, a fact partially concealed by the febrile speculation of the 1950s.

From Ideal Types to Concrete Reality

In reality, the behavior of collectors is not necessarily as consistent as an ideal-typical classification would suggest. Pure types are rare, mixed types much more common. Many collectors buy for prestige, and it is not uncommon to buy works to own as well as to speculate on. Matters become even more complex when we examine how the behavior of collectors evolves over time.

Mixed Types

The collector who buys both established older painting and fashionable new painting is following accepted social values. This type of collector avoids risks and subscribes to what I shall unblushingly call "bourgeois taste." One collector commented: "I own some eighteenth-century works, some impressionist paintings, and, as for the moderns, some Marquets and a few works by poetic realists. Nothing nonfigurative." [C89] In calling such taste bourgeois I simply mean that the bourgeois is influenced by conventional contemporary judgment, whereas the artist, with his sights set on future glory, has his mind fixed on posterity, for which invention and novelty are the qualities that count.[25]

Other collectors, less influenced by conventional values, seek cultural prestige by buying avant-garde art or older art rediscovered by enterprising art scholarship. They aim not to perpetuate old values but to establish new onces. Such collectors are generally aesthetes.

Socioeconomic prestige is combined with cultural prestige in many ways. Haphazard modern art collections reflect on collector's determination to be current. The typical "society" collection reflects the influence of both fashion and snobbery. By making extreme choices a collector can place himself at the pinnacle of both the socioeconomic and cultural prestige hierarchies—witness the collections of certain very wealthy collectors of avant-garde art. Douglas Cooper commented on the collection of Elie de Rothschild:

> Baron Elie's collection is interesting in that it is constantly growing and developing, confronting past and present. It is also in the hands of a young Rothschild who possesses to the full the family's sense of tradition and yet seeks to advance with the age by trusting to his taste and his speculator's instinct. . . . Elie de Rothschild has no preconceived tastes, and his likes are neither static nor old-fashioned. Though he may appreciate the historical side of some of the pieces that he owns or purchases, he lives in the present, and his collection is an intrinsic part of his daily life.[26]

His personal collection is notable for its ultramodern paintings: "Above all he likes to make forays into the sometimes speculative art of the present day."[27]

Collectors' Personal Histories

The collector's taste does not develop arbitrarily. There is a hierarchy of cultural values that collectors must ascend rung by rung. Many begin with accessible, easily interpretable, largely decorative painting and proceed to more difficult painting that can be understood and judged only in terms of sophisticated artistic and intellectual values. In literature, too, the novice often prefers sentimental narrative and only later progresses to more sophisticated forms, and in music the neophyte frequently begins with program music before attempting to appreciate more difficult works. As the collector's taste becomes more sophisticated, he moves from the realm of subart, where taste is arbitrary,[28] to that of fine art, where an established hiearchy exists.

Contemporary collectors of modern painting often retrace the steps of the artists themselves. Historically, art gradually liberated itself from extra-aesthetic functions and became an autonomous activity, an end unto itself; representative images—allegorical or symbolic-were supplanted by "plastic objects." How rapidly a collector acquires sophistication depends on his personal experience, social background, and education.

> At the beginning I didn't really know what it was all about. When I moved into my home, I bought reproductions for their decorative value. Then I moved from the decorative to the plastic. [C50]

> For a long time my great love was impressionism. It took me a little while to take the step and familiarize myself with modern art and the freedom it takes with respect to nature. Now I understand what painting is in itself. I learned about painting not from books but from painters. . . . It took me a fairly long

time to take to cubism. I was converted at Maeght's show of early abstract art. I then became a fan of the cubists. At the Salon d'Automne in 1945 I saw a lot of Picassos, but they seemed really strange to me. I'm still a bit hesitant. Unfortunately, my interest in cubism came too late. It was too expensive. A collection like mine is put together before the artists became expensive. [C29]

I began collecting at the age of twelve or thirteen. My first collection was of drawings and illustrated books. I loved pictures. At fifteen or sixteen I liked Dufy and Vlaminck. At twenty my attention was drawn to more modern art by various people involved in the art world. I became interested in Klee and Kandinsky. [C46]

Even within a given school, collectors first flock to the most accessible artist before moving on to the "greatest," meaning the most innovative or most accomplished. They seek the best work from the best periods of single artists. Daily intimacy with painting and the inevitable comparison that goes along with collection encourage the collector to become increasingly selective.

At one of the Kahnweiler sales after the First World War I bought a Picasso painting of the head of a Negro. Later, at the Quinn sale in New York, I bought a large gouache by Picasso, also the head of a Negro, this one with the head lowered and arms crossed. The two lived peacefully side by side for a number of years. But one fine evening war broke out between them. I was forced to choose. I began to have doubts about the oil, which gradually lost its expression. By contrast, the gouache gathered strength; its mystery deepened. I sold the painting. But its rival's conquests were not yet finished. It drove eight minor Picassos out of my room. I found I could no longer keep them, because the gouache made them redundant. Today it's the only Picasso I own. It is satisfied, and so am I.[29]

My principle is ultimately to collect few paintings, just the best works of the most important painters. I have many things, but I've made choices. Unfortunately I own only one Picasso: Picasso was already expensive when I began collecting. I sold most of my Légers, but the two I kept are extraordinary. . . . I sold my other surrealists, including one quite expensive but facile work, and bought this very beautiful pre-1930 Max Ernst, which contains everything, everything that followed, V. and the rest. He was the leader of the pack. [C57]

As tastes evolve the manner of aesthetic consumption also changes. The collector aspires to be worthy of the works he owns. "Painting is too complicated for me. When I'm in my room at night and only the paintings are illuminated, I ask myself sometimes if I am worthy of them." [C57] Some collectors seek to make themselves worthy of their collections by extending or acquiring knowledge of art. Their great fear is that they should be

compared with the bourgeois philistines against whom the romantic painters railed. And their great ambition is to see themselves, and to be seen by
others, as aesthetes—the word often carries an unconscious historical reference to the "art for art's sake" movement of the nineteenth century.

> I've thought a lot about the history of art. I've learned a great deal in amassing
> this collection. [C55]

> You have to work on the question, study it with books, systematically. When-
> ever I go to Paris, whenever I have official business at the ministry, I go look at
> paintings. [C24]

> I know the National Museum of Modern Art quite well. I've been to the major
> shows several times. I come to Paris on purpose when there is a show. [C22]

> Before the war I had older paintings, but I got rid of them. My interest in paint-
> ing really began in 1947–1949. My taste has evolved since then, and I'm
> ashamed of my early purchases. I've tried to educate myself. I've attended lec-
> tures and joined a group that arranges visits to museums and artists' studios. I
> go to the public auctions and buy little anywhere else. I keep a file of critical ar-
> ticles and prices on the various painters. [C36]

It is more difficult to interpret unambiguously the changing tastes of collectors of contemporary painting. In the 1950s the typical collector moved
from traditionalist art to progressive art. Starting points vary: some inherited important collections; others purchased "classical" collections or fashionable contemporary paintings in the figurative mode. But at some point
these collectors became "disaffected with figurative art" and shifted their
allegiance to "today's painting," to "art in its nascent state," to "the painting of our time," or to "living painting" (to mention a few of the most commonly occurring phrases).

> I have always been interested in the arts. My family was very much involved in
> music and the arts. . . . I was sensitive to art, music, and architecture—it all
> goes together. I was interested in Italian and Flemish painting. I started buying
> contemporary painting. My first purchase, in 1945, was a landscape. I still have
> that painting in my bedroom along with some eighteenth-century paintings that
> I inherited. My first modern purchase was a large abstract painting by Nicolas
> de Staël in 1950. I saw it in a gallery and was thunderstruck. I went to his stu-
> dio. He became a very good friend. . . . Since I move in literary circles, I have
> many friends who are artists. Through them I came to know the younger,
> newer painters. [C37]

> I graduated from agreeable paintings to paintings with content. In 1945–1946 I
> bought classic paintings by Renoir, Gauguin, Cézanne, and Rouault. But I

nosed about; I wanted something else. I did the galleries—now they come to me. It was through other collectors that I found my way. . . . I've done some speculating. I sold nineteenth-century paintings. I bought a whole lot of H. at a very low price and sold it to buy newer works. [C34]

Forty years ago I liked very bad paintings. I began collecting seriously in 1950. I bought paintings that I liked: Vertès, Derain, Kisling, Valtat, Asselin, Chabaud. Then a major dealer took a hand and educated my taste. [C57]

The progressive collector's behavior thus seems to be governed by the logic of taste: more accessible paintings are bought first, then more complex paintings that require some cultural background to understand. But there is always ambiguity. This is not a period of firmly established aesthetic norms; there is no uncontested hiearchy of artistic values. Hence there is no guarantee that bolder collectors are not mistaken in interpreting rejection by the majority as a guarantee of greatness. Many more advanced collectors may not be recognized as connoisseurs by posterity. It may be that outward signs of revolutionary work are misleading; obscurity thought necessary may be mere systematic and deliberate artifice. Be that as it may, the progressive collectors of the 1950s have declared their independence from socially accepted norms.

In today's market the role of the collector is crucial. "Collectors make the necessary effort because they're the ones who foot the bill." [P246] Whether the art market flourishes or flags depends on the number of collectors, on their disposable income, and on their willingness to spend money on art. Until 1962 demand was high, thanks to generally favorable economic conditions and the great prestige attached to ownership of art (even before there were special provisions in French tax laws to favor collectors).

Those who collect established painting adhere to the hierarchy of values established by art historians. To be sure, every era looks at the past with new eyes, and it is an undeniable fact that taste changes over time. Nevertheless, periodic revisions of taste are primarily the work of specialists. Collectors follow, some more quickly than others, depending on their level of culture and interest in the work of art historians and curators.

As for contemporary painting, buyers are influenced by the people socially responsible for establishing the hierarchy of values and for shaping systems of thought and belief, those who wield what Auguste Comte called "spiritual authority." In arts and letters they are the intellectuals and creative artists. The new norms are first adopted by the narrow circle of those who create them; later they are imitated by others. Negro masks and tribal artifacts were found in artists' studios and writers' apartments long before they appeared in the apartments of fashionable people.[30]

Art and taste rarely evolve simultaneously. The history of taste and the history of aesthetic forms are not identical; the two coincide only in rare periods, when the creators of an aesthetic message adhere to the same system of values as their audience. Ever since impressionism it has been clear that the world view of artists is very different from that of the bourgeoisie buying their works. This disparity was camouflaged—but not eliminated—in the period from to 1952 to 1962 by the activities of art speculators and snobs, who drove up the prices paid for the works of living artists. In its vast majority the bourgeois class remains faithful to traditional aesthetic/moralistic attitudes and attached to an eclectic range of anecdotal and academic art. The art most likely to become fashionable is that which incorporates enough innovative tendencies to appear original but does not call into question widely accepted aesthetic and moral values.

6

Painters

Broadly speaking, market demand has replaced patronage as the moving force behind artistic production. Since the impressionists the market has not only distributed finished works but also influenced unfinished ones.

In pre-Revolution France, the patron who commissioned a work of art was also its buyer. The dominant strata of society granted social recognition to an artist and his work. For an artist, social success meant receiving a commission from a prominent aristocrat or, better still, the king. The privileged classes anointed chosen artists and, to the extent that they established values recognized by society as a whole, gave the artist a social role. This mode of social integration is no longer available. The dominant group no longer accords social recognition, as it did in a hierarchical society of orders; instead, money now plays a key part, offering proof of success and social prestige.

This raises a number of questions. What tribunals are authorized to pass judgment on the "greatness" of an artist? How impartial is this judgment? Does a wish to enforce a kind of aesthetic orthodoxy enter into the question? Is there collusion between the judges of aesthetic quality and those who set the prices for works of art? How are prices determined? Does market selection bear any relation to the quality of the work? Are the painters whose work commands the highest prices likely to be judged great by posterity? And finally, how do painters see their lot in industrial capitalist society?

I have classified artists by date of birth. (Those born in the period 1900–1920 were placed in one group; those born after 1920 in another.) I have also classified them according to artistic tendency (conservative or progressive). Some degree of arbitrary judgment was involved; however, to minimize this, I limited my sample to artists whose artistic positions were clear and unambiguous. In the end, the sample consisted of four groups of thirty painters each. The artists range from the unknown to the well known, and the prices quoted for their works span a similarly broad range.

Stages of Recognition: Typical Careers

The situation in the late nineteenth century was relatively clear: on one side were the academic artists, with credentials from official institutions and an assured market; on the other side were independent painters, without credentials and, unless they could find a dealer, without hope of finding clients for their work. In the worst of situations the independent painter was condemned to a wretched life of poverty, at least in the early stages of his career.

Today the situation is more complicated. Considered in global terms, the artist is caught between two forms of society. In the Soviet Union painting is subservient to ideology, and the career of the artist is controlled by government agencies. Young students in state schools are choosen at age twelve to receive art training along with their regular course of study; this additional training prepares them for the competitive examination for entry into the state school of fine arts at age eighteen. Upon graduation they either become art teachers or join the artists' union and devote themselves to full-time painting. From then on they collect official prizes, and a few culminate their careers as members of the Academy of Fine Arts.[1]

In the United States there is no national school of fine arts or official academy. Artists are trained in private studios, and their works are shown in private galleries or museums (usually private foundations). Their careers depend on their ability to attract buyers. In schematic terms, then, we have on the one hand a situation in which the artist's career is subservient to ideology and dependent on the favor of official institutions, and on the other hand a situation in which careers depend on the market.

Freedom of artistic creation is taken for granted in France. Careers of two types coexist: some artists enjoy official recognition that ultimately leads to membership in the Academy of Fine Arts; others proceed independently, and the ultimate sanction is success or failure in the marketplace. These two types are not independent: academic careers can bring market success, and painters successful in the market are increasingly winning institutional recognition. Both types of career follow predictable patterns.

Catalog writers, art critics, and museum curators are aware of the fascination that an artist's curriculum vitae can exert on the spectator (not unlike the fascination exerted by a painting's pedigree). The artist's training (or lack thereof), the different stages of his career, and the official institutions certifying his quality are scrupulously noted. The point is always to guarantee the quality of the work by noting the quality of its author, unless the name itself is sufficient, as in the case of Picasso. This expression of value is socially mediated: status, rank, privilege, official position, and power—objective qualifications—must be present for the work to be judged. Only the magician can perform valid acts of magic; only the noble can perform acts of valor; only the physician can save lives. It is important to understand the concrete context in which a qualification is expressed and recognized as legitimate, for this reveals the real meaning of the qualification and the social setting in which it makes sense.

The objective factors that accredit a person as a painter are similar in all sectors of the market: number of shows, number of works owned by museums and collectors, awards received, prices paid for works. But beyond these factors we see a clash between two different types of aesthetic, two different philosophies. In one, aesthetic praise is reserved for those paintings that respect reality and embody accepted artistic values. The painters' earnestness, painstakingness, personal merit, and sincerity are also worthy of note, as are the institutions that have trained and recognized them. In the other aesthetic, praise focuses on the artist's freedom and authenticity; recognition, moreover, is afforded by nontraditional and supranational institutions.

The Artistic Career and the Academy

Art instruction in France is offered by the National School of Fine Arts in Paris, seven other national schools, and sixty municipal schools. Admission to the National School is determined by the results of an annual competitive examination; tuition is free. Students can be admitted only if they will complete their studies by the end of their thirty-fifth year. The course of study is at least three years, with degrees awarded in painting and sculpture. Approximately 3,700 students are included in the system as a whole. Courses are taught by *patrons,* who are not allowed to impose any notion of Beauty; the relation between technique and aesthetics is not simple. Juries are generally conservative and hostile to technical innovation, given that they are made up for the most part of professors who wish to maintain their positions. Study at the School of Fine Arts offers many advantages: free studio space and models, free shows at the Maison des beaux-arts, subsidized meals, and access to important prizes and scholarships.

Every year the Academy offers various prizes and awards, some quite modest, to selected artists. The most important prizes are the traveling fellowships, such as the Casa Velazquez Prize and above all the Prix de Rome. The latter—awarded every year to a painter, sculptor, or engraver, not necessarily a student at the School of Fine Arts—enables the recipient to spend three years and four months at the Villa Medici in Rome. Awarded by members of the Academy of Fine Arts and professors of the School of Fine Arts, the prize generally goes to students who exemplify the values of those institutions. Efforts by the Ministry of Cultural Affairs to "de-academicize" artistic education and change the selection process for the Prix de Rome have been thwarted by entrenched opposition.

Winners of the Prix de Rome are free to choose careers in teaching or devote themselves fully to creative work; some combine teaching with studio work. Among artists whose work responds to existing demand they enjoy a high status. Their clients' tastes are unadventurous and predictable, differing from the tastes of people who buy paintings from street vendors only in that they require their artists to possess more illustrious credentials. The culmination of this type of career is election to a seat in the Institute.

The Artistic Career and the Market

The "official" artist combines awards and honors with the financial advantages of a ready-made clientele and access to government commissions. By contrast, the artist who works for the market is free to break with tradition. He does not need to please juries of professors. Nevertheless, the "free" market has itself become increasingly organized and rationalized over the years. Artists must overcome a series of hurdles if their careers are to advance. Yesterday's impoverished garret painter has been succeeded by today's new mandarins.

Legend has it that young painters with true artistic vocations instinctively opt for freedom. They avoid the official art schools on the grounds that they are inimical to free expression and pursue their art in solitude, occasionally seeking the advice of recognized masters or chosen comrades. In reality, however, even nontraditional painters often spend a year or more studying at the School of Fine Arts in Paris or in another state-supported art school.

Artists win praise for being self-taught.

> Because he believes that the only true knowledge is that which we incorporate in our actions, Degottex, who is self-taught as a matter of fact and by his very nature, has paid little attention to the lessons of past masters. He has spent little time dallying in the museums, eager as he was to burn the bridges of Western culture and painting behind him; for these, it seemed to him, cut him off from the totality of human reality.[2]

If a painter has studied at an official art school, any technique he may have learned is praiseworthy only if left behind.

It's crazy how hard it is to forget the tricks and devices that they're always harping on in the schools. You have to be stubborn and have an unusually clear head to stay clear of all that facile knowhow. It takes some people a lifetime to forget what they've learned, and it's so easy to make do with ready-made formulas that are so widely used. But Dodeigne resisted the influence of his father and the art schools. That took courage, considering the life-sized nude that won him a medal and an honorable mention at the 1942 French Artists' Exhibition.[3]

Along with the autodidact's pride in being self-taught and the critics' tirades against the evils of academic art training, shamefaced artists are wont to confess dreary years spent learning to paint in state-supported art schools. They argue either that the material rewards were simply too good to pass up or that they needed to acquire a certain level of technique before they could develop their own style.

I am a self-taught painter. [P260]

I learned to paint by myself, working in independent studios. [P293]

I worked alone and never attended art school. In the schools all the professors are failed painters looking for cushy bureaucratic sinecures. [P219]

Painting cannot be taught. There is a Chinese proverb that says, Anything worth learning cannot be taught. The only worthwhile lesson comes from within.[4]

I spent three years at the School of Fine Arts in Toulon and a year at the School in Paris. The truth is, I didn't learn very much. [P218]

I attended the School of Fine Arts in Toulouse. There is no school worth going to any more. [P296]

School has its advantages for artists from poor families. There are scholarships and models. [P248]

I went first to a school of fine arts in the provinces and then to the one in Paris. I was registered as a student for thirteen years, during and after the war. The school is a great thing for a kid from the provinces. It has a cafeteria and scholarships. You have to pay to go to a private academy. Besides, the state schools are safe; they kill only the weak talents. A potter who has genius but no technique will turn out primitive stuff. If he knows how to center his piece, mount it, and turn it, he still won't get far if he has no ideas in his head. The thing is to surpass yourself, always to go beyond what you've already done. [P270]

The career of the market-oriented artist is similar to that of the academic artist; the only differences are the institutions that judge the work and distribute rewards. For example, the nonfigurative painters who took part in the show held on 10 May 1941 of "Young Painters in the French Tradition" had to wait until after the war to win recognition; the same was true of the abstract and surrealist painters of the same generation. They began to earn money and win prizes only after reaching the age of maturity. After the Second World War nonacademic painters began to win recognition from new institutions, including modern art museums and galleries outside France.

International expositions, in general patterned after the Venice Biennale (first held in 1895), also played a part. Of particular importance were the Biennale of São Paulo (established 1951), the Documenta Show at Cassel,[5] and the Paris Biennale (established 1959 and limited to artists under thirty-five years of age). The most prestigious prizes—the Biennales, the Guggenheim, and the Carnegie—were awarded by international juries of artists, critics, and curators. International competition and market pressures inveitably played a role. Diplomatic maneuvering is generally easier to spot than economic pressure, which is carefully camouflaged. As Sir Herbert Read has written: "The institutions in question cannot possibly be unaware of the role they played in causing market prices to rise, but their motives are surely disinterested. . . . Yet here we touch on a subtle aspect of the problem: the hidden effects of publicity on impartial minds. . . . In this jungle warfare the award of a prize can constitute a decisive advantage."[6] More skeptical observers delight in pointing out that the award of a prize to an artist often coincides with the publication of a lavish book on the artist's work by a member of the jury, or that jury members often favor artists whose work they have championed for years.

Academic careers unfold under the aegis of the government and its state-supported schools. Honors are distributed by institutions insulated from the marketplace but prisoners of their own traditions. From generation to generation, the major institutions have remained the same. Although the market system, developed in the late nineteenth century in opposition to official art, is an open system, it is hard to deny that collusion exists between those who set prices and those who award prizes. Over the past twenty years, however, the market system and the official state system have become more and more similar. In the market for traditionalist painting, influential dealers have arranged for prizes to be awarded to painters by juries composed of critics rather than professors. As for progressive art, international institutions award prizes that have become essential to the career of every successful modern painter. Thus, nonacademic art also has its prizes and medals.

Such honors are not without influence on prices, and it is not always clear that the awards themselves are not arranged by some economic pressure group. "*Pretium,* or price, occurs in the medieval concept of the *pretium justum,* or just price, the equivalent of today's concept of market price; but the same word also means prize, in the sense of honor or praise."[7] The artist succeeds in two ways: by winning the recognition of authoritative judges and by earning a high price for his work. These two forms of success are not unrelated; each tends to confirm the other.

Modes of Economic Integration

Types of Contract

Readers interested in a full treatment of contracts should refer to the work of Philippe Vergnaud, who has carefully studied the various types of contract between painter and dealer.[8] The dealer who signs an exclusive contract with an artist gains the right to sell all the artist's work for a specified period of time within stated geographical boundaries (for example, throughout the world, in Europe only, or exclusively in France). The dealer is thus able to monpolize sales of the painter's work.[9] In nonexclusive contracts the painter reserves the right to sell part of his output to other buyers. He simply grants the dealer the right to buy a certain proportion of his work, with or without prior inspection. At regular intervals (for example, every three months), the dealer is allowed to select a specified number of the painter's finished canvases.[10] Other terms vary from contract to contract. Some contracts stipulate that the dealer will purchase paintings at regular intervals, while others allow the dealer to take canvases on consignment with payment of an advance to the painter. Still others provide for regular monthly stipends to the painter, the sum total of which counts as an advance against future earnings.

The distinction between consignment and outright purchase is not always clear. In the simplest case, the painter leaves his canvases with the dealer on consignment. The dealer's only obligation is to sell the consigned work should a buyer appear. The dealer then collects a commission on the sale. Or the dealer may buy finished canvases outright. Paul Durand-Ruel and Ambroise Vollard customarily bought "lots" of paintings, which they then sold whenever and at whatever price they saw fit. A more complex situation arises when a dealer wishes to control an artist's future output without incurring liability for value-added tax.[11] Some dealers accept paintings on consignment, sell to the highest bidder, and pay the artist an irregular stipend. Others buy a specified minimum number of paintings per month. A schedule of prices, agreed upon in advance, varies according to the type of work (drawing, gouache, or oil painting) as well as size.[12] Sometimes the dealer agrees to pay a certain price per point for a minimum number of points each month, and a higher price for any points beyond the agreed minimum. A nonfigurative painter less than thirty years old describes his system: "He pays me 1,000 francs per point up to sixty points per month, and 2,000 francs per point for anything above that. That comes to between 100,000 and 150,000 francs per month. Collectors pay 3,000 francs per point." [P275]

The dealer's commission is theoretically 33 percent (or less when the dealer acts merely as an agent). As the dealer lays out more for publicity and shows, his percentage goes up. The longer the period that elapses between payment of the painter and sale to the client, the higher the dealer's profit. Consider the following interviews, the first two with figurative painters in their fifties, the third with a nonfigurative painter in his forties, the fourth with a nonfigurative painter in his sixties.

He takes a commission of 33 percent on consignment and 50 percent when he buys outright. [P290]

He agrees to pay so much per painting and so much per month. Every month I receive a check, and every six months we settle accounts. He keeps 50 percent [P226]

For that painting I got 125,000 francs (2,500 francs per point). It sold for 400,000 francs (8,000 francs per point). [P227]

When he sells immediately, he multiplies the price eight- or tenfold. When he holds a painting for two or three years, the price may be multiplied twenty or twenty-five times over. [P206]

How can you explain to the people, and in the first place to painters, that the dealer who wants to recover the heavy cost of monthly stipends, publicity, mailing invitations, framing, and so on is obliged to charge the client five times as much as he pays the artist for a painting. With that kind of markup, people are quick to conclude that art dealers must be crooks.[13]

An artist may sign a contract with more than one dealer. Often French and foreign dealers will enter into joint agreements with an artist; sometimes several Paris galleries will undertake to sell paintings by an artist whose work is too costly to be monopolized by any one dealer. Such agreements are the prerogative of the dealers. An artist unwilling to sell all his work to one gallery can insist on a joint contract or reserve the right to sell part of his output to another dealer, either French or foreign; the artist stipulates, however, that the other dealer will respect the prices established under the initial contract.

Does the nature of the work influence the type of contract between artist and dealer? The question is difficult to answer. Dealers in what I earlier called non-art are under no obligation; they do not represent a particular style of painting but merely sell a commodity, for which they receive a 33 percent commission. The dealer who sells progressive painting for which no prior demand exists must attempt to establish new values; this is a matter of long-term investiment, and few dealers will undertake such a risk without securing a monopoly or at least a substantial proportion of an artist's output. Monopolistic and oligopolistic practices are more common in the progressive than in the traditional sector of the market. It is hard to give concrete figures, however. Dealers tend to be equivocal on the subject. They will often claim to have an "ongoing" relationship with an artist, but this does not always mean they are his exclusive representatives. In any case, contract terms vary so widely that the meaning of an exclusive contract is hard to pin down in any precise way. Bearing these caveats in mind, I estimate that approximately 320 contracts between artists and dealers were in force in Paris in 1961, and of those more than 200 involved the work of progressive painters.

The Legal Value of the Contract

Whether verbal or written, every contract imposes legally binding obligations on the parties, although it is more difficult to prove a case in court when the contract is verbal. When a dealer or artist repudiates a verbal or written agreement, he implicitly affirms that his word or his signature has no value. In practice broken contracts rarely end up in court; it is interesting to ask why.

French law (article 33 of the law of 11 March 1957) stipulates that "an agreement to deliver all future works is null and void." But it is easy enough to bring futures contracts into conformity with the law by limiting their duration; generally the artist agrees to deliver all his work for a fixed period, usually three years, to the dealer.

Nevertheless, the art dealers I interviewed frequently denied that their contracts with painters had any legal validity. They insisted that the moral obligation outweighed the legal obligation. The contract, they maintain, is a "gentleman's agreement." What really matters is personal loyalty and the value of one' word. Legal agreements simply pervert personal relationships. This emphasis on extraeconomic, extrajudicial bonds, on a code of honor older than the legal code governing mercantile relations, results from the widespread and more or less conscious tendency of participants in the art market to conceal the true economic basis of market transactions. Dealers also emphasize their warm feelings for their painters and the emotional nature of the relationship. In doing so their aim is to separate the artist-dealer relationship from its economic and legal context.

> My contracts with artists have been most amical and trusting. I pay so much per month and assume all costs. The art supply shops send their bills to me. Our understanding is not written down. It is based on trust. It also depends on awareness of our mutual interests. [D143]

> All contracts are moral contracts. If a painter loses confidence in a dealer, that's all there is to it. The accord between painter and gallery must be total. The relationship is one of friendship. [D109]

> Artist-dealer relations cannot be studied in terms of law or economics. There is no legal relationship between dealers and painters. It doesn't exist. [D142]

> I'm interested only in human relations. Emotion is everything. [D131]

The artists, on the other hand, emphasize that the parties to the contract are not equally powerful; the coercive aspect is uppermost in their minds. If a dealer violates his part of the bargain, the painter feels powerless to protest because the dealer may hold large numbers of his paintings and because dealers generally stick together. These factors outweigh any legal protections available to those whose production is more than just a commodity but the expression of a creative personality.

> Going to court is out of the question. I'm not sure that he would try to sink me, because that would cost him, too; but he has the means to do it. [P206]

> Anyway, if you went to court, you'd be done for. It wouldn't be easy to find another dealer. Dealers are very tight in that way. [P252]

Painters and dealers agree that lawsuits are rare. "A young legal scholar has just written a book on contracts between art dealers and painters. I find the book somewhat naive, because I've never seen a case in which a lawsuit resulted from violation of a single agreement. The whole business depends on good faith. There have been lawsuits, but only after the death of a painter or dealer: Vollard, for example."[14] Both parties may nevertheless seek to resolve disagreements in an amicable way. Under French law, obligations incurred under private contract affect only the signatories.[15] As long as the contract is not publicly registered, only the parties know what clauses it contains. If a contract involves both parties in violations of tax laws, going to court could prove embarrassing. One dealer commented: "No, we cannot bring suit, for obvious reasons. We know where too many bodies are buried. He [the painter] earned so much a month and declared approximately that amount as his income. You can't imagine the contortions I had to go through to make sure his real income didn't appear on the books." [D166]

Thus, in theory, the contract between artist and dealer is legally binding; however, in practice, both sides behave as though it did not exist. Contracts are not worthless, but the ambiguous status of the object (commodity or work of art) and the complications due to tax laws combine to make enforcement of contract terms a risky undertaking.

Painters Receiving Monthly Stipends

Under French law, monthly stipends received by a painter are not considered wages. Legally, the painter is not subject to the will of the dealer; the dealer cannot specify the subject of the artist's work or its size or the painter's rate of output. Nor can the dealer insist that the artist work in certain premises or oversee performance of the work. Nevertheless, the payment of a monthly stipend does have much in common with ordinary wages. The sums paid to begining painters are just enough to allow them to live: the "iron law of wages." If the artist paints more than the contractual minimum number of paintings, he is paid at a higher rate for each additional "point," much as the blue-collar worker is paid extra for overtime. The monopoly contract has transformed the art market: what was a "circulation process" has become a "production process," and the "unproductive" artist has become a "productive" worker. Marx defines this distinction:

> Milton, who wrote *Paradise Lost* for five pounds, was an unproductive laborer. On the other hand, the writer who turns out stuff for his publisher in factory style is a productive laborer. Milton produced *Paradise Lost* for the same reason that a silk worm produces silk. It was an activity of *his* nature. Later he sold the product for five pounds. But the literary proletarian of Leipzig, who fabricates books (for example, Compendia of Economics) under the direction of his publisher, is a productive laborer; for his product is from the outset subsumed under capital, and comes into being only for the purpose of increasing that capital. A singer who sells her song for her own account is an unproductive laborer. But the same singer commissioned by an entrepreneur to sing in order to make money for him is a productive laborer; for she produces capital.[16]

One artist told me: "I have no complaints about my dealer. He's a good boss." [P248] On 2 December 1918 the dealer Léonce Rosenberg wrote Picasso in terms that give a good idea of what Picasso must have written to him to provoke such a response:

> In speaking of relations between artists and dealers, you mentioned the class struggle. There is class struggle between bad workers and bad employers, but

for people of high moral caliber there is never struggle, only conciliation. The dealer, you say, is the enemy. Yes, for artists of inordinate pride and ambition. In any case, this enemy has in the past saved many an artist from oblivion and starvation . . . and, as you yourself have said, such favors can never be forgiven![17]

A contract with a dealer is undoubtedly of great economic importance. It enables the artist to show his works to potential buyers. For the client the dealer serves as a guarantor of quality. "Who's his dealer?" is the first question asked by collectors uncertain of their competence to form an opinion about an artist. A first contract with a relatively modest dealer is a painter's introduction into the market. A contract with a major gallery is a certification of the artist's work and the best way to gain access to the high-priced international market.

The contract liberates the painter from clerical chores and economic worries. The dealer negotiates with clients over prices and protects the painter from annoying but necessary collectors.

I don't like selling directly to collectors. I'm sick of it. It's very unpleasant. [P230]

The dealer's social role is extremely important. It is very difficult to sell yourself. You always ask too little. And then you're stuck. It's always less than you would like. [P296]

I'm satisfied with my dealer because I don't like collectors. The only good thing about the dealer is that he gets the collector off the painter's back. [P297]

To be honest, I have to say that we all want a gallery to rid ourselves of clerical chores and publicity, for which the dealer assumes responsibility. And then we want to protect ourselves; we don't want collectors to come visiting. Whenever one shows up, it's a day of work lost. You lose three hours from anxiety just waiting for him to come. If he doesn't like the work, you're angry, and if he does, you're excited. A painter can't be everywhere all at once. [P284]

Nevertheless, painters look upon contracts as a form of servitude, even in the absence of objective constraints.

It's all right to be at the mercy of society but not of one individual. [P276]

When I come for my money, I feel like a kept woman. [P261]

Until I found a dealer, I wasted a lot of time cooling my heels in outer offices. The danger is that after you find a dealer, he'll treat you like a horse that needs to be run. The dealer uses his whip and spurs. [P285]

He takes every picture I paint before the paint is dry. [P222]

Because defending the artist's work is not necessarily the same thing as defending his interests (at least not initially), the artist is exploited. The marketing strategy most profitable to the dealer is not necessarily the one most profitable to the producer. Competition among novice painters for dealers—and hence for the ability to live and work and show their paintings—gives dealers a decided advantage. Not until a painter is well known is he in a position to bargain with the dealer for better terms, such as greater freedom to sell his paintings and higher prices.[18] He may also seek out a new dealer and go with the higest bidder. (In the past, of course, painters were no more loyal to their patrons, abandoning one for another wealthier or more celebrated.[19]

Painters without Contracts

The beginning painter with no outlet for his works often attempts to sell his paintings directly to the public. Initially he may have no choice other than to barter his work for needed paints and supplies or for food, clothing, or medical services. Through personal contacts he may then seek additional clients. These early clients are later looked back upon as "friends," disinterested lovers of art, as distinct from other collectors who are merely the dealer's clients.

I have no dealer. My friends buy my work. I feel close to them. [P244]

A few of the collectors who buy my work are friends of mine We're very close in a spiritual sense. They are cultivated people who happen to be wealthy. They feel out of place in society, marginal, and painting is an outlet for their spiritual energies. Other collectors I don't know and don't want to know. The gap between them and me is too wide. [P218]

I don't know any collectors except for my pals from the old days. I don't know the clients of the gallery I'm with now; if I run into them, it's by chance. [P261]

Some of the collectors who bought my paintings when they were less expensive sold them when the price went up, God only knows to whom—Americans, probably. Yet they told me that they cared about the work, that they would hold on to it, that they had feelings for it. My dealer's prices are very high. None of my old friends can afford my work; even foreign museums find the prices too high. I can't sell anything any more. [P206]

Many painters, particularly among the traditionalists, continue to sell their own work even after they have established a reputation. Some set up shop in tourist centers and spa resorts and sell paintings there. Others rely on personal contacts; in this spouses often play a major role. Such strategies work well enough in local markets. Nevertheless, dealers remain essential if an artist wishes to establish a national or international reputation.

A dealer can also work on behalf of an artist without a contract, serving simply as a sales agent. Painters who have not signed a contract giving a dealer the exclusive right to buy their work (or right of first refusal) consider themselves to be "independent." They may avail themselves of the services of a number of dealers (entering into temporary agreements for shows and exhibitions, for example) without establishing a permanent relationship.

> I've had more than forty shows, but I have no contract. I am opposed to dealers who work in partnership with foreign dealers and try to lay down the law. I have some very loyal clients, collectors who own ten or twelve or twenty of my paintings, and one who owns thirty-six. I have contacts with galleries in France and abroad; I give them paintings to show or to sell, but without a contract. You need luck to become famous without a contract, but you've also got to have what it takes. Painters on contract are like bureaucrats, paid by the month, not true creators free to do as they please. They are forced to turn out so many paintings every month and to have a show at least once a year. . . . It's all business. [P219]

> I've always managed to earn my living by painting and yet remain independent. My commercial base is Paris. I sell exclusively to F.E. He's the only great dealer, but we have no fixed arrangement. He buys and sells; I prefer to be free. He takes care of things, preparing shows and so on, only in France. I have dealers in other countries as well—Belgium, Italy, Scandinavia—and I sell to collectors in South America. Every two years I show thirty paintings in Italy: all are sold. Things are exactly the way I want them to be: no compromises. [P246]

> As soon as I felt powerful enough, I didn't need a contract. [P230]

These statements by "independent" artists should no doubt be interpreted with some caution. While some artists do in fact choose independence others boast of independence all the more loudly because they have no other choice: "If you had come two or three years ago, you would have found me fiercely opposed to dealers and contracts. Now that I have a contract, I've changed my tune. It's like pedestrians and drivers." [P276]

Independent painters seem to have fared better in the art-market crisis of 1962 than painters whose fortunes were bound up with those of a gallery. Ever since Durand-Ruel signed contracts with the great impressionists, the contract has been the cornerstone of the art market. As such, its value depends on market conditions. In periods of prosperity, such as the years immediately following World Wars I and II, the number of artist-dealer contracts increased; in hard times (1884, 1930, 1962), the number decreased. Although a contract can bring an artist security in good times, it is no guarantee when the economy turns sour.

Careers of Market-Oriented Painters

Social and economic conditions influence the careers of each generation of artists in different ways. Artists born around the turn of the century built their reputations slowly; prices for their paintings rose only after they had made a name for themselves. By contrast, artists who entered the market after World War II saw their careers take off relatively rapidly.

Most painters born in the first fifteen years of the twentieth century found the process of making a name for themselves slow and difficult. Some were forced to do work other than painting in order to survive. The Depression hit while they were still young, and many did not begin to live off their earnings from painting until they were forty or fifty years old.

I was born before the First World War. My background is modest. My family was neither enthusiastic nor hostile [about my decision to paint]. It's only in books, I think, that you find families totally opposed to an artistic vocation. It's just that parents worry a lot about the insecurity of the artist's life; they're willing to go along if you take courses that lead to good jobs, as in teaching or architecture. I dropped out of high school when I was around fifteen. I attended the Estienne School for four years, studying engraving. Schools like that train artisans rather than artists, but they play a very important role. Then I went to the School of Fine Arts for a year. I had a traveling fellowship from the government for two months, and the following year a year's traveling fellowship from the city of Paris. . . . When I returned, the depression was on and it was impossible for a new painter to find an audience, let alone buyers. We showed our work to one another. The Salons were an event because you could see what your buddies had been up to. Later I won the Prix de Rome. My first one-man show came when I was thirty-five. . . . During the war my painting sold, thanks to the black market. I was selling almost a painting a month. In 1942–43 I sold a twenty-point painting for 4,000 francs. Today a painting the same size goes for 400,000 francs. By the end of the war I was making enough from painting to support myself and my family. But I wasn't really free from money worries until I was forty-five. I have an agreement with a dealer, but I don't have many shows. I'm beginning to use my knowledge of technique to advantage and to organize my work a little better. I also have shows in the provinces and abroad in the United States and Switzerland. . . . I'm still with the same gallery. It's better to have roots somewhere. Otherwise the clients lose track of you, unless you're one of the big names. Most people who buy my paintings know only the dealer. I take no interest in what becomes of my paintings. Collectors? I know a few. Doctors, pharmacists, industrialists. . . . It's not important to me that I'm in somebody's collection. . . . I feel that I've had a lot of luck. [P238: figurative painter born in 1912]

I had a dealer before the war. I didn't make a cent, but there was plenty of atmosphere. People called it the cradle of art. I was one of a group of painters. I thought we were together for life. . . . I showed paintings at all the Salons: Autumn, Independents, and so on. What was I doing for a living in those days? All sorts of things. I worked in art supply shops. I tried working for the government. I gave lessons. Now people come to me asking for lessons, but I don't want to teach. Just before the war I won a prize, the only one I've ever won. For a while I lived on the prize money. I had a contract with a major dealer from 1942 to 1948, and then with another dealer from 1948 to 1960. . . . Now I'm independent. [P206: nonfigurative painter born in 1904]

Until 1952 I did all sorts of work. I even pressed clothes. Anything so as not to betray my destiny. [P219: abstract painter born in 1904]

I've done everything: music, fabric decorations, you name it. I didn't earn enough from painting to live on until 1953, when I was forty-seven. [P222: abstract painter, born in 1906]

My first painting was bought by Jeanne Bucher. I was in my early twenties. It was during the Great Depression, a very hard time for young people. During the war I did all sorts of things: illustrating and so forth. After that I had money. In 1947 a dealer came to see me. That was when I started earning a regular living. I began selling at age forty. I produced little, and it wasn't easy. [P301: nonfigurative painter born in 1908]

I did other kinds of work in order to live: comic books, political caricatures, page layout. I've been showing my work regularly since 1945, when I was thirty. I sold my first painting in that year, but I didn't really start living off painting until 1953; that's when I quit working as a layout artist. [P263: nonfigurative painter born in 1915]

It would be easy to multiply examples of this kind. Although it is not possible to determine precisely how much painters earn from their painting, an objective indicator of success is to note when a painter quits working in other occupations (a measure independent of maturation of the work or critical approval). Artists born around the turn of the century did not achieve commercial success until the postwar market boom. It should be noted, however, that traditionalist painters trained by state-supported institutions were supported by government commissions and hired to do book illustrations and scenery for theater and ballet. They were also able to teach and engage in other activities which, as one of them put it, "were expressions of their art, not alternative occupations." [P266] But painters of the same generation who chose to challenge established taste had no choice but to work in areas totally unrelated to painting. For a long time their lives were difficult in a way unknown to later nontraditional painters, the most fortunate of whom achieved market success at the same time as their elders.

In 1951 I had a show, which didn't cost me anything, along with some Americans in a very small gallery. I was noticed by a critic who praised my painting in a daily newspaper. We became close friends for a while. This critic was associated with Soulages, Schneider, and Hartung. He showed them my work. Schneider was a member of the Salon de Mai committee. I was invited to exhibit at the Salon de Mai in 1954. At the opening I was noticed by an English dealer, and I made a deal with him. He organized a show for me in 1955. The English dealer brought a French dealer with whom he often collaborated to see my work, which he looked at for a year. In 1956 he included me in a group show. After that I agreed to verbal contracts with him and several foreign dealers. The terms were never written down. Once a year we sit down and look at the situation and raise prices a little. Mine have been rising slowly. [P284: abstract painter born in 1924]

Another painter, a pal of mine, introduced me to a well-known painter who introduced me to an art critic. That same well-known painter also introduced me to a gallery, which gave me my first show. It was a small left-bank gallery and the show didn't create much of a stir. The second show, like the first, came about through a combination of circumstances. A painter friend of mine had bought one of my paintings and the director of a left-bank gallery saw it in his home and gave me a show. In the meantime I participated in a number of Salons and in the Réalités nouvelles and Comparaisons exhibitions as well as in a number of small group shows. Things slowly got rolling, and after the second show the situation improved quite a bit. By the time I was thirty-five I had an exclusive contract with a right-bank gallery, and I was able to live on what I earned by painting. [P297: abstract painter born in 1925]

Every case is special. . . . I took courses at the School of Decorative Arts. . . . As far as I'm concerned, there aren't a whole lot of ways to succeed. The important thing is to show what you do so that as many people as possible get to know and like your work. For a painter who has talent and knows how to exploit it, it takes five or ten years. For a painter who has talent but doesn't know how to exploit it (and the two gifts rarely go together), it takes ten to fifteen years. You hang your paintings wherever they're willing to have you. The first step is the unjuried Salons like the Independents, but to be noticed in a show of that size you have to be one of the twenty or thirty best painters. You're lucky if five critics know your name, and when you're unknown critics will generally give you no more than a mention in their articles. After that you move on to the juried Salons. Reputations are made mainly by other painters, who notice young and still unknown artists with talent. Of course there are also a few well-informed collectors who buy directly from novice artists, and it's possible that a critic will fall in love with the work of a young painter. One break leads to another. But in the end it's usually other painters who make or break a newcomer's reputation because people listen to what they say and ask their advice. Then a dealer invites you to participate in a group show. After that you compete for prizes, and then you're invited by a gallery to hold a one-man show. In my case, I exhibited at the Independents in 1940 when I was twenty years old. I was mentioned in *Arts,* but that's not enough. During the war I worked in a factory. Then I showed my work at the Salon d'Automne and the Salon de la Jeune Peinture. Other painters noticed my work. I showed my paintings everywhere. Dealers took canvases on consignment. Occasionally I sold directly to collectors. I took part in group shows. I won several prizes, including the Populist Prize and a National Fellowship. My first one-man show came in 1950. I signed first with one dealer, then with another. . . . I've been living on my earnings from painting since around 1952. I used to do other kinds of work: apart from the wartime factory work, it was generally decoration of one kind or another. In 1950 I sold three paintings. Little by little, my earnings from painting began to overtake my earnings from decorating. The process was so slow I was hardly aware of it. [P256: figurative painter born in 1920]

In this area all generalizations are misleading. I am well aware that some painters born in the 1920s are still awaiting their "big break" as I write. There is no doubt, however, that many painters of this generation did achieve market success between 1950 and 1955 while still in their thirties. For them the period of relying on another line of work, a wealthy friend, or a spouse's income was much shorter than it was for artists of the previous generation.

By contrast, for the generation of painters born in the 1930s success again seems to require a longer period of waiting. The art market has taken a downward turn, and these younger artists are suffering from the speculative excesses and inflationary prices of the 1950s.

It is useful to distinguish three types of market success. The healthiest is probably the career that progresses slowly, with prices rising gradually as the artist's work matures. Then there is the accelerated career artificially fabricated by skillful managers. Finally, there is delayed success, compensation for a long period of neglect. The latter two types usually involve some sort of commercial push. Many hurdles must be leapt by any artist who achieves world renown, but the process is sometimes accelerated by judicious investment and the use of influence. It is possible to promote bad painters as well as good ones. From the end of World War II until 1962 conditions were ripe for the creation of new stars: the economy was booming, and the painting "craze" ensured that publicity would yield at least short-term benefits. In the long run a painter's success depends on the originality and quality of his work, but in the short run fads, snobbery, speculation, and a certain aura around a man can generate market interest. Promotion is aimed at the short term, but no reputation can survive without enduring qualities. A shrewd dealer can raise an artist quickly to great heights, only to see him plummet just as quickly into oblivion.

The Artist's Standard of Living

The artist's standard of living depends on the nature of the society in which he lives as well as on the way in which works of art are evaluated and sold. In order to grasp how artists feel about the conditions in which they live, however, we must examine not only objective factors such as these but also the ideas they have about themselves and their society, that is, their ideology.

The Ideology of Freedom

The Renaissance ideology of the charismatic artist, confirmed and sublimated by the ideology of romanticism, is still with us today. From the humblest to the most celebrated, the artist is seen as having not just a profession but a vocation. He sees his work as a creative endeavor and anxiously clings to the hope of genius.

Painting is in no sense a job or a trade. It is a vocation. [P294]

Painting is my daily bread; it is body and soul. To be a painter is to have such feelings. [P205]

What good would life be to me if I couldn't paint? Either I paint or I die. [P211]

I know what I am. [P275]

Artists naturally speak of their work in aesthetic terms. They talk about art and about *their* art. They see artistic creation as a direct expression of liberty: "I am wedded to the freedom of creation" [P265]; "The vital thing is to paint, to confront one's work directly." [P297]

Similarly, the only constraints on their freedom that artists will admit are those stemming from the development of their work: "The program is determined in a sense. You draw your inspiration not from yourself but from the work you have already done" [P304]; "You have to follow where your painting takes you." [P256] The artist who responds to social demands rather than to intrinsic creative needs is condemned to being a bad painter:

The young painter attempts to do something new. But painting defines itself in terms of necessity, not novelty. Novelty is something that comes later. Modern art had become academic because it rates fashion ahead of necessity. Young painters want to be innovators no matter what the cost. Such an attitude is just as academic as obediently doing whatever the master teaches. There is also another kind of academicism, what I might call auto-academicism, which is responsible for the majority of failures: failures not with the public but of the painter to live up to the promise implicit in his work. Students fail by remaining epigones of the master, adding nothing to his work, turning out works of competent craftsmanship and nothing more. But there is a radically different kind of failure, more characteristic of our era: the failure of those who elect on principle to oppose all outside influences, who want to do something new at all cost, and who ultimately paint without inner compulsion. As an antidote I advise young painters to live with painting, to live as painters. [P223]

Painters often invoke the nature of a painter's relation to painting in judging his work. For the true artist the moral imperative is to abide by aesthetic rather than social norms. Painters will say of one of their number that he is "uncompromising" or "unyielding," that he "has always been sincere" or "honest," a "true painter," a "pure artist."

You can do anything, anytime: so says André Breton. If that "anything" doesn't stem from some inner necessity, then the work is facile. The artist needs a more sober outlook. He requires a personal ethic. [P228]

The work has to grow from within. If an artist gives in to pressures other than those of painting, he makes himself vulnerable. It's a question of temperament, of the quality of the artist, of the quality of the man. . . . Some painters made a lot of money very quickly. The quality of their work fell off. The work of a particular period has to be seen in the context of the painter's work as a whole; the latest paintings throw new light on what went before. When the later works are a failure, the early works are seen in a new light. People see that the worm was already in the fruit. [P206]

While not incompatible with awareness of the constraints of the marketplace, the ideology of creative freedom governs artists' judgments of a painter's social success or failure.

Types of Strategy

In the short run a painter's success or failure depends not only on the intrinsic quality of his work but also on the system by which artistic products are evaluated and traded. Artists are reluctant to generalize about their situation. They know that there are many different ways of being an artist.

This variety is due in part to the diversity of painting itself, but just as much to the diversity of artists' attitudes toward the market system, which range from outright rejection to one form or another of adaptation. Artists respond to the objective rules of the game in many different ways. As different as their strategies are, they must take account of the individualistic ideology of art, which is as much a part of their objective situation as the economic system itself. The artist is torn between two conflicting sets of demands, which can be summed up as follows: a man has to live, hence he must earn at least a modest living; at the same time he wants to secure his salvation. Thus every strategy for approaching the market has its own rationale to justify the authenticity of the work.

At one extreme we find artists who are contemptuous of the means by which success can be achieved. Consciously or unconsciously they wish to emulate the outcast painters of the nineteenth century. They play to lose and discourage any attempt to lend them a hand. They are "in love with failure and lie down on the tracks whenever they hear a train about to start." [D166] In the most extreme cases they refuse to submit their work to the judgment of others, like the hero of Balzac's *Chef-d'oeuvre inconnu*. To identify such failure-obsessed neurotics we must pay attention not just to what they say but also to what they do. For artists who do not succeed in the market, polemics against the system may be simply a defense against failure. The inequality of rewards becomes bearable if the system is thought to be unjust. The experience of the late nineteenth century proves that lack of success, whether voluntary or involuntary, can actually lend luster to art.

Today's artists take a pessimistic view of success, a view inherited from the nineteenth century: success in this world is not, as Calvinist doctrines would have it, a mark of election in the next. It is rather a sign of failure in the eyes of posterity. The outcast painter of the nineteenth century cannot be accused of having prostituted his talent, since he painted solely for generations to come. Instant success is suspect and compromising; it casts doubt on the authenticity of the work and on its power to endure. Lack of success can be regarded as proof of the honesty of the artist and presumptive evidence in favor of his genius.

In contrast to artists who play to lose are those who attach symbolic value to success and therefore play to win. They reject the model of artist as outcast in favor of the model of artist as prince of the arts. Taking into account the external factors that determine success in a particular field of art at a particular time, the "shrewd"[20] artist adopts the most efficient strategy. Experts in practical sociology, artists during the boom years adapted their conduct to the needs of marketing and publicity. They learned how to use part of their time for public relations to enhance their reputations.

Making yourself known is a matter of waging all-out war against everyone else. On the one hand you have the people in charge of official institutions. For them, if you don't have the Prix de Rome, you're nobody. They're not open-minded, but at least they believe in their history. I forgive those who go the way of the Institute. On the other side things are even worse. They're just as closed-minded, and it drives you crazy. You say to yourself, "Why not me?" At first it's maddening. No matter how much faith you have in yourself, you end up getting more bitter. I am a proletarian, from a family of workers. A part of me badly wants to make it. I'm not an aesthete. I want no part of living in misery. That's a bourgeois fashion. I'm for living in comfort, not to mention the fact that in order to paint you need to have the means to live. . . . You have to do what you have to do. Collectors can be important to your career. They hang your paintings along with others, and, when they have a dinner party, the guests see it. I think of the time I wasted playing the clown at the T.'s, but they were great; they bought my work when I really needed it, and I'm very grateful to them. Critics? If I wanted a film by So-and-so on television, I'd find out where to get invited to dinner so I could meet him. Friends are also important, the ones you have a drink with at the Coupole in the evening. It was friends of mine who introduced me to my first dealer. And it was friends who got me into the Salon de Mai for the first time, when I was thirty-five years old. I wound up with a contract, an exclusive contract. I have only one dealer; he's the one who contacts the foreign dealers. He's not a bad guy, a sort of boy scout. Look, the market is a bunch of families, or, rather, of neighborhoods. You have dealers, critics, and collectors. It all depends on human and artistic affinities. You have to get into one of those circles. I'm now a part of the system; you have to be. But it's a dangerous system for the guy who lets himself be had. [P270]

These remarks make it sound as though there is no connection between what an artist does to sell and publicize his work and what he actually paints. The painter who quickly and easily wins a place for himself on the market is not unaware that, seen from the outside, his strategy tends to discredit him because quick success is interpreted today as superficial and artificially contrived. Thus he needs to maintain, and to convince himself, that social and economic success is but a means to an end: the accomplishment of his work. If he set out to make a name for himself, it was only to ensure that his painting would have admirers and he would be able to work in independence. The self-promoting painter often sounds cynical because he is critical of a system he has been able to manipulate. He talks, as an artist, about the art of success.

Where once intrigue and personal connections were the surest path to success, a flair for business and public relations proved even more valuable in the postwar period. Another winning strategy was that of the artistic daredevil. In a technocratic and utilitarian society there seems to be a compensatory need for kind of magicianship, and some painters have been showmen enough to succeed in filling this need. By pursuing ecstatic experiences, dressing in unusual ways, or behaving eccentrically, they attract attention to themselves. Such behavior may be the outward sign of genius, or it may be a mere publicity stunt. The artist may be inspired, or he may be a wheeler-dealer whose only ability is to profit from making a spectacle of himself. To justify his behavior the painter-showman may resort to such extremes of eccentricty that his behavior ceases to be profitable, thus proving that it was not a rational strategy but an inner necessity. If the artist's charisma is powerful enough, he may not even feel the need to justify himself.

Such charismatic behavior implies that the artist is rejecting all external sources of legitimacy and relying exclusively on himself. These "sacred monsters" of art immediately set themselves up above the normal channels of distribution and use a system of their own devising. Until the Second World War Picasso never participated in any Salon. His biographers agree that he showed no deference to his various dealers. Painters sure of their artistic vision do not distinguish between the means—winning a place in the market—and the end—artistic creation. Whatever they do, their behavior defines what it means to be a genuine artist.

It is not always easy to distinguish between the self-promoting, daredevil, and charismatic strategies. All three transform the painter into a star. The greater and more rapid the success, the more suspect it is.

Overnight success is dangerous. You mustn't be too shrewd. You have to have common sense and know when to say no. [P223]

Young painters are often killed off in embryo. They're not passionate about painting, and they lack a sense of great adventure. They're not strong enough to resist. It's very dangerous. [P200]

Dealers support painters who produce. They are very keen on productivity. For young painters it's a temptation, especially when they're urged to redo what people have liked. [P226]

Integration into the system is supposed to cause the artist to submit to objective market constraints, which can influence his output in both quantitative and qualitative senses. When an artist's paintings are selling well, he may be inclined to shift into "mass production" of works in his current style, which can quickly degenerate into mannerism. But such perversion of the work is not an automatic consequence of market integration. Success can also lead to awareness of the economic realities and suspicion of other market actors. Painters may realize the importance of keeping their goods scarce and controlling their supply, so that they will refuse to increase their output or allow too many paintings to accumulate in the hands of a single dealer or collector. As they become more suspicious of other market actors, they will use their services but remain wary of possible manipulation.

If some painters play to win and others to lose, there is a third group in the middle. These painters do not see rebellion as a viable strategy. Hence they submit to living on modest incomes and doing other kinds of work while continuing to paint. Often they enjoy a *succès d'estime* among their peers before attracting the notice of a broader public, usually fairly late in their lives. Even if they are ultimately taken up by the market, they seem (when viewed from outside) less compromised by it. The quality of their work is guaranteed by the qualifications of the judges who admired it before it earned high prices. Recognition by other artists is reassuring (despite errors of judgment that some great painters have made about the work of others—errors that figure as part of the folklore of art).

> In 1932 Bonnard came to my show. He said some wonderful things to me. They had no practical effect but were of immense spiritual comfort. . . . What counts for me is the opinion of other painters. The only thing that matters is what other painters think, Vieira da Silva for example. The fact that Bonnard thought my work was good gets around. Yes, the important thing is the judgment of painters. [P206]

> What counts is recognition by young artists. [P222]

> I would like for some museum to stage a retrospective show of my work, not to sell but so that young painters can see it and react to it. [P249]

If an artist has done a great deal of painting before achieving commercial success, he cannot be suspected of having succumbed to the influence of the marketplace. Artists are so conscious of this that they frequently point out the years they spent in purgatory prior to being discovered:

> The risk is really something. My wife and I lived through an astonishing period. We managed to live, but meanly, very meanly, from the time I was thirty. We sold a few drawings for very little money. We lived on practically nothing, without feeling that we had failed or turning bitter or going begging. Doing what you like is already quite a reward. I was doing what I liked. . . . Every sale brought me one more defender. We were very poor until 1950. I made about as much as a semiskilled laborer. [P248: abstract artist born in 1911]

Painters relate to the system in various ways, ranging from refusal to adapt to passive adaptation to active adaptation. Refusal to adapt leads to a devaluation of success and a withdrawal into the ideology of the artist as outcast. Active adaptation implies a high value placed on success and acceptance of an ideology of election. Between these two extreme attitudes is a third, which shares characteristics of both. In a sense, the ideology of the artist as outcast is merely a pessimistic version of the ideology of election. It makes sense to ask whether the adoption of different strategies by different painters can be explained in psychological or psychoanalytic terms. Without seeking to pinpoint the deep determinants of each type of behavior, I shall simply make the commonplace observation that no strategy is immune to all forms of external constraint and that all artists are alienated—some by success, others by lack of it; some by poverty, others by wealth.

No matter how the system of art distribution is organized, the artist's problem is to secure his independence, which can never be taken for granted. Renaissance artists often treated their patrons haughtily or disdainfully and so earned an independence not normally present in the patron-protégé relationship. Today, each painter attempts to gain his independence from the market system in a manner determined by his temperament. To distinguish between those who succeed and those who do not, between the prophets and the charlatans, demands consideration of the finished work. Even without an uncontested hiearchy of aesthetic values, it is surely possible to come to a judgment in cases where artistic creation has clearly been sacrificed to profit. Nevertheless, numerous more doubtful cases remain in which the only possible judgment is subjective.

As artists are well aware, art exists as an independent force only to the extent that artists respond more to the inner exigencies of the work than to external constraints.

> The present economic system is trying, but it does not prevent aesthetic selection. Socially, that's irritating. It's almost impossible to live with. But inwardly, no. The painter's freedom is more private, more inward than that. [P303]

> All that is secondary, a mere epiphenomenon. Painting interests me more than money, and I do my painting. [P265]

> Painting holds its own. The best works have vitality. [P220]

> The quality of painting and the tenacity of painters are far stronger than the influence of any dealer. [P206]

Utopias

Although painters deny that market constraints impinge on their creative freedom, they nevertheless aspire to play a social role denied them by existing institutions. To the image of the artist working for private bourgeois clients they prefer that of the artist integrated into a unified society. They

contrast the easel painting, an object of individual pleasure and speculation, with monumental art and large-scale murals that express collective
ideals and serve as a backdrop to social life. Isolated from the broad public by the esoteric nature of their art and contemptuous of the bourgeois
philistines who buy their works for the wrong reasons, innovative artists
dream of a society in which they would be recognized not by the wealthy
few but by society as a whole.

> The market is not a good way of integrating the artist into society, and I reject
> it. What the market offers is integration through money and only through
> money. It leads to anonymous and soulless relations with other people. For the
> painter, the prospect is devasting. The painter needs to be in touch with social
> reality as a whole and not with some financial abstraction. Of course, it takes
> considerable effort to avoid being caught up in it all; it's a hard fight. The trag-
> edy is that if you refuse, you're no longer part of society at all. . . . Art is a
> form of solidarity. I am for a collective art. What the present era needs is to
> transcend the easel painting both formally and socially. It needs architecture.
> We must move toward more reasonable functions for art. [P228]

> I am against measuring painting by its market value. I want painting to be popu-
> lar, accessible to everyone. [P260]

This nostalgia for a lost unity, far from being novel, revives an ideology
that has had its adepts since the days of John Ruskin and his disciple William Morris, who advocated a return to the craft traditions.

> The artist should be rooted in the world in which he lives. And if he has a
> strong temperament, his work becomes a message, an eternal thing. But the
> painter as he exists today is a historical species destined to disappear from the
> face of the earth. There will be no more painters, only men who express them-
> selves by plastic means and who participate in other, more direct arts, in closer
> contact with society, such as architecture. By taking part in collective projects,
> these artists will contribute their deepest feelings about men and society. But
> they will be anonymous. They will no longer be stars as they are today. The era
> of the stars is over.[21]

In an age when the most vital painting challenges prevailing social values and the artist lives in contradiction with the taste of the majority, taking refuge in all-out individualism, social integration is a utopian notion. It
is also incompatible with the ideology of election inherited from the Renaissance and the ideology of freedom and risk inherited from the nineteenth century. It is not at all clear that most artists are willing to return to
the anonymity of the cathedral builders.

I chose this profession with all its risks. You don't become an artist in the same way you become an auxiliary mailman. [P247]

I am for freedom with all its risks. [P208]

Persecution provides a powerful pair of lenses. Money and material comfort prevent you from sharing the experience of persecution. You can't paint in comfort. To do so is a professional error, just the same as it would be an error for a drunken pilot to step into the cockpit of a jet. You lose your position as a social observer and activist. [P249]

Material difficulties are in a sense the gauge of freedom. [P292]

The problem is that artists tend to focus exclusively on the best in every system and fail to consider the social context. Esoteric modern artists profess to want to work for "the people" like the artisans of the Middle Ages; or they wish they could enjoy the glory reserved for artists in the age of aristocracy, forgetting the constraints imposed by necessary commissions; or they dream of the freedom of the outcast artist, forgetting the insecurity that went with it.

The artist, as we have seen, can choose to follow either a career sanctioned by official state institutions or a career sanctioned by the market and private international institutions. In either case he must compete for honors and material rewards. The choice of one or the other is dictated by the nature of the work that the artist undertakes.

Between 1945 and 1960 the art market flourished to such a degree that most painters were able to live in comparative security, while a few earned considerable fortunes. The pace of commercial success accelerated. The early stages of an artist's career continued to be difficult, moreso for revolutionary than for conservative artists, but the length of that difficult period was shortened. Individual differences between artists make it hard to generalize. Some flourish in a competitive market system, while others are condemned, perhaps by themselves, to remain marginal.

The art world is not an idyllic place in which the artist can live "for" his work rather than "from" it, free of all external constraint. Not all collectors are enlightened and disinterested. Not all critics are understanding interpreters. Not all dealers combine a passion for painting with a passion for good art. Once the painting leaves the artist's studio it becomes a commodity, and the artist is exposed to the forces of the marketplace and the influence of those who control it. During the art market boom, it became obvious that success imposes its own constraints. Now that the boom is over, the artist's insecurity is again on people's minds. The painter's well-being is at the mercy of the economic climate. If an artist's work satisfies existing demand, he can earn a living; otherwise his lot is hard. Some are more adept than others at meeting the demands of the marketplace. The market transforms aesthetic judgments into prices, thereby influencing the painter's relation to his creation and thus, to some degree, the creation itself.

Yet every system of artistic production and distribution constrains the artist in one way or another. To judge the situation of contemporary artists fairly, we would have to undertake comparative study, examining how other societies treated their artists and interpreted their art. No system is perfect. As one painter rightly remarked: "I see no system of organization that does not require some concessions on our part." [P203]

Transactions

III

Artworks as Commodities

First we must define what it means for a work of art to be treated as a commodity. As moveable property, easily sold and transported and lending itself to secret transactions, the easel painting is a prime object of financial manipulation. Yet it is no ordinary commodity. Capable of giving pleasure indefinitely,[1] paintings are different from other consumer goods and durables, which are by nature subject to obsolescence. Painting is unique, irreplaceable, and unproductive. With other types of goods, advertising is sometimes used to make an item irreplaceable, but with painting irreplaceability is a given. Painting, like gold, is an unproductive investment that can be used for purposes of protection or speculation. Unlike gold, however, it cannot be traded on an exchange; it must be sold privately or at auction.[2] Prices of artworks are set at the time of transaction and are determined exclusively by the market.

From Junk to Masterworks

To bring out some peculiar features of the market for contemporary painting, the main focus of this book, I shall begin by looking at two extremes of the art market. By examining the market for old masters on the one hand and sidewalk painters on the other, I can abstract from the question of aesthetic value. The works of the sidewalk painters can be assumed to be of no aesthetic value, while the aesthetic value of the old masters can be assumed to be beyond question. Both therefore differ from contemporary painting, concerning which aesthetic judgment interacts in complex ways with market values, and buyers cannot avail themselves of the benefits of hindsight.

Economic Questions and Market Dynamics

Among the key economic questions: What factors determine changes in the price of an artwork? Are prices set in Europe or in the United States? Are the prices of old, modern, and contemporary painting related? Are there any patterns in the way changes in art prices relate to changes in the overall economy or to other circumstances? What economic laws govern the various sectors of the art market, and how well does the art market conform to various market theories proposed by economists?

Analyzing the dynamics of the art market yields much quantitative data. It would be pleasant if these data could be considered reliable and objective. Unfortunately, where the art market is concerned, this is not the case. The only publicly available price data pertain to paintings sold at public auction; this information is of limited significance for contemporary painting.[3] Prices paid for works sold privately are difficult to pin down and vary widely. At any given time a given work may be up for sale at several different prices: one for anonymous buyers, one for museums and a select group of collectors (i.e., a painter's presence in an important collection is good advertising, and dealers are willing to sacrifice financially to obtain it), one for brokers or resellers (the so-called dealer price), and one leaked to journalists for publicity purposes (the tendency here being to overprice, since a painter's status is associated with his place in the economic hierarchy). Much mystery surrounds the sale of old masters. Once shown, they immediately lose value, hence dealers generally keep only "display pieces" in their windows; important works are sold in secret. As for contemporary works, dealers often conceal from their painters the names of the collectors interested in their work, both to avoid being bypassed by direct contacts between painter and client and to ensure that, if the artist changes dealers, lists of clients will not be passed to a competitor. Confusion is deliberately maintained: the murkier the water, the better the fishing. There is no way to study the private art market or the wartime black market other than to gather as much information as possible and then attempt, with all due caution, to draw some general conclusions.

Paintings and Prices

The art market is particularly difficult to study. Any price index is an abstraction. Averages often conceal as much as they reveal, and economists have learned to distrust them. While price indices can be useful, they are misleading in the case of painting. Two paintings of equal size by the same artist are never identical and may not have anything in common; they may differ in period, subject, or degree of finish. Artists nowadays are commonly paid so much per point for newly painted work, yet it is very difficult to gauge the real value of work by living artists.

Other factors affect the price of contemporary art as soon as it leaves the studio. Works by a single artist can sell at widely different prices, and the prices of different works need not vary in the same way. Works by Picasso are not sold "by the point"; each painting is judged and evaluated independently. For the relatively unknown painter, moreover, the auction price may be a long way from the market price. Thus the only valid comparisons are between prices paid for the same work at different times, and these are hard to discover. For want of an alternative, I have compared prices as well as I could (stating in each case how the comparison was made) in order to arrive at a rough estimate of the general trend. To correct for changes in the value of the franc in my price comparisons, I have used a "deflator" factor, based on an average of the wholesale and retail price indices.[4]

The Market for Junk Painting

Viewed abstractly, the market for junk painting seems to conform fairly well to the classical model of pure competition. The number of suppliers is large, as is the number of buyers, and none exerts dominance over the market. The product may be considered homogeneous: one "doe in a forest" can easily be substituted for another. Any painter who wants to set up shop to sell his or other painters' works can do so wherever and whenever he wants. Yet observation of reality suggests that this model is far too simple.

Product Similarity and Techniques of Differentiation

Sidewalk painters (as I shall call the producers of cheap, "subartistic" paintings—"junk" in the parlance of the trade) turn out large numbers of canvases according to strict formulas as to subject and style. "This type of work accounts for most of the painting done in the West. To this group one might add nine-tenths of the works shown in the Salons by aspiring artists, who cannot believe that anyone can love art as they do without having the gifts needed to practice it."[5] In the eyes of connoisseurs, junk paintings are interchangeable objects capable of satisfying only the most vulgar taste. The buyer is less interested in the aesthetic value of the work than in its decorative or prestige value, that is, in qualities having little to do with the uniqueness of the work.

Since there is nothing intrinsic to differentiate such paintings from one another, distinctions are created artificially by those who sell them. They work hard to suggest that the products are distinctive rather than homogeneous and that differences of quality do exist.

One criterion of differentiation has to do with the manner in which the paintings are sold, whether by the painter himself or by a dealer. The artist who sets up his easel on a square in Montmartre and sells his own work takes the simplest possible course. Although nearby galleries object to the presence of these sidewalk painters, the city authorities believe they are a picturesque addition to the neighborhood, a worthy tourist attraction. Any painter who wishes to sell his wares on the streets of Paris must obtain a license from police headquarters.

Sales through dealers are affected by several factors: the location of the dealer's shop, the elegance of the display, the personality of the dealer, and, in the case of unknown painters, the presence or absence of works by better-known colleagues, serving to guarantee the "quality" of the gallery.

At all levels of the market sellers seek to differentiate their wares. The sidewalk painter avails himself of a loud voice and a glib tongue to prove to the passerby that, in spite of appearances, his paintings are not the same as those of his neighbor. The old artist may look like a tramp, but he carefully explains to his client that he has not skimped on either material ("excellent canvas," "vivid colors") or technique ("highly polished," "very good workmanship") or training (he removes from his pocket a medal won at a Salon, though it is hard to tell which one). Finally, he seeks to prove that his work is unique: "Three of us do almost the same thing, with the same colors and roughly the same thickness of paint, but each one has his speciality. Mine is the morning dew." Each painter points out the detail that distinguishes his work from that of other sidewalk painters; he works hard to perfect his particular trademark and faithfully reproduces it in all his painting.

Even in shops where paintings are piled one on top of another among other cheap goods, the salesman is always careful to indicate that the price depends, if not on the painting, then at least on the artist. There are many ways of differentiating artists: by subject (this one specializes in scenes of hunting), technique (thick paintwork costs more), or training (eg., membership in the Société des artistes français is a credential that adds to the price). In any case, the salesman attempts to convince the buyer that no two painters are alike. The price of a painting by a given painter depends on its size. In dealers catering to a wealthy clientele, the buyer's attention is often drawn to the decorative qualities of the work (here, "salon painting" refers to large pieces suitable for hanging in a living room). Ultimately, however, it is the painter's name that counts. "Everything depends on the painter." The tourist galleries of Montmartre are no different, and dealers like to emphasize the possibility of windfall profits. There are no clear-cut boundaries between the market for junk painting, the market for serious contemporary painting, and even the market for recognized works. Any number of galleries straddle the divide.

Even though all junk painting is more or less equivalent, painters and dealers do their utmost to differentiate their wares. The techniques used are not unlike those developed by dealers at a more exalted level of the market in their efforts to monopolize the work of a particular painter or school. The clients, who have little knowledge of painters or markets, tend to take seriously the artificial differences created by the sellers. Yet there is only so much that sellers can do to inflate prices, since potential buyers of this kind of painting are people of limited means.

Competition among Many Buyers and Many
Sellers

Junk painting is bought by workers, peasants, artisans, merchants, office workers, and technicians, even by the less cultivated members of the bourgeoisie. Lacking the privileges of the wealthy and educated, these kinds of buyers know little about painting and, except for a few with unusually good taste, generally settle for works of poor quality. Of course, those who buy such works do not think they are inferior. In these circles, tastes in art are like preferences for one color over another; judgment reflects nothing more than personal predilection. What is more, lack of taste is not incompatible with a genuine need for art, and no one can deny that these paintings produce in their artistically illiterate buyers emotions of an aesthetic order. Aesthetic emotions, like passions, can be aroused by the most foolish of things without thereby being foolish in themselves.

Buyers of junk paintings are no more immune than buyers of expensive art from the desire to own pretty things or status symbols. Some bad paintings are decorative; others serve as souvenirs. Sometimes they become part of the furniture of the house, like copper pots and carved wooden chests. But they are never purchased as investments: painting is least contaminated by money at this lowest level of the market. Uncultivated art lovers of limited means evince profound respect for the humblest works of art. The painting derives its prestige from the "artist," that inspired master of his trade. Those who buy junk art respect painting far more than they do photography, which is classed as technology and seen as something that anyone can do without special training. Yet they expect nothing of painting except that it reproduce reality and reflect the interests of the buyer: the fishmonger buys still lifes of fish, while the Auvergnat living in Paris buys pictures of the pink heather of his native province and the farmer's son working in the city buys pictures of the sheep and cows of his youth. Shrewd painters take their motorcycles out to the country and set up their easels in front of some prosperous farm, hoping to entice the owner into buying a portrait of the old homestead.

No matter what the buyer's motives or how intense his desires, he will not pay more than he can afford; art, after all, is not a necessity but a pleasure or a status symbol. The demand for junk painting is therefore, in the jargon of economists, income-elastic (i.e., as income increases, so does demand for this kind of art); its price is whatever the kind of buyer it attracts is willing to spend. Price may depend on location, owing to differences in income and attitude between buyers of lower and higher socioeconomic status. The bourgeois buyer is affected by such things as the elegance of the dealer's gallery and the lavishness with which paintings are displayed. In the eyes of the general public if not of specialists, there is added security in buying from a gallery that shows works not only by unknowns but also by painters of some stature. Bourgeois buyers tend to believe that the higher the price, the better the painting.

Price has a great influence on the sale of art, just as it does on the sale of consumer goods, but the effect is the opposite: higher prices attract buyers, not only because some buyers like to make a show of spending money but chiefly because the buyer who is not a connoisseur sees the price of a painting as something to admire about it. Middle-class buyers are not really making different artistic choices from buyers of more humble background, but they do wish to distinguish themselves. Art dealers in the more fashionable neighborhoods know how to capitalize on this wish.

Junk painting is sold in a variety of settings. In Paris the artists themselves sell junk paintings on the streets. Dealers can be found along the boulevards de Strasbourg and du Palais-Royal and the Champs-Elysées, as well as in the larger department stores. In the provinces the market is supplied by local and itinerant painters. Paintings are sold by furniture stores and especially by souvenir shops in tourist spots. Because of the large number of sellers and the relatively small volume of each one's business, the sellers remain quite independent. In each region or neighborhood there is usually a tacitly fixed price level, pegged to the means of the clientele. Dealers behave as though they have no influence on this price level; not only are there so many other dealers, but also the similarity of the merchandise offered for sale is more important in the final analysis than the differences. The price level is not determined by production costs; rather, it is fixed by what potential buyers are willing to pay for luxury consumer items.

Prices

The prices charged by painters hawking their wares in the squares of Montmartre in 1964 were:

Formats	Price (unframed)	Cost	Price of frame
No. 8 (46 × 38 cm) figure	200 F	20 F	70 F
No. 20 landscape (73 × 54 cm) seascape (73 × 50 cm)	450 F	50 F	130 F

The average price per point is around 20 F at Paris street fairs, large art dealers on the boulevard de Strasbourg, in tourist cities like Cannes, Deauville, and Vichy, and in the major department stores. The same types of paintings can be had at more out-of-the-way provincial markets for 10 F per point. Yet for strictly comparable paintings prices are two to three times as high in more fashionable neighborhoods such as the Champs-Elysées and Palais-Royal areas and in dealerships that offer other types of painting along with the junk.

At a given point of sale, other charges may be added, not usually for the subject but often for paintings in particular formats or for the works of artists with particularly impressive credentials. A small trompe-l'oeil still life (size 3, 27 × 22 cm) painted by an artist who has been awarded a medal by the Société des artistes français and who is dead (death, signifying an end to further works by the artist, often causes prices to rise) goes for 900 F on the boulevards. Similarly, publicity costs incurred by galleries that attempt to "launch" new artists result in prices of from 100 to 200 F per point for paintings that are hard to distinguish, aesthetically, from those sold at street fairs in Montmartre.

There is no hard and fast distinction between outright "junk" dealers and their more ambitious colleagues who try to pass off what they sell as genuine art. The question is really one of clientele. Between the client who buys a "Ballerina" for 10 F a point and the one who pays on the order of 400 F a point for a "Parisian Girl" by Jean-Gabriel Domergue (1889–1962, elected a member of the Institut de France in 1950), the major difference is one of income.

The art market is like a pyramid with a broad base. At the lowest level supply is abundant and artistic quality almost nil. Large numbers of sellers compete for the business of large numbers of buyers. Yet the classical model of pure competition does not apply. Supply and demand do not automatically come into balance: there is a great deal of friction in the operation of market mechanisms. All participants, particularly the clients, have at best fragmentary knowledge of significant market factors and are unable to appreciate aesthetic value (or lack thereof). Sellers work to differentiate similar goods. High prices attract at least the higher-income buyers. Competition hinges on product variety rather than price. Even in this relatively competitive sector of the market, some monopolistic practices are evident; their importance increases as we move to market sectors dealing in works of higher quality.

The Market for Established Painting

In rough terms, "established" painting refers to art by other than contemporary artists. Hence the supply of established painting is fixed, whereas that of contemporary painting is highly elastic. People invest in established painting for the long term rather than for speculation. Unlike contemporary painting, established painting is perceived as a safe investment. The collector of contemporary painting gambles both aesthetically and economically; this is not the case with the collector of established painting, for history has already made its selection. Because of its uncontested legitimacy, established painting offers a maximum of prestige coupled with a maximum of financial security. Limited supply, security of investment, and prestige value all tend to drive up the prices paid for established paintings.

But these are generalities. When we look in detail at the market for established painting, the picture becomes far more complex. The rubric "established painting" covers both old masters and modern works. Those who deal in old masters constitute a world apart, isolated from other sectors of the art market. Many old masters are neither signed nor dated; identifying them requires much scholarly detective work. The highest levels of this sector of the market are dominated by a few dealers of international reputation and a handful of auction galleries. Prices paid for masterpieces are so high that only a very few buyers can afford them: very wealthy individuals, museums, and foundations are the only clients. Ninety to ninety-five percent of the sales made by major French dealers are to foreign buyers. "Old masters" include such widely varied merchandise that it would take another book to study this sector of the market in detail; my remarks here are simply for purposes of comparison.

The market for modern masters is in many ways similar to the market for old masters. Powerful dealer dynasties hold large stocks of impressionist works. There is general agreement as to the relative quality of these paintings, which have already achieved a place in the history of art. Nevertheless, the modern sector is more open than the old masters sector owing to the activities of many dealers and brokers. It is not isolated, moreover, from the market for contemporary art.

Theoretical Analysis of the Market for Old
Masters

The most important point to make about the market for old masters has to do with the uniqueness of the "product." Every painting is unique and irreplaceable and comes with its own set of references. There is usually fairly general agreement about the importance of a particular work, as well as its author, in the history of art. The condition of the painting, which may have undergone restoration, is certified by experts. Its pedigree is well-established: when and in what studio it was painted, who has owned it, where it has been shown, scholarly works in which it has been discussed. Thus the "merchandise" has been carefully evaluated, and the prospective client knows what he is buying. There are, of course, dubious cases. When experts disagree about the attribution of a work, the buyer is in a less comfortable position. The judgments of art historians are taken as a kind of guarantee.

Since the painters of established paintings are dead, supply cannot be increased by decision of the market factors.[6] Works of art are not impervious to physical damage, so that supplies may actually decrease over time. Innumerable paintings have been lost in natural and manmade disasters. What is more, works are often lost when painters fall into temporary eclipse. While new conservation techniques have helped to protect works of art against the ravages of time, the very same policies of the museums have withdrawn many paintings from the commercial marketplace. Old masters have ceased to be commodities and have become cultural goods. To continue to view them as economic quantities, as so much "frozen capital," is hopelessly nostalgic. For example, the creator of a Renaissance painting could hardly have forseen that his work, commissioned by one individual, would now be viewed by millions, but history cannot be undone. When such paintings first became social goods, their status was quite ambiguous; those days are now long gone. How much the artist was paid by the man who commissioned the work is of little importance now, and how much the museum paid to acquire it is equally insignificant. These sums do not enter into the significance of the work as art. Once excluded from the market, the cultural good can no longer be reduced to economic terms.

Scarcity is of course a matter of degree. Some old masters were more productive, others less. The most important paintings were the first to disappear from the market. And so on. It is now considered right and proper that masterpieces should be the property of the community rather than of individuals. In other words, aesthetic quality in part determines scarcity. Thus qualitative judgments affect supply as well as demand. The strategy followed by those who sell old masters is to limit supply in anticipation of future revisions in the scale of aesthetic values; such revisions are sometimes predictable, while other times they may be precipitated by deliberate effort.

A few dealers dominate the market for old masters. There is no law preventing dealers from entering the old master segment of the market. But older firms, well endowed with capital and reserves of paintings, enjoy official support and wield great influence. It is therefore very difficult for younger, relatively undercapitalized firms to enter the market. The only way for them to survive is to work as agents of the larger firms, and this means submitting to the wishes of rival dealers. In the old-master segment the titans are still in control; the situation is one of closed oligopoly. The major firms can influence the market in two ways: by placing on sale only a fraction of their holdings and by stimulating demand. Of course, demand is stimulated not so much by dealers themselves as by art historians and museum curators. Dealers generally follow the interests of these specialists, unless they can somehow arouse new interests. Those in the art business are well aware that historical studies and major museum shows awaken the public's interest in particular kinds of painting, leading to a re-evaluation of the accepted scale of values.

Each seller makes up his mind to sell in light of the prices offered by prospective buyers. The decision is based, however, on certain calculations about the future. In other words, it is not only current prices (determined chiefly by public auction sales) but also anticipated future prices that govern supply. A dealer will choose to place a work in storage if he anticipates that prices will rise in the future; there is relatively little risk in doing so with old masters, which maintain their value quite well even in periods of depression. Conversely, a dealer will sell immediately if he anticipates that changing tastes and fashions will cause prices for a given type of work to drop. Temporary fads for a particular style can lead to excessively high prices being paid for relatively minor works, but it is difficult to maintain such prices over the long run. The supply curve is also affected by deliberate dealer decisions to limit supply. Within certain bounds, however, supply is elastic with respect to price.

Once the decision to sell is made, the collector or merchant finds himself the sole seller of a unique work, hence a monopolist in the strict sense of the word; he is theoretically free to ask whatever price he pleases. It is well known, however, that monopolists never actually have as much power to fix prices as they appear to have. Income sets limits on total demand. In addition, other dealers are free to offer other old masters for sale; while these are not strictly speaking interchangeable, they may satisfy the same need for a safe investment or a prestige purchase. The uniqueness of the work of art makes every sale monopolistic, but the complexity of them prospective buyers' motives reintroduces elements of competition.

The first task of the dealer is to identify paintings likely to be put up for sale. By unscrupulous means some will attempt to outmaneuver their rivals to gain control of an old masterpiece, since sales of major old paintings are few and far between. Having obtained the painting from its former owner, the dealer will then try to sell it to a limited number of potential buyers, whom he knows personally. He does not set them openly in competition with one another, for to do so would be to take the bloom off the painting. He will show it to someone whom he thinks in a position to buy the work. If that first attempt is unsuccessful, the dealer may "bury" the painting for a time before approaching anyone else. When the price and the moment are right, he will sell.

In economics, the situation is one of a small number of buyers (oligopsony) dealing with a single seller (the monopolist). The buyers compete with one another, driven by their desire to possess the painting; this introduces an element of irrationality into the transaction. Of course, the desire for ownership makes no sense unless coupled with the means to buy. The market takes no note of desire unless it is combined with the power to purchase; cash must back desires before they can be satisfied. The beggar who desires a diamond has no influence on the price of diamonds. Similiarly, the art lover who passionately wants to own a Rembrandt has no influence on the price of Rembrandts unless he has the money to buy one. The price of a painting depends on the amount that one person is willing to pay in order to demonstrate his superiority over his rivals. The effect of such competition is most evident at public auction sales, but it also exists in private transactions.

Thus the individual demand curve does not follow the classic pattern of the economic textbook. Since the desirability of the "commodity" is a function of the distinction and prestige attached to ownership, desire increases with increasing price. Thus, in the upper reaches of the art market the individual demand curve is the inverse of the classical demand curve. Demand for painting is not limited by satisfaction of desire, as with normal consumer goods. It is not governed by the law of decreasing utility. Human needs "fall into two classes—those needs which are absolute in the sense that we feel them whatever the situation of our fellow human beings may be, and those which are relative in the sense that we feel them only if their satisfaction lifts us above, makes us feel superior to, our fellows."[7] Needs of the second class are characterized by insatiability. As one wealthy collector rightly observes: "One can't sit on two sofas at the same time or consume thirty pounds of caviar a day. But one can always buy more paintings." (C45)

The only thing that can prevent a person from satisfying the desire for art is lack of money to buy it. The demand for painting, whether fabulously expensive or ridiculously cheap, is highly elastic with respect to income. Taxes, by reducing the number of people in a position to bid on old masters to a few hundred worldwide, have greatly reduced overall demand. It is no accident that two of the highest-priced paintings sold in recent years—Rembrandt's *Aristotle Contemplating the Bust of Homer* and *Portrait of the Artist's Son*—went not to private collectors but to American foundations.

Given a market in which one seller confronts a limited number of prospective buyers, the selling price is determined by the sum that each buyer is willing to pay in order to win out over his rivals. Collusion among buyers is practically nonexistent. Indeed, competition rather than collusion is the rule whenever a masterpiece is sold. Buyers know how scarce old masters are, and they also know that history's judgment is on their side. Since they know what they are getting, they need no special flair for art.

We know little about the prices paid for museum-quality paintings that are sold privately. High prices are concealed for tax reasons, while low prices are concealed for commercial reasons. Broadly speaking, it is reasonable to assume that prices paid for works sold privately are roughly comparable with those paid at public auctions. Note, however, that since it is mainly demand that determines prices, the latter may fluctuate rather considerably around the average. There has been a tendency for private buyers to pay even more than buyers at public auctions for comparable works. Well-informed sources estimate that the highest prices paid for art since World War II have been in private sales by collectors to museums or foundations, followed by gallery sales and public auction sales.

Price Stability: Old Masters as Investments

Unlike contemporary painting, established works of art may be considered safe investments. As dealers say, "Buy today's painting: it will go up. Buy yesterday's painting: it won't go down." Periodic revisions of taste do, however, affect the value of older painting. Which paintings are most likely to resist such fluctuations?

A collection of old masters brings aesthetic pleasure and prestige to its owner; it also represents a considerable investment. The owner does not expect this investment to produce income, but he does quite reasonably believe that he will protect his fortune against inflation and taxes; what is more, appreciation of his capital may well outweigh the income sacrificed in purchasing the works.

Established art is a good long-term investment. Nominal prices rise steadily. What is more, old masters are an increasingly scarce commodity. In today's economy overproduction is a constant threat; even diamond producers have to worry about its effects. But there is no danger of overproduction of works winnowed by time. Normally, therefore, the value of *true* works of art tends to increase relative to ordinary consumption goods. The trend is quite regular, moreover. While it is true that during a boom art prices may rise less than leading stocks, they also decline less during periods of depression.[8]

The evaluation of older works of art depends on the work of general historians as well as by prevailing ideas of the beautiful. The judgments of art historians are therefore subject to change. Methods change, and research opens new vistas. Moreover, creative artists change their contemporaries' ways of looking at past art: "The work of an old master is not given but conquered and, as it were, recreated by dint of great effort."[9] This recreation bears the stamp of the value system within which the art historian operates.

Today's aesthetic values have led art historians to rediscover artists who long suffered from a neglect that scandalizes modern observers. Vermeer, El Greco, Uccello, Hieronymus Bosch, and Georges de La Tour are all artists "discovered" within the past century. These spectacular resurrections had corresponding economic consequences.[10] Changes of attribution, often as a result of revived interest in long neglected works, also have an impact on prices.

Let me remind the reader of two major reevaluations of the past. After a hundred years of neglect, eighteenth-century painting underwent a revival in France in the 1880s and in the United States in the 1910s; owing in part to the efforts of the Goncourt brothers, who wrote about it, as well as collectors and dealers, such as Nathan Wildenstein and the Duveens. Boucher's *La toilette de Vénus,* which was auctioned off for 587 francs in 1872, went for 133,000 francs just thirteen years later.[11]

Historians like Bernard Berenson (through his collection, writings, and expert counsel), museum directors like Wilhelm von Bode in Berlin, collectors like Jarves, and dealers like Joseph Duveen helped to promote Trecento and Quattrocento painting among first American and later European buyers in the late nineteenth and early twentieth century.[12]

By the time a particular school of painting attains the market limelight and commands outrageously high prices, innovative dealers have already discovered new curiosities. Following the Second World War, the art market reaped the benefits of scholarly research into eighteenth-century French and Italian painting during the first half of the twentieth century, and dealers realized huge profits on reserves that they began accumulating when the new trends in scholarship began to emerge.

First came the rehabilitation of baroque painting. The first major show took place in Florence in 1922. About the same time the publication of works by H. Voss and Roberto Longhi launched major scholarly debates on the baroque. Then came the revival of Caravaggio with the Milan Exposition of 1951 and innumerable epigones.[13]

After the revival of the baroque came that of mannerism. Discovered in the period 1925–1930 by M. Dvorak, Walter Friedlander, and others, mannerist painting was featured in several postwar exhibitions: "Fontainebleau e la maniera italiana," Naples, 1952; "Pontormo e il primo manierismo florentino," Florence, 1956; and, most important of all, "The Triumph of Mannerism," Amsterdam, 1955. Over the past ten years mannerism has given rise to a vast literature, in which bold extrapolations and audacious comparisons with modern art are not unknown; this has further added to mannerism's popularity.

The renaissance of classicism also dates from the postwar period. It began with an exhibition of the work of Guido Reni (Bologna, 1954). In England and France there were shows of eighteenth-century French painting (London and Paris, 1958), a Poussin colloquium at Bordeaux in 1958, and a Poussin exhibition (Paris, 1960). Also worth mentioning is the exhibition of eighteenth-century art held under the auspices of the Council of Europe in Rome in 1956–57.

No matter what the style on which interest was focused, attention extended to "secondary" artists to whom monographs and regional shows were devoted, especially in Italy. There were exhibitions of seventeenth-century Venetian art at Venice in 1959, seventeenth-century Emilian art at Bologna in 1959, and Piedmontese baroque at Turin in 1963.

Once public interest in styles rediscovered or reevaluated by historians was kindled by major shows, it was up to the dealers to turn these intellectual developments into profits. Just as the names of the English historians Dennis Mahon and Dennis Sutton are associated with the revival of interest in seventeenth-century Italian art, so, too, is the name of the dealer Colnaghi associated with the economic revival of the art of this period.

Major contemporary attempts at reevaluation involved not styles but genres of art. The 1934 "Painters and Reality" exposition, the "Still Life" exposition at the Orangerie in 1952, and Charles Sterling's book[14] helped to revive interest in still lifes. The genre of course admirably fulfills the decorative function that many buyers expect of painting: to make daily life more pleasant in apartments too small to permit hanging of paintings on a larger scale.

The reevaluation of certain styles and genres has not come without the effort of specialists such as art historians and curators. My purpose here is not to give an exhaustive account of recent scholarship and exhibitions, nor is it to trace price fluctuations in detail. I want, rather, to bring out the unwitting collaboration that exists between scholarship and commerce in rediscovering and marketing artists of the past. The judgment of connoisseurs is considered authoritative, but different generations of specialists have focused on different areas of the past. Various factors influence these changing interests.

Let us grant for the sake of argument that intellectuals are immune to the temptation to write about relatively inexpensive works of art in order to drive up prices. The impact of their work on the market is a consequence of their interests, not a cause. There is a natural tendency for historians to avoid well-trodden areas of the past, where it is unlikely that any attempt to alter the chronology or established hierarchies of taste will meet with success. They are attracted, instead, to poorly understood periods. Of those, they will naturally choose those aspects that accord best with their own value system. Their way of looking at the past ultimately depends on the way in which the creative artists of their own time have shaped aesthetic perception. Mannerism such as that of Giuseppe Arcimboldo (1530–93) or the group of Monsu Desiderio (*circa* 1590–1650) came into favor because surrealist art exalted the bizarre. The current interest in

Luca Cambiaso (1527–85) stems from his experimentation with "geometrization," a tendency made familiar by cubism.

I am not suggesting that our understanding of the past is condemned to relativism. The historical value of an artist or school depends on how the work of that artist or school influenced the history of forms and the development of style. Within the body of work done by a particular painter, moreover, certain paintings are of historical interest because they represent a turning point in that artist's development, the beginning of a new period in his career. No one would challenge the authority of an art historian when it comes to distinguishing between the works of a master and those of his followers or between the major and minor works of an individual painter. Within a given style, there is a hierarchy of values that firmly resists alteration by the concerns of the moment. Yet the place of a particular style within the universe of art can and does change in response to contemporary interests. The artist's place as an exponent of his own style is far more stable. No matter how perception changes, the great masterpieces of art have an extraordinary capacity to withstand changes of taste. Momentary disaffections and passing fads chiefly affect minor works.

Within each particular realm of art, history is the queen of sciences: it defines the hierarchy of historical values on which prospective buyers can base their choices. Although prices fluctuate as the relative value of different realms is periodically reevaluated, the masterpieces of each style remain good investments.

8

The Market for Contemporary Painting

It has become increasingly difficult to separate aesthetic from economic values, owing in part to the development of contemporary art itself and the uncertainty of aesthetic judgments concerning it, in part to acceleration of capitalist transformation of the art market. Art's involvement in the economy, with all the consequences of that involvement for the material condition of the artist, is most evident when we look at the market for new art. In my analysis I shall try to explain how the prices paid for works by living artists are determined, how they change, and what they signify; I shall also consider the relation between production and consumption.

Supply and Demand

The supply of contemporary painting, unlike that of old masters, is potentially unlimited. To maximize their own returns sellers (painters and dealers) can opt either to stimulate demand or to limit supply. Sellers seek to raise the value of what they are selling. In the case of painting, this value is determined by demand, which depends on the judgment of the critics and the choices made by social leaders. Sellers therefore compete for the recognition of the critics; failing that, they will seek publicity in various ways to draw attention to what they sell.

Publicity

To a man, every art dealer I questioned claimed to despise advertising. Some maintained that advertising was used only by the more "commercial" dealers who sold not genuine painting but mere "luxury" decoration. The latter returned the compliment, maintaining that the success of abstract art was due entirely to publicity.

I refuse to resort to advertising. [D156]

I do no advertising of any sort. [D166]

I attach no importance whatsoever to advertising. [D125]

The word advertising should not be used. It's a question of propagandizing in favor of something one believes in. [D131]

The choice of words in the last quote is not without significance. If the purpose of advertising is to attract customers, the purpose of propaganda is to win adherents to an ideology (whether political, social, religious, or artistic). In the case of art, "propaganda" purposely draws the attention of the public and prospective buyers to an artist's work. Although the purpose is always the same, the nature of the propaganda varies according to the social characteristics of the targeted individuals. In other words, sales techniques depend on the nature of the clientele, which in turn depends on the type of painting offered for sale.

Art galleries generally do not maintain public relations departments. Dealers will often hold receptions at the gallery, or they may ask one of their clients to do so. Cocktails are served at openings, and fancy parties are held, sumptuous enough in some cases to recall the art patrons of the past but always linked to some utilitarian purpose.[1] The décor is geared to the clientele. In modern art galleries the tone is generally sober, with neutral carpets or mats, bare walls, functional lighting, no furniture. The point is not to impress the visitor with a sumptuous interior but to surround the art on display with a sacred aura. A prolonged wait in a room as bare as a Protestant church in which simple wooden easels stand ready to receive unseen paintings helps to condition the client psychologically. Usually decorated with such items as eighteenth-century commodes and Persian rugs, galleries handling more traditional works offer solid bourgeois comforts.

Some of the newer galleries systematically resort to publicity by scandal, but overuse of this device has diminished its shock value. Scandal works only if it triggers a snobbish response; word of mouth then travels through high society and does the trick. "The important thing is word of mouth among the right group of snobs. The group varies from gallery to gallery, but in Paris there are any number of art coteries that play a crucial role." [P261] The names of leading "art world personalities" can easily be gleaned from the lists of patrons of such exhibitions as the Biennale de Paris and the Salons des Peintres témoins de leur temps. These people play a major role in creating reputations.

Quantitative manipulation

For the producer a classic problem of economics is how much to produce. For the art dealer this problem takes the following form: what painters to choose, and how many? A producer of ordinary goods bases his decision on the relation between selling price and production cost. Strictly speaking, the production cost of an artwork is a meaningless term, but dealers do incur costs in acquiring art and these must of course be taken into account when he considers how much to charge his clients. The dealer also has fixed costs such as rent, lighting, maintenance, insurance, and administration, as well as variable costs including "wages" paid to painters and advertisers. At best the dealer can estimate his total costs. He cannot, as producers of economic textbooks do, estimate his average unit cost or marginal cost (the cost of producing one additional unit), owing to the nature of the merchandise. In other words, the art dealer cannot behave like an industrialist and adjust the artist's productivity to market demand.

The dealer's ability to make rational predictions ends where the artist's creative freedom begins. The dealer's initiative is limited to three areas: allocation of capital resources, limitation of supply, and manipulation of prices. He can spend more on publicizing an artist's work and thereby hasten the process of recognition (as many dealers did after World War II). Or he can allocate most of his resources to acquiring paintings to be placed in storage for fairly long periods while awaiting a rise in price (a technique at which Ambroise Vollard, among others, was a past master). It is possible to make a rational choice between these alternatives on the basis of aesthetic judgment. With some artists it is better to strike while the iron is hot, so to speak, because the work happens to correspond to some passing notion of what Beauty is; with others it is better to wait, because one feels sure that the work will ultimately find its place in the hierarchy of values recognized by history.

In the short run doubt is of little consequence. With paintings as with stocks the market is a game of mirrors. What counts is not the reality of things but how market actors perceive that reality. This is a subject for game theory.

This battle of wits to anticipate the basis of conventional valuation a few months hence, rather than the prospective yield of an investment over a long term of years, does not even require gulls amongst the public to feed the maws of the professional; it can be played by professionals amongst themselves. Nor is it necessary that anyone should keep his simple faith in the conventional basis of valuation having any genuine long-term validity. For it is, so to speak, a game of Snap, of Old Maid, of Musical Chairs—a pastime in which he is victor who says Snap neither too soon nor too late, who passed the Old Maid to his neighbour before the game is over, who secures a chair for himself when the music stops.[2] These games can be played with zest and enjoyment, though all the players know that it is the Old Maid which is circulating, or that when the music stops some of the players will find themselves unseated. Or, to change the metaphor slightly, professional investment may be likened to those newspaper competitions in which the competitors have to pick out the six prettiest faces from a hundred photographs, the prize being awarded to the competitor whose choice most nearly corresponds to the average preferences of the competitors as a whole; so that each competitor has to pick, not those faces which he himself finds prettiest, but those which he thinks likeliest to catch the fancy of the other competitors, all of whom are looking at the problem from the same point of view. It is not a case of choosing those which, to the best of one's judgment are really the prettiest, nor even those which average opinion genuinely thinks the prettiest. We have reached the third degree when we devote our intelligence to anticipating what average opinion expects the average opinion to be. And there are some, I believe, who practise the fourth, fifth, and higher degrees.[3]

The launching of new artists is done with this same kind of short-term mentality.

In the short run, then, the strategies of trading in art are not unlike those of trading in stocks. But in the stock market, when it comes to the long run, objective criteria become important; dividends more or less accurately reflect economic reality. In painting, judgment ceases to be subjective only in the very long run, where the judgment of history comes into play. In the interval between the short run and the very long run, art dealers are free to manipulate supply. The monopolist dealer can also manipulate prices to some extent, within limits set by overall demand.

The Behavior of Buyers

Art buyers divide into several groups, between which there is little communication. The most impenetrable divide separates the buyers of figurative painting from the buyers of abstract painting. Within each major group there are usually several subgroups, which may overlap but remain highly distinctive. Members of each group do their utmost to stress the originality of the "product" that interests them in order to ensure that no other product can be substituted for it.

Each gallery has a small core of loyal supporters on which it lives. [D125]

A gallery has its clients. A painter, if he has a reputation, has his. It adds up. [D159]

Each group of buyers receives advice from one or more galleries. Because a dealer provides an implicit guarantee of quality, buyers will pay more to purchase from a gallery than they might pay if they were to buy at public auction or directly from the artist (assuming no exclusive contract exists between the artist and a dealer).

Finally, for a substantial proportion of buyers, the price of a painting is one factor that influences their judgment of it. Art is often bought for show, as Thorstein Verblen has pointed out. Other psychosociological factors are also at work. Buyers are generally more influenced by a reference group than by the group to which they actually belong, hence they aim high. The demonstration effect (which induces dissatisfaction with one's possessions when one is exposed to goods of better quality) is very important; taste develops according to its own laws, and buyers tend to become increasingly selective in their purchases. Furthermore, given the confusion of values that currently prevails in the world of art, confused buyers who admit their incompetence to make up their minds see high prices as a guarantee of aesthetic quality. "It is easier to sell a successful painter at 50,000 F than a young unknown at 1,000 F." [D166] Although high prices can be very attractive to individual buyers, income determines overall limits; demand is highly income-elastic. Very few French buyers are able to pay more than 10,000–50,000 F for a painting, but foreign buyers can pay more.

It is impossible to find buyers for paintings that sell at 500–600 F, because the clients want to buy known painters. If his paintings go for 20,000–30,000 F, however, that's too much. French clients in general spend between 2,500 and 5,000 F. To go from stage A (500–600 F) to stage B (2,500–5,000 F) requires the help of a dealer, but the painter plays a part. He has to paint enough but not too much, his painting has to have some weight, and in some cases it needs to be potentially scandalous. At stage C, where things really get expensive, it's the foreigners who buy. [D120]

The clientele of the leading contemporary-progressive galleries is between 80 and 95 percent foreign.

We do 95 percent of our business with foreigners. [D142]

In our business, export counts for far more than what we sell in Paris. [D108]

The bulk of the paintings is sold to foreigners. Buyers from around the world visit all the galleries. There are many more foreign than French buyers. It's not a question of money; it's that the French are not particularly moved by painting that ruffles their habits. They could have bought Kandinsky watercolors ten years ago for 300,000 francs. Now (1959) they cost two million. The buyers are mainly Americans, Swiss, and, since the war, Belgians. Among the French it's mainly businessmen, bankers, foreign exchange dealers, and movie producers. [D159]

A young, progressive dealer summed up the situation in 1959: "We see more French than Americans. We sell more to the Americans than to the French." [D177]

Excluding the speculators or gamblers, buyers of contemporary painting fall into two classes. Most behave like people who buy junk painting: they buy what they like based on what they can afford to spend on luxury purchases. The only difference is that they can afford to spend more than the clients of the sidewalk painters, because their incomes are higher. The rest behave like buyers of established painting, except that their incomes are lower. They, too, are looking for painting that occupies a place of honor in the hierarchy of aesthetic values. Since, however, there are no objective guarantees of value in contemporary art, they look for other guarantees: the dealer's competence, seriousness, and good reputation, and the comfort of a high price.

The Markets

Monopoly of Production

Every artist monopolizes his own production; there is no other source of supply. This monopoly is unaltered by the fact that today a series of paintings is often more representative of a painter's work than any single picture. Every artist monopolizes his "invention," whether or not it degenerates into "mannerism." Creators are distinguished from followers by the degree and variety of their inventiveness. The painter also has a monopoly over his signature, which gives proof that a work represents his intention and thus confers upon it existence as an aesthetic object. To be sure, several factors have modified these conditions of production in recent years: the diminished importance attached to techniques requiring a long apprenticeship; praise for speedy work; reliance on what has been called "objective chance"; and the acceptance afforded to ephemeral works designed to surprise the spectator rather than provide lasting pleasure. Yet none of these things has altered the basic fact that the artist monopolizes his own production. The most one can say is that the emphasis has shifted from the uniqueness of the individual painting to the uniqueness of the individual signature.

Painters can either sell directly to buyers or make use of intermediaries. If intermediaries are used, the painter is free, if he wishes, to grant his agency a monopoly over sale of his production. He may also offer one dealer a right of first refusal.

Distribution

The dealer who signs an exclusive contract with an artist obtains a monopoly over that artist's production. The artist's monopoly as producer is incontestable and inviolable; the dealer's is conditional. Exclusive contracts are generally limited in geographical extent and always in duration. Worldwide exclusive contracts are rare because they require substantial investment; the law of 11 March 1957 requires that exclusive contracts be for limited duration only.

Oligopolistic distribution is the most common practice. Several dealers together acquire a monopoly of an artist's production, each within a specific region of the world (e.g., France or Europe). In some cases, each dealer acquires a worldwide or regional monopoly of one type of production (e.g., watercolors and gouaches or oils). In any case, the result is a situation of oligopoly rather than monopoly. Oligopoly is all but inevitable when a painter becomes so successful, and consequently high-priced, that no one dealer can afford to buy his entire output. The parties to such oligopolistic arrangements are not antagonists; they cooperate closely with one another and generally agree on prices so as to maximize everyone's profits. In the traditionalist sector of the market, contracts with artists are less common, hence monopolies and oligopolies are also rare.

Sellers can usually count on a large number of potential buyers for paintings whose prices are below a certain threshold (in the tens of thousands of Francs). Beyond that threshold the number of buyers decreases rapidly. To the extent that a dealer is able to control prices, he must determine whether he prefers a broader market or a higher price. Yet even when the dealer controls the supply of an artist's production, he may have less control over prices than at first appears to be the case.

The best picture of monopolistic mechanisms comes from looking at the most speculative segment of the market. The dealer who enjoys a temporary monopoly can control price. He works closely with a small number of collectors. Each buyer buys in large quantities and seeks to obtain a monopoly. The number of participants is small, but their financial resources are large. The monopolists are not conspiratorial (as those who doubt the aesthetic value of the work may believe), but they do form a coalition in the economic sense of the word. When we take a broader view of the art market, however, the monopolistic model breaks down in several ways.

Competitive Elements

Underlying economic competition in the art market are differences of opinion as to aesthetic value. The major division today is between what is usually (and, I repeat, misleadingly) described as figurative and abstract art. Economic conflict, or the battle to attract buyers, is camouflaged by vehement aesthetic dispute; the surreptitious transition from economic interest to artistic ideology reflects either bad faith or intellectual confusion. However important the passion for money may be in determining human behavior, the bitterness of artistic dispute is due not so much to pure self-interest as to sectarian ardor and the will to win. All the interviews reveal that people unaware of the extent to which their tastes are sociologically conditioned will fiercely defend their own preferences, which they consider a reflection of their innermost being.

From 1945 until 1962 modern art enjoyed a resounding commercial success. Demand for modern art came from a small but wealthy segment of the population, which Maurice Rheims dubbed the "financial wing" of art. Yet during the same period modern art was the subject of constant polemic. In France, the art establishment remained conservative until at least 1958. Reviews devoted to abstract are generally made it a matter of policy to ignore figurative art, whereas profigurative reviews and weeklies frequently ran campaigns against abstraction which can be summed up in the slogan, "Abstract art is dead." These reviews were generally published at least once a year, usually in the fall but occasionally in connection with special events such as the first Paris Biennale in 1959 or the recession in the United States economy in 1962.

The attack on abstract art rested on three arguments: artistic, political, and economic. First, abstract painters were accused of ignorance of technique, from which the conclusion was drawn than abstract painting is a fraud. Second, abstract painting was said to be un-French, "American," or "international." And third, to buy abstract painting, it was argued, was to buy something as ephemeral as the wind.

> Abstract painting is a decorative mode of expression. There is no test by which it can be judged. It is the realm of subjectivity in which "anything goes." Abstract painting is killing French art. It is international, American, whatever you want to call it, but not French. [D157]

The word *art* is applied to all sorts of things, and anything called art is treated with respect. The key, the pass to respectability, is the word art, not the work itself. The dealer is Tartuffe and the client is Monsieur Jourdain. Today's aesthetic is the result of speculation. The bourgeoisie became interested in painting in order to imitate the refinement of the aristocracy, but they brought with them their concern with money. Painting adjusted to the situation by means of "despiritualization." The business is in the hands of fairly primitive people. They enjoy a prestige above that of the stockbroker for doing more or less the same kind of job. In the old days, with big dealers like Lebrun, commercial interest and personal taste were the same thing. Taste was a verity. Today there are no verities. . . . Abstract painting does not sell by itself. You have to go out and sell it, force people to buy it. It's painting for pedants. Abstract art reflects the evolution of society and the economy. Parvenus feel obliged to respect social conventions by taking an interest in art. Abstract painting is a great liberation for semicultured people. It is a social phenomenon justified by commercial success. The merchandise is easy to manufacture. The artists try to find a style. The dealer buys all their work for 100,000 francs a month. The painter turns out twenty paintings a month. At the first show thirty paintings are sold for 200,000 francs. The bourgeois come, look around, but don't buy. A year later the same gallery will stage a second show. In the meantime the gallery has paid the painter 1.2 million francs. It may have spent another 2 million or more on publicity and the like. So now the paintings are priced at 450,000 francs. Fifteen are sold, which is enough to provide a return on the capital invested. The third year the contract is upped to 1.8 million. There are shows in Paris, Zurich, Munich, and New York. Publicity costs increase. The paintings are priced at around 1 million. It's a sell-out. The rise is meteoric for three or four years, and then the artist falls back into oblivion. [D132]

Abstract art was promoted by the Americans. To promote painting as they did is like manipulating the stock market. A few people get together, raise twenty million francs, print some nice catalogs, and the thing is done. There is a conspiracy in favor of abstract art, a conspiracy connected with capitalism, the Americans, the Jews, and the immorality of our time. It is also the work of intellectuals, those parvenus of the mind. The sons of concierges who get degrees in philosophy are more dangerous than the newly rich. They'll write anything about art in order to keep from being put down by the snobs, and the herd will buy without understanding in order to keep from looking like idiots. What they all lack is an inherited culture. I am for figurative painting because I am French, and only the French do decent figurative painting. [D179]

As is clear from these interviews, the debate is highly impassioned. Some of what is written in the reviews and weeklies reflects the competition among influential dealers for business. But beyond that there is a dispute about aesthetics and, even more, about value systems.

The conflict between abstract and figurative art should not be allowed to obscure dissension within each camp. There is also rivalry between lyrical and geometrical abstraction, which gives rise to commercial competition. When Pop Art was taken up by all the American galleries in Paris, exponents of other schools rallied in response. The "new figurative art" is not only taking over existing channels of distribution but also looking for new ones.

In a monopoly situation, the most acute competition probably results from innovation. Economists since Schumpeter have called attention to this powerful form of competition, which, though deadly in the short run, can be most fruitful over the long haul.

> Economists are at long last emerging from the stage in which price competition was all they saw. . . . But in capitalist reality as distinguished from its textbook picture, it is not that kind of competition which counts but the competition from the new commodity, the new technology, the new source of supply, the new type of organization. . . . This kind of competition is as much more effective than the other as a bombardment is in comparison with forcing a door, and so much more important that it becomes a matter of comparative indifference whether competition in the ordinary sense functions more or less promptly.[4]

Willingness to assume the risks of innovation by signing contracts with revolutionary artists drove some dealers into bankruptcy, but the shrewdest prospered. In recent years, as the public's capacity to absorb novelty in art has increased, the risks of innovation have diminished. For nearly a century the art world has been reshaped by what Schumpeter calls a perpetual whirlwind of innovation.

In the traditionalist sector competition through innovation is less in evidence, however. To a limited extent it does exist and can produce brief fashions. Yet the quip that "to be a figurative painter requires talent; to be an abstract painter requires genius" fairly accurately captures the reality: uniqueness of style is more essential in abstract than in figurative art.

Price Competition

Economists speak of a *parallel market* when goods are sold outside the fixed-price official market. Strictly speaking, this situation does not exist in the art market; but market actors do themselves refer to a parallel market for art, and it is in this sense that I shall employ the term here to refer to that segment of the market not controlled by monopolist dealers and dominated by resellers, brokers, and collector-dealers. The existence of a prosperous parallel market alters the way in which the monopolistic system functions. The prices that monopolistic dealers attempt to enforce are not respected in the parallel market, where price competition is the rule. Early collectors who acquire paintings at low prices and brokers who obtain paintings at dealer prices can sell them at competitive prices on the parallel market.

Imagine an abstract painter whose works sell in Paris in 1950 for 1,500 francs per point. At this point his work is admired by a few initiates but has no buyers. He is taken up by a Parisian coterie with contacts among wealthy collectors; the group includes admirers, collectors, speculators, brokers, patrons, and traders. The exact classification may be difficult to pin down. As one painter [P227] put it: "He is a collector-dealer. The word may seem pejorative, but it isn't. What I mean is a collector who takes a very active role, a patron of the arts." To get back to my example: the painter's reputation gradually grows beyond the small circle of speculators and attracts the attention of Paris collectors on the lookout for "what's happening." Minds are made up when internationally renowned experts confirm the painter's talent and American museums begin to buy his work; a major dealer takes him on. Prices of his work continue to rise, going from 1,500 to 50,000 francs per point in five years. His dealer now has an exclusive contract with him and sets the price of 50,000 francs per point. But his earlier paintings can still be had on the parallel market for 20,000 francs per point. At this price early buyers can still make substantial profits.

If a dealer succeeds in temporarily controlling the price of a painter's work, he can attempt to maximize his profits in several ways. He may keep prices relatively low in the hope of increasing demand. Or he may store paintings acquired at low prices, buy back those in circulation, limit supply, set prices high, and select buyers who he can be sure will not quickly resell. If circumstances are favorable (owing to a fad for an artist's work, an "aura" of the artist, or a fever of speculation), the dealer may try to sell many works as quickly as he can and drive prices up rapidly. In this case, rising prices will attract speculators seeking quick profits, and owing to the existence of a parallel market the dealer will find it difficult to maintain control over prices for long. The dealer's best strategy is not necessarily in the best interests of the artist. (See my previous analysis of the relations between painters and dealers.)

It is clear that the market for contemporary painting is one of "imperfect competition." What this technical term of economics means is that supply and demand are not "atomic." In other words, the scale of operation of both buyers and sellers varies widely; there are many small dealers and buyers, few large ones. Entry into the market is restricted, moreover. (The prospects of profit are uncertain, and there is imperfect mobility of the "factors of production," namely, the painters, some of whom are bound by contract to existing galleries.) Not all market actors are rational economic calculators. Finally, the major reason why imperfect competition exists is that the "product" is by its very essence nonfungible. Product competition is far more important than price competition.

But art monopolies are also imperfect, even if this is at first less obvious. According to the traditional theory of Cournot and Marshall, an absolute monopoly is one in which a single vendor offers a product to buyers with a fixed set of demand schedules which the vendor cannot influence. Nothing like this exists in the art market. If, however, we take *monopoly* in the eytmological sense to mean "unique vendor," and if the essence of monopoly is control of supply, then monopoly is the natural condition of the art market (required at the production level by the nature of the work of art and reinforced at the distribution level by the exclusive dealer contract); the organization of the market is simply arranged in such a way as to take maximum advantage of this. Although the market for contemporary painting, particularly that of living artists, is highly monopolistic, elements of competition are present. Pure monopolistic mechanisms function only sporadically.

The theory of monopolistic competition, one of the major achievements of economic science in the period between the two world wars,[5] provides the best account of reality. According to the traditional theory of monopoly, monopoly and competition are not simply opposites but mutually exclusive. To prove that competition exists is to prove that monopoly does not, and vice versa. Hence many regard the notion of "monopolistic competition" as a contradiction in terms. This is unfortunate. The new theory shows that competition and monopoly do not exclude one another and that both are required to explain prices in an intelligible fashion.

Boom and Bust

The vogue for art in the 1950s is comparable to earlier enthusiasms in Rome in the first century, in Florence in the late fifteenth century, in Holland in the seventeenth century, and in Paris in the 1770s. A variety of circumstances contributed to an overall rise in prices. A prosperous economy, the encouragement of speculation owing to the absence of any capital gains tax, the interest in painting of all sorts on the part of many different kinds of people, and the social prestige attached to ownership of painting all played a part. The increasingly common use of exclusive artist-dealer contracts also contributed. What dealer would have risked investing large sums to promote a new painter without assurances that he would be able to sell the bulk of what that painter produced?

Prices rose in all sectors of the contemporary art market. The rapid increase of prices for Bernard Buffet's paintings signaled the new trend. Information that I have been able to obtain suggests that the first collectors of Buffets paid between 1,000 and 5,000 francs per painting just after the war. The large canvas that won the Critics' Prize on 25 June 1948 is said to have been sold by the Galerie Saint-Placide for 50,000 francs. At the Buffet retrospective held by the Galerie Charpentier in January 1958 (110 oil paintings, 20 watercolors and drawings), the smallest paintings sold for between 800,000 and 1 million francs.

As for the most revolutionary modern painting, speculation was rampant. Many of the founders of abstract painting achieved commercial success only posthumously. After many years of struggle, artists born around the turn of the century saw prices of their works rise a hundredfold in a short time. Artists born in the 1920s achieved such spectacular success in their thirties and forties that some people believed in the coming of a golden age of painting.

The most noted names in contemporary painting did not achieve simultaneous success. Kandinsky, Mondrian, and Klee preceded Robert Delaunay and Kupka. Bissière achieved commercial success not before but after his pupils, the "young painters in the French tradition."

I have gleaned a number of examples of rapid price increases from my conversations with collectors and dealers. Of course, these are just indications of the overall trend, and I make no claim that my treatment of the subject is exhaustive. I take no account of variations in prices of works by a particular painter owing to differences in size or date of completion. I cannot be sure, moreover, whether quoted auction prices represent actual sales or redemptions by the seller.

Consider, then, the work of Alfred Manessier, who was born in 1911. One 1954 canvas (115 × 115 cm) was purchased from a dealer in that same year for 570,000 francs. At a show organized by the Galerie de France in late December 1959, prices ranged from 500,000 to 10 million francs.

Hans Hartung was born in 1904. In 1945 his paintings sold for around 50,000 francs. In October 1953 a collector paid a dealer 180,000 for one of his paintings (100 × 65 cm). In 1959–60 canvas (80 × 80 cm) sold for 40,000–50,000 francs. In 1960 a painting was auctioned by the Park Bernet Galleries in New York for $3,915 (58,870 F).[6]

In 1950 a collector paid a gallery 45,000 francs for one painting (size 30) by Serge Poliakoff (1906–69). Another confided that at a somewhat later date he acquired "quantities" of paintings at prices ranging from 80,000 to 150,000 francs. A third collector acquired a painting (size 50) in 1953 for 180,000 francs. At the Bing Gallery show in 1956, prices ranged from 150,000 to 750,000 francs. In 1957, at the retrospective show organized by the Galerie Creuzevault, the price per point ranged from 40,000 to 50,000 francs, depending on the format.

Marie-Hélène Vieira da Silva was born in 1908. In September 1955 a painting of his size (size 20) was sold by a dealer for 220,000 francs. Prices at that time ranged from 200,000 to 500,000 francs and by 1961 had risen to amounts between 40,000 and 60,000 [new] Francs.

Pierre Soulages was born in 1919. According to the review *Connaissance des arts* (15 June 1958), his paintings were worth twenty times as much in 1958 as in 1950. Reitlinger reports that his *Abstraction* sold for $3,255 (44,788 Francs) on 27 April 1960 at the Parke Bernet Galleries in New York.[7]

Later to be affected by the trend toward higher prices were Jean Dubuffet (born 1901), Jean Fautrier (1898–1964), and Henri Michaux (born 1898). Prices for the work of these men, especially Dubuffet, shot up rapidly. In 1954 the Galerie Drouin sold a Dubuffet canvas (size 40) for 200,000 francs. A gouache and ink (33 × 25 cm) went for 20,000 francs. Gerald Reitlinger reports two auction sales at Parke Bernet in New York on 27 April 1960: *L'Ame des sous-sols,* $4,820 (66,323, F) and *Grand Jazzband,* 1944, $9,650 (132,784 F).[8]

In 1956–57 a large early watercolor by Henri Michaux (66 × 50 cm) was sold by a gallery for 60,000 francs. Another watercolor (41 × 30 cm) went for 40,000 francs. A gouache (50 × 33 cm) sold for 45,000 francs. A "mescaline-induced" drawing (33 × 24 cm) was sold for 30,000 francs. An ink painting went for 75,000 francs. In 1959 a watercolor (64 × 50 cm) was priced at 250,000 francs. In 1964 watercolors and gouaches sold for between 5,000 and 6,000 Francs, ink paintings for between 7,000 and 8,000 Francs. Prices multiplied nearly tenfold in seven years.

Thus, prices rose gradually from 1945 to 1950, while modern art struggled to achieve commercial recognition. By 1950 prices were moving upward at a more rapid pace, and between 1954 and 1956 the rate of increase became dizzying. Prices continued to rise until 1959–60, when the postwar boom apparently peaked; they leveled off somewhat from 1960 to 1962. The last artists mentioned did not see prices paid for their work begin to rise until 1956 or 1957, but at that point the rate of increase was quite rapid.

Following the trail toward higher prices blazed by their elders, younger painters (born between 1920 and 1925) saw their large-format paintings selling by 1959 at prices between 300,000 and 750,000 francs, occasionally even higher. Mathieu was born in 1921. One of his large paintings sold for 1 million francs. Gerald Reitlinger reports a sale for $1,350 (18,576 Francs) at Parke Bernet in New York on 27 April 1960. Paintings by Antoni Tàpies (born 1923) that were worth 4,000 francs per point in 1958 sold for 12,500 francs per point in 1960. In April 1959 an exhibition of his work was held at the Stadler Gallery; the largest paintings (210 × 175 cm) sold for 1.25 million francs.

Prices paid for the work of artists who died prematurely, such as Wols (1913–51), Nicolas de Staël (1914–55), Jackson Pollock (1912–56), and Jean Atlan (1913–60), increased especially rapidly, partly as the result of various "conspiracies" and partly because death put an end to further supply, helping to drive up prices. Paintings by de Staël went for around 50,000 francs in 1944–45. Prices began to rise while he was still alive, moving slowly from 1947 to 1950 and more rapidly after that. In 1953 his paintings were going for 1 million francs, in 1954 for 1.5 million, and by 1958–59 for between 5 and 10 million. One collector [C17] told me that in 1960 he turned down an offer of 13 million old francs for a size 30 de Staël that he owned. Daniel Cordier remarked on a "30-point painting by de Staël that I bought for 6,000 francs in 1945, resold for 40,000 francs seven years later, and then saw on sale ten years later [in 1962] at Fels's for 15 million."[9] Similarly, Jackson Pollock's paintings became the object of feverish speculation after his death. In 1945 a painting of his sold for 50,000 francs. By 1955 the price had risen to 1 million; by 1958–59 it ranged between 5 and 15 million. Both de Staël and Pollock knew hard times before achieving success (which came while both men were still alive). Both died tragically. Above all, both were revolutionary artists who exerted a powerful influence on the work of their contemporaries. Their work was strong enough to withstand the weakening of the market, and prices for their painting have since continued to rise.

The increase in prices paid for the work of the more revolutionary painters has been particularly spectacular because they started so low. But prices of other kinds of painting have also gone up. An article in *Réalités* (January 1958) refers to "artists who are successful enough to sell their works for 500,000 to 1,000,000 francs: Borès, Brianchon, Carzou, Chapelain-Midy, Clavé, Derain, Desnoyer, MacAvoy, André Marchand, Pignon, to name only ten (in alphabetical order)." Prices for paintings by Yves Brayer ranged from 100,000 to 1 million francs depending on size (*Connaissance des arts,* January 1957). Larger paintings by Lorjou were priced at between 2 and 3 million at his October 1959 show at the Galerie des Beaux-Arts. Paintings by successful young figurative painters born in the 1920s increased from the 25,000–200,000 franc range in 1955 (depending on size) to the 60,000–500,000 franc range by 1958; in 1960 some were bringing prices as high as 500,000 to 1 million francs.

Both figurative and abstract paintings have sold well in the past decade. There are of course exceptions to this general rule; some artists have remained on the sidelines, from lack of publicity more than lack of talent. It is easy to understand the success of painting that breaks no new ground and does not force spectators to confront bizarre and hostile new forms. What is pardoxical about the art market in the 1950s is that bold and sometimes offensive new painting achieved very high prices, higher than those paid for traditional painting. The situation was the opposite of that in the last thirty years of the nineteenth century, which Van Gogh described:

> As I said to Gauguin in my last letter, if you paint like Bouguereau you can hope to make money, but the public will never change; it likes only slick, sweet things. Painters with more austere talent must not count on living from their work. Most of the people intelligent enough to understand and love impressionist paintings are and will remain too poor to buy them. Will G. or I work less because of that? No. But we will be obliged to accept poverty and social isolation as a result. [10]

Traditional painting, supported by the taste of the majority, has proved less vulnerable than innovative painting to the weakening of the art market, however. The dizzying increase in the price of innovative art, sustained in part by speculation and snobbery, reached the point where cultivated buyers could no longer afford to buy what they were capable of wanting.

Even though the prices paid for contemporary paintings may seem exorbitant, they cannot compare with the inflation-adjusted prices paid for fashionable paintings in the late nineteenth-century. At the Steward sale in 1887, *Friedland* by Ernest Meissonier (1815–91) sold for 900,000 francs (or approximately 1,400,000 Francs), more than the highest amount ever bid for a Picasso.

The "Crisis"

Since 1962 the boom climate has given way to one of caution and even suspicion. Dealers have maintained their prices, but demand has fallen off. The disparity between auction prices and gallery prices has increased. Quite a few artist-dealer contracts have been terminated, because dealers, faced with slow sales, have been unable to continue regular payments to their artists. In 1963 a number of galleries would have closed their doors had it not been for purchases by the government, the city of Paris, and a few generous and wealthy collectors.

The immediate cause of the problems in the art market was the financial crisis that hit Wall Street in May 1962. Though short-lived, the crisis apparently crystallized a latent uneasiness. For the art market there were worrisome signs. In July 1962 abstract paintings by Nicolas de Stael and Miro were withdrawn from sale at Sotheby's in London for want of a buyer. Major American collectors such as Robert Lehmann, Huntington Hartford, and Daniel Bright unloaded their nonfigurative paintings. These and other signs were interpreted in the circumstances as bad omens. Prices were slack on the Paris Stock Exchange from 1962 to 1965, and some fortunes were undoubtedly affected. Stockholders suffered a crisis of confidence, which extended to paintings, always viewed by some collectors as similar to stocks. The phenomenon proved contagious. When stocks go down, the most aggressive French art buyers—bankers, foreign exchange dealers, and businessmen—tend to retrench. The phenomenon is not new: the impressionists suffered from the financial disasters of 1884, and artists in the 1930s suffered from the effects of the Depression. Of course the problems stemming from a stock-market crash are not of the same magnitude as those stemming from a lengthy depression; they do not affect the art market as a whole, but only the more speculative sectors of the market.

Not all contemporary painting dropped in price. The hardest hit segment of the market was the most speculative. Because the prices paid for innovative painting had risen most rapidly, they also fell most precipitously. Most affected were painters whose work was expensive but still dubious in the eyes of buyers because it had not yet withstood the test of time. Demand for such work dropped much more sharply than demand for the work of young painters that was still relatively inexpensive. Hence the small left-bank galleries found it easier to survive than some right-bank galleries that occupied a higher echelon in the market hierarchy. "The effects of the crisis on me were not particularly severe, because I sell young and relatively inexpensive artists. Such painting is still a luxury item, of course, but it's not ridiculously expensive. My painters are well enough known to attract clients but not famous enough to be that expensive. It would take a worse economic downturn to affect my business."[D129] The most vulnerable galleries were those that stood above the "tryout" galelries for the avant-garde but below those selling firmly established art.

It was inevitable that speculation on rising prices (which some dealers actively encouraged and others did nothing to prevent) would ultimately fall flat. Feverish "bull markets" are inevitably followed by panic as prices fall. It was imprudent to allow prices of contemporary artists to rise so high. For one thing, it is hard for a living painter to resist the temptation to overproduce if demand for his work is high.[11] The risk of inflation is further increased by the nature of some modern art, which emphasizes speed of painting and the role of chance in creation. As long as demand for painting grew independent of prices, "rising" young painters could produce and sell as much as they wished without running the risk that increased supply would drive prices down. Rising prices reflected the higher value placed on modern art by buyers and were therefore relatively independent of the number of paintings in circulation. In times of inflation buyers preferred paintings to liquid assets. But when the French devaluation of 1958 and the stabilization plan of 1963 succeeded in steadying prices, the inflationary psychology was broken and demand became elastic with respect to price. Artists could no longer sell as many paintings as they wished at whatever price they wanted.

The fact that the monopoly price was manipulated upward during the market boom had important consequences later. As long as demand is increasing, a monopolist can raise prices with apparent impunity. But when demand wanes he cannot lower prices in the hope of broadening the market because nonexpert buyers equate price with aesthetic value; lowering prices therefore calls the aesthetic value of an artist's work into question. At public auctions in recent years buyers have been able to buy paintings for one-tenth the amount that paintings by the same painter cost in a gallery (5,000 as against 50,000 Francs). Although neither price reflects the true value of the work, the gap between them is interpreted as a worrisome sign by prospective buyers who see price as an index of aesthetic worth.

The art dealer differs from the industrial producer: he cannot lower prices. When a manufacturer launches a new product of which he is the sole producer, he can set the price very high (banking on novelty to attract buyers). Later, when the market is saturated at the high initial price, he can lower his price to attract new buyers. Increased demand compensates for the decreased margin of profit. But art dealers cannot lower the prices of certain painters; they can (and doubtless some do) try to promote the less costly work of epigones. But, at best, the strategy is only partially successful. It is not difficult to find paintings for which very high prices are asked but for which there is no demand; without demand, the price is meaningless. For painters as well as dealers the wise course was to resist pressure to raise prices or at any rate to limit supply in order to prevent the market from becoming saturated.

Thus, some investors forgot the basic rule that even the best investment can be priced too high. The modern art market also faced other difficulties. In France, at least, most modern art was bought not by art lovers but by speculators, often inexperienced in the purchase of art and quite fickle in their tastes, ready to drop a "declining" investment in favor of another. High prices misled people into thinking that for the first time since 1870 artists whose work did not conform to established taste were at last understood by the market and capable of attracting buyers. The "crisis" pointed up the ambiguities in the motives of those buyers. Some American and French dealers went out of business, flooding European auction houses with their stock. Meanwhile, speculators began to sell off their holdings. The decline in prices accelerated.

As anxiety mounted, the Paris art market faced stiff competition from abroad. Art galleries had proliferated in the United States; *Art News* (November 1962) listed 200 in New York alone. The New York School was very popular: American collectors, museums, and foundations had abundant cash to spend; the United States tax code encouraged donations of art; American dealers signed contracts with European artists; "buy American" was the day's watchword. Until recently, American buyers had been quite useful to French dealers because they had plenty of money to spend and were receptive to all kinds of art. For Americans now to supply their own art was undeniably a threat to the French market. Compounding the threat was the fact that the Americans used the considerable means at their disposal to win international recognition and customers for their artists. American capitalists backed European galleries, American firms opened European branches, and American dealers set up shop on the Left Bank in Paris.[12]

Growing awareness of American competition unleashed chauvinistic campaigns in the French press, which denounced "American imperialism," the "American fifth column," and "foreign plots" against the School of Paris. Artistic nationalism is neither a useful nor effective response to foreign competition; it has no effect on the balance of power. In any case, the French art business had to defend itself against more than just competition from New York. In London a very active modern art market has grown up over the past fifteen years. Galleries in Basel, Zurich, and Geneva profited from Switzerland's central location and reserves of capital. The German market is decentralized: Berlin, Munich, Hamburg, Cologne, and Dusseldorf all play important roles. Prosperity in the Ruhr has increased the number of art collectors in the Rhineland. Finally, there is a very active art market in Italy, especially in Milan and Turin (where art is sold to major industrialists) and in Rome. The Italians apparently work closely with American and English galleries. France's claim to world leadership in painting and as a supplier of art—a claim based on the history of painting in the nineteenth and early twentieth century—has been put in doubt by the development of an international style and by the nature of economic competition on the international marketplace.

The "crisis" has apparently had a more profound effect on innovative art than on conservative art. Particularly hard hit were those artists who went along with the speculators, especially those who experienced sudden commercial success while still in their thirties. "Until I was thirty I lived in difficult straits; from thirty to forty I lived in opulence; and now at forty I have to start all over again." [P217] Is it reasonable to say that the crisis has had a beneficial healing effect, that it has been harder on bad painters than on good ones, worse for frauds than for authentic talents? None of these propositions is supported by available evidence. But it is clear that the economic difficulties have had an immediate impact on the lives of artists.

9

Summary and Conclusion

Although the contemporary art market is highly monopolistic, competition still plays an important role. Each painter monopolizes his own production. He can sell his work either directly to collectors or indirectly through one or more distributors. Buyers cannot rely on a historically validated hierarchy in making their choices. Price is therefore a factor in the evaluation of contemporary painting, along with the guarantees offered by dealers and critics. If a dealer holds, even temporarily, all of an artist's work, he is free to set prices as he chooses.

Prices and Dealers

Yet there are limits to monopoly power. Prices set by a dealer who both restricts supply and stimulates demand are subject to challenge in the parallel market or at public auction. In the long run the arbitrary nature of monopoly prices becomes apparent as demand for the artist's painting wanes. The price of an established work of art is meaningful; it is the amount actually paid by a buyer competing with other buyers to own the work. The prices paid for junk art are also meaningful; they are just sufficient to absorb the consumer surplus. Since works of comparable quality fetch comparable prices, these prices are valid at different points of sale, with minor variations. By contrast, the price of contemporary art is largely unpredictable. Initially, it is determined by supply and demand, but both supply and demand are artificially manipulated. Supply is affected by the strategies of painters and dealers; demand is manipulated by various psychological devices. At a later stage, gallery prices are often arbitrarily set, with no relation to actual demand. That such prices are meaningless is evident from the fact that comparable works by the same artist sell for widely varying prices at different locations.

Aesthetic uncertainty runs high in the contemporary art market, where even connoisseurs disagree and where coalitions of interested parties form to influence sales for purposes having nothing to do with aesthetic considerations. Contemporary paintings just introduced to the market are highly speculative investments, since their artistic quality has not been tested by time. In the short run prices depend on the opinions of dealers and buyers. From 1945 to 1962 steady economic growth and enthusiasm for painting encouraged speculation on the work of younger artists. Within a short time young painters were selling their works for fabulous prices and had achieved considerable reputations; they represented "growth investments" whose yield far surpassed that of other alternatives. But a brief change in the economic climate was enough to destroy the illusion that new art was a safe and profitable place to put one's money. The postwar frenzy of speculation brought inflation to the world of art (or renewed it, since a similar inflation occurred after World War I). The current disarray makes one wonder about the operation of a market that seems to have no regulatory mechanism other than crisis, which takes such a severe toll on the unfortunate artist.

Changes in Price and Market

To conclude this analysis of market transactions, I want to examine the extent to which changing prices for works of art reflect changes in the market's estimation of their worth. It bears repeating that, given the nature of the art business, all quantitative data should be treated with caution.

Six Painters

I have selected six painters as representative examples. Among the impressionists, Renoir (1841–1919) experienced the quickest commercial success; his work also conforms most closely to bourgeois expectations, in view of his prestige and amiable subject matter. Boudin (1824–1898) was a precursor and Loiseau (1865–1935) an epigone of impressionism. I have also selected three living artists (identified as I, II, and III), all born in the 1880s. The first and the third are typical of the innovative tendencies of the first half of the twentieth century, while the second typifies more conservative tendencies. (I have respected the anonymity of the living artists because it is not necessarily in their interest to have it known how much their earnings have increased.)

It was of course impossible to trace the price of a single painting over the course of several public sales. Hence I have compared prices for representative paintings comparable in terms of date, size, and subject; results are therefore approximate. Consider the following[1]

	Price paid	(*adjusted to reflect value of franc in 1961*)
Renoir 1		
Young Girl Reading 62 × 54 cm, Paris 22 June 1948	9,050,000 f	199,100 F
Young Girl in the Fields ca. 1900 London, Sotheby 6 December 1961	453,090 F	453,090 F
Renoir 2		
Roses 19 × 22 cm, Paris 22 December 1947	160,000 f	5,760 F
Roses 18.5 × 30 cm, Geneva Motte Gallery, 25 May 1963	50,850 F	47,036 F
Boudin		
River Banks 48 × 73 cm, Paris 14 February 1947	200,000 f	7,200 F
Banks of the Loques 47 × 75 cm, London Sotheby, 10 April 1962	68,650 F	66,179 F
Loiseau		
Millstone 54 × 50 cm, Paris 20 June 1947	15,100 f	544 F
Millstone 1906 54 × 65 cm, Geneva Motte Gallery 2 November 1963	14,125 F	13,181 F

In making these comparisons I would have liked to have used the year 1949 as my initial reference year, as is generally done by economists. The choice of that year is a good one: it avoids the unusual circumstances of the wartime and immediate postwar years yet comes before the inflationary trend of the 1950s and the art boom triggered by the Cognacq sale in 1952. But I was unable to find enough transactions in 1949 alone, so I have instead recorded prices from the years 1947, 1948, and 1949. For comparison I chose the period 1961–64. The graph shows the percentage price increase for each painter.

Coefficients of Price Increase

The coefficient of increase, based on constant (1961) francs, is smaller (2.28) for a large work by Renoir than for a smaller work (8.17). It is lower for a painting by an impressionist master than for works by precursors or epigones of impressionism (9.19 and 24.23, respectively). The variation reflects the great recent interest in impressionism and anything related to impressionism. The highest percentage increase is for a painter who followed the trail blazed by the impressionists. As supplies of masterpieces dwindled, buyers turned to lesser masters. Bear in mind, however, that the initial prices for these painters are very different. A large Renoir went for 253,990 Francs, a Boudin for 58,979, and a Loiseau for 12,637. A large painting by a major master brings the largest absolute profit, if not the highest percentage increase. Relative values are the same at the beginning and the end of the period, suggesting that with the benefit of some historical hindsight a hierarchy of values with speculation cannot alter does come into play. The role of chance is limited.

As for the living painters surveyed, the coefficients of increase ranged from 2.25 (I) to 6.31 (II) to 280 (III). It is particularly low for the artists whose status as grand masters was recognized before the base period of the comparison, and particularly for the one artist (III) who was long neglected before finally winning recognition as a twentieth-century master. Absolute prices range from 128,250 Francs (I) to 80,000 Francs (III) to 36,229 Francs (II). Relative values have changed: the ranking was I, II, III at the outset and I, III, II at the end. The greatest percentage increase was for the work of the painter whose status changes during the period under consideration. The greatest absolute increase was for a painting considered a masterpiece from the beginning. The change in relative values favored innovative painting.

Conclusion

The price of a painting cannot be determined by computing its production costs. The cost of raw materials is ridiculously small compared to the cost of a painting. It makes no sense to try to compute the value of the labor embodied in the painting; to do so is to treat a unique object as though it were an item of mass production. The Austrian economist Böhm-Bawwerk tried to refute the Marxist labor theory of value by examining the special case of sculpture and painting, but Marx never sought to apply to works of art a model based on reproducible objects.[2] The economic value of a painting results from demand for it as a work of art, which is a function of its presumed artistic quality. Though treated as a commodity, the painting does not cease to exist qua work of art. The uniqueness of the art market stems from the fact that, taste being subjective, there is no group of experts with the authority to establish a hierarchy of values capable of serving as an objective basis for prices.

In the market for older, more established painting, two sets of objective factors lacking in the modern art market come into play. If price is determined by demand, supply (that is, scarcity) is also a consideration. In addition, since experts can often achieve consensus as to the relative importance of various artists employing the same style, historical value bolsters aesthetic value.

The supply of contemporary painting is potentially unlimited. Critical judgment is uncertain, especially since modern painting aims to be independent of nature, ideal models, and the rules of genre. Sellers contrive to create artificial conditions similar to those that govern the market for old masters; that is, they limit supply to create scarcity, and they enlist connoisseurs and critics to attest to the value of the work. Different opinions are heeded in different circles, however, and rival institutions compete in judging the work of painters of different schools. A characteristic feature of the present is the dominant role played by the market in the distribution of works of art. Aesthetic judgment takes a back seat to business in an age where art takes many forms, ranging from hidebound academicism to recherché modernism. Through an obscure dialectic, aesthetic judgment justifies sales promotion, and commercial success justifies aesthetic judgment. As a result, the disinterestedness of the judgments of dealers, critics, and buyers is open to question. It is not always clear that the people who launch a new painter really believe (or have reason to believe) in his work. Strategies for establishing reputations are similar whether the painter is good or bad. But since society does not currently agree on a single set of values, two rival groups of specialists—conservatives and progressives—clash constantly.

Economic and Historical Values

In the midst of this confused situation the painting of our time is being created. Gradually history is winnowing the crop. The economic value of older painting depends on its historic value, whereas the economic value of contemporary work depends on a provisional estimate of its aesthetic worth, subject to manipulation by market actors.

According to my analysis (confirmed by comparison of price trends over time), the forces that determine the price of older painting are not the same as those that determine the price of contemporary painting. The investment value of an old master is largely independent of the value of other investment instruments. The old master comes with the guarantee of history and is therefore able to hold its value despite temporary fluctuations in the economy. By contrast, the contemporary painting is much more affected by fluctuations in the value of other investments; indeed, it is particularly vulnerable when the economy turned down. But the differences between the old masters market and the modern art market are not of kind but of degree; a subjective theory of value governs the art market as a whole. Demand—a subjective affair, unstable and manipulable—plays a decisive role; thus, irrational factors are important in determining art prices, and it would be irrational to attempt to eliminate them.

Structure of the Art Market

However irrational the behavior of market actors, the market itself continues to function and to a certain extent becomes more rational. The structure of the art market depends on the type of work. For junk painting the market consists of many buyers and many sellers (*polypole*), while the market for old masters is a closed oligopoly. The proliferation of artist-dealers contracts in the contemporary art market has transformed the circulation process into the production process (to use Marxist terminology) and encouraged the development of an oligopolistic structure. The market for junk painting is largely competitive, while the market for old masters tends to be more monopolistic. As for contemporary art, the theory of monopolistic competition seems to provide the best explanation of the market structure. During the period of interest, price changes appear to have followed a discernable pattern. For established painting, consensus as to relative value tends to reduce fluctuations due to changes in the economy. Study of the ways and means of achieving commercial success has cast light on the evolution of prices of more recent works. The chaotic nature of the art market is all too often stressed. Without denying that irrational factors and accidents play a part, I have argued that it is still possible to discern an inner logic in the operation of the market.

The foregoing remarks reflect an economist's point of view, not uninfluenced by considerations of the sociology of artists and, secondarily, of art. Today's art market is different from yesterday's guilds and academies. Gone are the rigid regulations of the old guild system and the doctrinaire attitudes of the academy. Nevertheless, the market still exerts decisive influence over the work that artists do. The existence of the work of art qua commodity gives an economic dimension to relations among artists, critics, dealers, and collectors; the behavior of each group is governed by its own internal logic. When patrons commissioned paintings, relations between artist and patron were direct and personal; now the direct relationship is between artist and dealer. The dealer intervenes at the primary stage, when the artist is ready to put his work into the world, rather than at the secondary stage, after the painting has passed into the hands of the person who commissioned it. Whether the dealer merely follows taste and interprets preexisting demand or helps shape taste and create demand, his function is to integrate the painter into the market. Although some artists deal directly with clients and manage to survive, they are condemned to remain outsiders in a system in which the dealer's role is pivotal.

The market actors are not abstract economic agents but concrete social subjects whose values dictate their judgments and shape their decisions. The painter, creator of an aesthetic object, is also the producer of a commodity. As such he is exposed to risks: if forced to sell his goods too cheaply, he risks being unable to carry through his creative plans; more insidious, if he achieves commercial success, he risks altering his vision to fit the desires of the marketplace. Painters rationalize success and failure in terms that cast doubt on the verdict of the market: commercial success is contrasted with the succès d'estime, overnight fame is contrasted with the slow growth of a reputation, and success through compromise is contrasted with success through misunderstanding. The successful painter's feelings of satisfaction are not unalloyed with feelings of resentment against the means by which success was achieved, as well as doubts as to its significance. Regardless of artists' ideological doubts, however, appreciation of the work is currently reflected in price. Recognition is not bestowed by a privileged class whose values are accepted by all of society; success is measured, rather, by money, an objective gauge in a theoretically democratized society where no one group enjoys the prerogative of setting values for all.

The social constraints on the distribution and sale of artworks are intensified by economic pressures. Social and economic forces act on the artist through the marketplace and affect his relation to his work. The artist commits his work, and therefore himself, to social judgment. Hence he must confront society's image of himself as he contemplates his future work. The relation of artist to work is not unaffected by other peoples' ideas about painting and how much they are willing to pay for it. The miserable unknown living in poverty and the famous painter living in splendor have different attitudes toward their work.

Can we say more? Can we explain the underlying tendencies of contemporary art in terms of the conditions under which creation takes place? The sociology of the art market can do no more than analyze the constraints resulting from the fct that the work of art eventually becomes a market commodity; it tells us nothing about the work qua aesthetic object. The impressionists and early modernists remained true, so far as we can tell, to the inspiration that preceded their commercial success. Hence the history of art cannot be reduced to the sociology of artists. If contemporary art exists, it does so only to the extent that artists place the exigencies of form ahead of the exigencies of the marketplace. Proof of this assertion would require an aesthetic study of contemporary painting.

Appendix 1
Deflater coefficients (1961 = 1.00)

[The franc was devalued in 1961: 1 Franc = 100 old francs.]

Francs	1963: 0,925		francs	1929: 0,36
»	1962: 0,964		»	1928: 0,37
»	1961: 1,00		»	1927: 0,37
francs	1959: 0,0106		»	1925: 0,45
»	1958: 0,0112		»	1924: 0,50
»	1957: 0,0126		»	1923: 0,57
»	1956: 0,0132		»	1922: 0,69
»	1955: 0,0138		»	1921: 0,66
»	1954: 0,0138		»	1920: 0,50
»	1953: 0,0137		»	1919: 0,70
»	1952: 0,0133		»	1918: 0,78
»	1951: 0,0143		»	1917: 1,01
»	1950: 0,0175		»	1916: 1,33
»	1949: 0,0191		»	1915: 1,67
»	1948: 0,022		»	1914: 2,15
»	1947: 0,036		»	1913: 2,15
»	1946: 0,054		»	1912: 2,15
»	1945: 0,087		»	1911: 2,15
»	1944: 0,126		»	1910: 2,38
»	1943: 0,148		»	1909: 2,47
»	1942: 0,177		»	1908: 2,47
»	1941: 0,21		»	1907: 2,38
»	1940: 0,25		»	1906: 2,56
»	1939: 0,31		»	1905: 2,47
»	1938: 0,33		»	1904: 2,56
»	1937: 0,38		»	1903: 2,56
»	1936: 0,50		»	1902: 2,56
»	1935: 0,56		»	1901: 2,56
»	1934: 0,52		»	1900: 2,56
»	1933: 0,49		francs	de 1899 à 1890: 2,53
»	1932: 0,47		»	» 1889 à 1880: 2,72
»	1931: 0,43		»	» 1879 à 1870: 2,79
»	1930: 0,38			

Correction coefficients are computed as an average of the wholesale and retail price indices:

—For the period 1900–1961 I used the coefficients published in *Statistiques et études financières*, supplement 157, January 1962, p. 173.

—For 1962, 1963, and 1964, the coefficient is based on an average of the wholesale and consumer price indices (for 1962 and 1963, an index of 250 items sold in the Paris area; for 1964 an index of 259 items; both published by the Institut National des Statistiques et Etudes Economiques).

—For the period 1870–1899, coefficients are computed from the five-year averages wholesale price indices published in *Statistique générale de la France*, and from an index of prices of 213 items published in J. Singer-Kérel, *Le Coût de la vie à Paris de 1840 à 1934* (Paris: Colin, 1962), pp. 452–453.

Appendix 2
Designation and Dimensions of Canvases

Number	Portrait	DIMENSIONS Landscape	Seascape
0	18 × 14	18 × 12	18 × 10
1	22 × 16	22 × 14	22 × 12
2	24 × 19	24 × 16	24 × 14
3	27 × 22	27 × 19	27 × 16
4	33 × 24	33 × 22	33 × 19
5	35 × 27	35 × 24	35 × 22
6	41 × 33	41 × 27	41 × 24
8	46 × 38	46 × 33	46 × 27
10	55 × 46	55 × 38	55 × 33
12	61 × 50	61 × 46	61 × 38
15	65 × 54	65 × 50	65 × 46
20	73 × 60	73 × 54	73 × 50
25	81 × 65	81 × 60	81 × 54
30	92 × 73	92 × 65	92 ×60
40	100 × 81	100 × 73	100 × 65
50	116 × 89	116 × 81	116 × 73
60	130 × 97	130 × 89	130 × 81
80	146 × 114	146 × 97	146 × 89
100	162 × 130	162 × 114	162 × 97
120	195 × 130	195 × 114	195 × 97

Sizes are given according to the traditional measure in *points*. Dimensions are given in centimeters. The "portrait" format is higher than it is wide; the "landscape" and "seascape" formats are wider than they are high.

Appendix 3
Map of Paris Galleries

This map of Paris galleries does not indicate the type of works sold (old paintings, modern paintings, and contemporary paintings including those not considered "art" by reputable experts), nor does it note differences in sales methods. There is more quantitative than qualitative information, owing to the difficulty of ascertaining for each gallery total sales, type of work sold, relations with living artists, and so forth. Since precision is worthless without accuracy, I have simply indicated the density of galleries in each district of the city. Art galleries have traditionally been located in certain streets; dealers regard nearby galleries as useful for business despite the competition. Since clients are widely scattered, a local monopoly is of no advantage, whereas concentration in a small area increases the chance of attracting prospective buyers.

The art business moves from section to section as the city changes. (In the late nineteenth century, for example, the center of the painting market was in the rue Laffitte and the neighborhood of the Opera.) Dealers also change location as their business grows. At present the itinerary is as follows: from Montmartre to the avenue Matignon and from the Left Bank to the Right Bank. The center of the art market is now located in an area that includes the faubourg Saint-Honoré, rue La Boétie, boulevard Haussmann, avenue de Messine, avenue Matignon, rue de Miromesnil, and rue de Monceau.

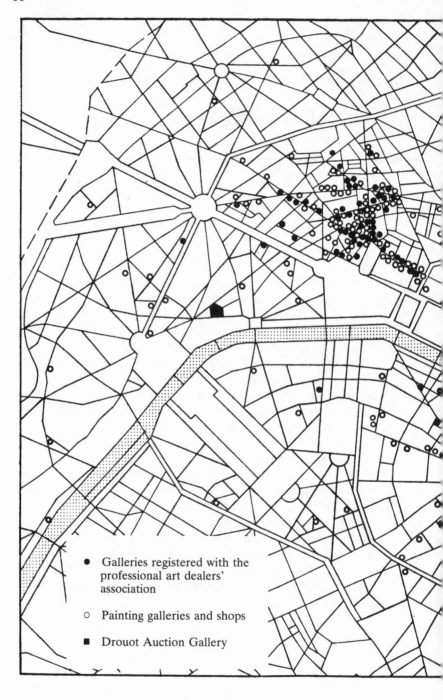

● Galleries registered with the
professional art dealers'
association

○ Painting galleries and shops

■ Drouot Auction Gallery

Appendix 4
Typical Contracts

---

1. Monopoly Contract between Derain
and Kahnweiler (1912)

Paris, 6 December 1912

Dear Mr. Kahnweiler,

In response to your letter, I agree to sell nothing to anyone except you and to give you everything I produce according to the following schedule of prices:

Canvases of		
	6	125 frs
	8	159
	19	170
	12	225
	15	150
	20	275
	25	300
	30	350
	40	400
50 & 60		500

These prices are to run from 1 December 1912 to 1 December 1913. We are therefore in full agreement. Please accept my warmest regards.

[signed] A. Derain
13, rue Bonaparte

2. Contract Offering Right of First Refusal between Raoul Dufy and Bernheim-Jeune and Vildrac (1920)

Between Messrs. Raoul Dufy, Bernheim-Jeune, and Vildrac the folowing agreement has been made:

For the amount of fifty francs per point, up to a maximum of fifty points, Messrs. Bernheim-Jeune and Vildrac agree to acquire half the production of Mr. Raoul Dufy, who agrees to sell to them up to a total annual amount of 40,000 francs. It is understood that Mr. Raoul Dufy is not required to produce a definite number of paintings and, further, that Messrs. Bernheim-Jeune and Vildrac are authorized to exceed the above-mentioned minimum purchase figure, to which they have committed themselves.

Mr. Raoul Dufy is free to dispose as he sees fit of those of his works acquired by Messrs. Bernheim-Jeune and Vildrac, but he agrees to offer them right of first refusal on all his production.

Division of the paintings acquired by Messrs. Bernheim-Jeune and Vildrac will be made either at the artist's studio or at one or the other of the two galleries, either by agreement or by lot.

This contract, which shall remain in force for one year from this date, is to be renewed annually. Any of the parties shall have the right, however, to end the association at the end of the year without conditions or formalities other than to make formal notification of the intention to end the contract two months in advance. The present contract has not been registered. Any party who may deem it appropriate to do so shall assume the costs of registration.

Done in three copies at Paris, 28 April 1920.

(This contract was renewed on 11 October 1921 for three years, with further renewals at three year intervals.)

3. Contracts between Matisse and Bernheim-Jeune (1909, 1912, 1917, 1920, 1923)

First Contract, 1909

Between Mr. Henry Matisse (42, route de Clamart at Issy-les-Moulineaux, Seine)

And Messrs. Bernheim-Jeune (15, rue Richepanse at Paris)

the following has been agreed:

ARTICLE I. Any paintings in the following sizes and intermediate sizes that Mr. Henri Matisse shall complete prior to 15 September 1912 he agrees to sell to Messrs. Bernheim-Jeune, who agree to buy them, regardless of subject, at the following prices:

Size				
50	1,875 frs		15	900 frs
40	1,650 frs		12	750 frs
30	1,500 frs		10	600 frs
25	1,275 frs		8	525 frs
20	1,125 frs		6	450 frs

Prices of paintings in intermediate formats ("landscape" and "seascape" and irregular formats) shall be proportional to their surface area and to these figures.

ARTICLE II. Mr. Henri Matisse shall receive, in additionn, twenty-five percent of the profit earned by Messrs. Bernheim-Jeune on the sale of these paintings.

ARTICLE III. In case Mr. Henri Matisse should sell one of these paintings during the course of execution, the difference between the prices stipulated above and the selling price shall be divided half and half between him and Bernheim-Jeune & Co.

ARTICLE IV. If Messrs. Bernheim-Jeune leave a finished painting in storage at Mr. Henri Matisse's studio and said painting is sold directly by him, the profits shall also be divided half and half.

ARTICLE V. The selling prices of paintings sold by Mr. Henri Matisse under the conditions set forth in articles III and IV shall not be less than approximately twice the prices indicated in Article I.

ARTICLE VI. Painted works that Mr. Henri Matisse himself considers to be sketches are not included in the terms of Article I or in the following articles. Any sketches that he may decide to place in circulation, however, shall be submitted to Messrs. Bernheim-Jeune. Each may be covered by a separate agreement. In case no agreement can be reached, Messrs. Bernheim-Jeune shall have the option, but not the obligation, to acquire full ownership of the sketch at the price set forth in article I.

ARTICLE VII. As soon as Mr. Henri Matisse has finished a painting, he shall notify Messrs. Bernheim-Jeune. Upon delivery of any painting he shall inform them of any discussions that have taken place concerning it.

ARTICLE VIII. Neither Article I nor any subsequent article has any retroactive effect on commissions for paintings accepted by Mr. Henri Matisse prior to the present agreement, to wit: a self-portrait, two size 50 paintings, a landscape of approximately size 20, and two paintings of approximately size 40.

ARTICLE IX. Mr. Henri Matisse is free to accept such commissions for portraits and decorations as he may receive directly, without giving rise to a claim on the part of Messrs. Bernheim-Jeune. The term "decorations" is understood to mean paintings of irregular format whose dimensions are strictly determined by the architecture of the room in which they are to be placed.

ARTICLE X. Messrs. Bernheim-Jeune shall receive a fee of 25% on commissions for such decorations and portraits as Mr. Henri Matisse may receive through their good offices.

ARTICLE XI. Either party to the contract may at any time cancel the present agreement for the remainder of the period it has to run by paying a forfeit of 30,000 francs and notifying the other party in writing.

ARTICLE XII. In case Messrs. Bernheim-Jeune pay Mr. Henri Matisse the forfeit of 30,000 francs as set forth in the preceding article, Mr. Henri Matisse would lose all rights to profits earned subsequently by Messrs. Bernheim-Jeune on paintings they already hold in storage at the time of said payment.

ARTICLE XIII. The present agreement is not registered. If, under any circumstances, either of the parties deems it appropriate to register the contract, that party shall assume the cost of registration.

Done in Paris in two copies, 18 September 1909.

Second Contract, 1912

Between Mr. Henri Matisse (92, route de Clamart at Issy-les-Moulineaux, Seine)
   And Messrs. Bernheim-Jeune (15, rue Richepanse at Paris),
   the following has been agreed:

ARTICLE I. Any paintings in the following sizes and intermediate sizes that Mr. Henri Matisse shall complete prior to 15 September 1915 he agrees to sell to Messrs. Bernheim-Jeune, who agree to buy them, regardless of subject, at the following prices:

Size				
50	1,875 frs		15	900 frs
40	1,650 frs		12	750 frs
30	1,500 frs		10	600 frs
25	1,275 frs		8	525 frs
20	1,125 frs		6	450 frs

Prices of paintings in intermediate formats ("landscape" and "seascape" and irregular formats) shall be proportional to their surface areas and to these figures.

ARTICLE II. Mr. Henri Matisse shall receive, in addition, twenty-five percent of the profit earned by Messrs. Bernheim-Jeune on the sale of these paintings.

ARTICLE III. In case Mr. Henri Matisse should sell one of these paintings during the course of execution, the difference between the prices stipulated above and the selling price shall be divided half and half between him and Bernheim-Jeune & Co.

ARTICLE IV. If Messrs. Bernheim-Jeune leave a finished painting in storage at Mr. Henri Matisse's studio and said painting is sold directly by him, the profits shall also be divided half and half.

ARTICLE V. The selling prices of paintings sold by Mr. Henri Matisse under the conditions set forth in articles III and IV shall not be less than approximately twice the prices indicated in Article I. This clause entails no reciprocal obligation on the part of Messrs. Bernheim-Jeune, who shall naturally do their utmost to sell the paintings of Mr. Henri Matisse in the best interests of both parties. In exceptional circumstances, they shall be permitted to sell the paintings for a price considerably less than twice the purchase price, in case where they have tried in vain to sell the paintings to collectors for some time, or when the paintings are sold to another art dealer, or when a concession on the price may result in finding new clients for the work of Mr. Henri Matisse.

ARTICLE VI. Painted works that Mr. Henri Matisse himself considers to be sketches are not included in the terms of Article I or in the following articles. Any sketches that he may decide to place in circulation, however, shall be submitted to Messrs. Bernheim-Jeune. Each may be covered by a separate agreement. In case no agreement can be reached, Messrs. Bernheim-Jeune shall have the option, but not the obligation, to acquire full ownership of the sketch at the price set forth in article I.

ARTICLE VII. As soon as Mr. Henri Matisse has finished a painting, he shall notify Messrs. Bernheim-Jeune. Upon delivery of any painting he shall inform them of any discussions that have taken place concerning it.

ARTICLE VIII. Mr. Henri Matisse is free to accept such commissions for portraits and decorations as he may receive directly, without giving rise to a claim on the part of Messrs. Bernheim-Jeune. The term "decorations" is understood to mean paintings of irregular format whose dimensions are strictly determined by the architecture of the room in which they are to be placed.

ARTICLE IX. Messrs. Bernheim-Jeune shall receive a fee of 25% on commissions for such decorations and portraits as Mr. Henri Matisse may receive through their good offices.

ARTICLE X. Either party to the contract may at any time cancel the present agreement for the remainder of the period it has to run by paying a forfeit of 30,000 francs and notifying the other party in writing.

ARTICLE XI. In case Messrs. Bernheim-Jeune pay Mr. Henri Matisse the forfeit of 30,000 francs as set forth in the preceding article, Messrs. Bernheim-Jeune would buy the rights to any paintings they might hold in storage for 20% of the purchase price set forth in Article 1 of the present agreement.

ARTICLE XII. The present agreement is not registered. If, under any circumstances, either of the parties deems it appropriate to register the contract, that party shall assume the cost of registration.

Done in Paris in two copies, 18 September 1909.

Read and approved,
[signed] Henri Matisse

Third Contract, 1917

Paris, 19 October 1917
Messrs. Bernheim-Jeune
15, rue Richepanse, Paris

Sirs:

The following will confirm the agreement we have just made:

I. For a period of three years starting 19 September 1917 I shall sell to you, and you agree to buy from me, half of all the paintings I produce from size 4 to size 80 inclusive at the prices indicated below, which, in each format, are uniform for the dimension "Portrait", the dimension "Landscape," and the dimension "Seascape":

Formats	Prices
80	6,000
60	5,000
50	4,500
40	4,000
30	3,500
25	3,000
20	2,800
15	2,500
12	2,000
10	1,800
8	1,500
6	1,200
5	1,000
4	800

The schedule for works in irregular formats shall be calculated proportionately.

II. I agree not to sell to any third party, dealer, or collector any unfinished painting.

III. The division set forth in paragraph I shall be accomplished as follows: I shall inform you whenever a pair of paintings of identical or similar format is completed, and the selection will be made by lot.

IV. Concerning the half of the paintings that belong to me, I agree not to sell any to any other dealer at a price less than 30% above the prices indicated in paragraph I. If, however, the sale is of the entirety of my half of the paintings, the supplement shall be reduced to at least 20%. You agree not to sell any of the paintings in your half for less than 40% above your purchase price.

V. I am permitted to accept commissions (decorations, portraits, easel paintings), for which you shall have no claim of commission unless I receive said commissions by your good offices, in which case you shall receive 25% of what I am paid.

Whether I receive commissions directly or through you, said work shall count as part of my half if it involves works of a format included in paragraph I.

VI. Our agreement is not registered. If, under any circumstances, either party deems it appropriate to proceed with registration, that party shall bear the cost thereof.

Please accept my best wishes.
[signed] Henri Matisse

Fourth Contract, 1920

Between Mr. Henri Matisse, route de Clammart 92, Issy-les-Moulineaux,
    and Messrs. Bernheim-Jeune, rue Richepanse, 15, Paris, the following has been agreed:

ARTICLE I. For a period of three years starting 19 September 1920 Mr. Henri Matisse agrees to sell outright, and Messrs. Bernheim-Jeune agree to buy, half of all the paintings that Mr. Matisse produces from size 4 to size 80 inclusive at the prices indicated below, which, in each format, are uniform for the dimension "Portrait", the dimension "Landscape," and the dimension "Seascape":

Formats	Prices
80	9,000
60	8,000
50	7,500
40	6,500
30	5,500
25	4,800
20	4,500
15	4,000
12	3,500

10	3,000
8	2,500
6	2,000
5	1,800
4	1,500

The schedule for works in irregular formats shall be calculated proportionately.

ARTICLE II. Mr. Henri Matisse agrees not to sell to any third party, dealer, or collector any unfinished painting.

ARTICLE III. The division set forth in paragraph I shall be accomplished as follows: Mr. Henri Matisse shall inform Messrs. Bernheim-Jeune whenever a pair of paintings of identical or similar format is completed, and the selection will be made by lot.

ARTICLE IV. Concerning the half of the paintings that belong to Mr. Henri Matisse, he agrees not to sell any to any other dealer at a price less than 30% above the prices indicated in article I. If, however, the sale is of the entirety of Mr. Henri Matisse's half of the paintings, the supplement shall be reduced to at least 20%. Messrs. Bernheim-Jeune agree not to sell any of the paintings in their half for less than 40% above their purchase price.

ARTICLE V. Mr. Henri Matisse is permitted to accept commissions (decorations, portraits, easel paintings), for which Messrs. Bernheim-Jeune shall have no claim of commission unless Mr. Matisse receives said commissions by their good offices, in which case they shall receive 25% of what he is paid.

ARTICLE VI. Mr. Henri Matisse has the right to keep for himself four paintings per year to be chosen by him from the part of his production covered by this contract.

ARTICLE VII. Mr. Henri Matisse is prohibited from selling the paintings mentioned in article VI so long as this contract shall remain in force.

ARTICLE VIII. The present agreement is not registered. If, under any circumstances, either party deems it appropriate to proceed with registration, that party shall bear the cost thereof.

Done at Paris in two copies, 23 August 1920.

Read and approved   Read and approved
[signed] Bernheim-Jeune   [signed] Henri Matisse

Fifth Contract, 1923

Between Mr. Henri Matisse, route de Clamart 92, Issy-les-Moulineaux,
    and Messrs. Bernheim-Jeune, rue Richepanse, 15, Paris, the following
has been agreed:

ARTICLE I. For a period of three years starting 19 September 1923 Mr.
Henri Matisse agrees to sell outright, and Messrs. Bernheim-Jeune agree
to buy, half of all the paintings that Mr. Matisse produces from size 4 to
size 80 inclusive at the prices indicated below, which, in each format, are
uniform for the dimension "Portrait", the dimension "Landscape," and
the dimension "Seascape":

Formats	Prices
50	11,000
40	10,000
30	8,250
25	7,250
20	6,750
15	6,000
12	5,250
10	4,500
8	4,000

The schedule for works in irregular formats shall be calculated proportionately.

ARTICLE II. Mr. Henri Matisse agrees not to sell to any third party,
dealer, or collector any unfinished painting.

ARTICLE III. The division set forth in paragraph I shall be accomplished as
follows: Mr. Henri Matisse shall inform Messrs. Bernheim-Jeune whenever a pair of paintings of identical or similar format is completed, and the
selection will be made by lot.

ARTICLE IV. Mr. Henri Matisse is permitted to accept commissions (decorations, portraits, easel paintings), for which Messrs. Bernheim-Jeune
shall have no claim of commission unless Mr. Matisse receives said commissions by their good offices, in which case they shall receive 25% of
what he is paid.

ARTICLE V. Mr. Henri Matisse has the right to keep for himself four paintings per year to be chosen by him from the part of his production covered by this contract.

ARTICLE VI. Mr. Henri Matisse is prohibited from selling the paintings mentioned in article VI so long as this contract shall remain in force.

ARTICLE VII. The present agreement is not registered. If, under any circumstances, either party deems it appropriate to proceed with registration, that party shall bear the cost thereof.

Done at Paris in two copies, 25 August 1923.

Read and approved   Read and approved
[signed] Bernheim-Jeune   [signed] Henri Matisse

4. Exclusive Contract Signed in 1957 by an Abstract Painter under Thirty Years of Age and an Art Dealer

Gallery X
A Corporation Capitalized at ———
Paris

Between Mr. L. D. residing at . . . . . . , Paris, and Gallery X, Paris, represented by its director, Mr. A. T., the following has been agreed:

Mr. L. D. grants exclusive rights to his work, completed and yet to be completed, to Gallery X for a period beginning 1 January 1957 and ending one year after the first show to be organized by Gallery X on his behalf. This show, which shall last three weeks, shall be held by 15 June 1957 at the latest. This exclusive agreement, which is valid for private collectors as well as French and foreign galleries and which also applies to all shows that may be organized during the term of the agreement, shall be renewable by tacit agreement for one-year periods. The parties reserve the right to rescind the present by registered letter three months prior to the expiration of each period.

In exchange for this exclusive right, Gallery X shall pay Mr. L. D. a minimum of fifty thousand francs per month as an advance on a certain number of paintings, gouaches, or drawings (at the gallery's option), according to the price schedules listed below, to date from 1 January 1957 until aforesaid exlcusive right is terminated. The surplus shall be paid to Mr. L. D. according to the same schedule. For his part, Mr. L. D. agrees to furnish the gallery a sufficient number of paintings, gouaches, or drawings each month to cover at a minimum the fifty thousand francs that he is guaranteed according to the following price schedule.

As a special agreement, valid solely for the first period, the gallery will sell, at the gallery's customary dealer price, to Mr. H. D., brother of Mr. L. D., paintings that he will sell directly to personal friends (and not to any dealer).

Price Schedule

1. Drawings

   P.F. = 65 × 50

   G.F. = 75 × 56 on drawing paper

		P.F.	G.F.
a.	Black and white drawings (pencil or india ink	3,000	3,500
b.	Color drawings	3,500	4,000
c.	Spiral drawings	4,000	5,000
d.	Light composition using paste, other materials, or marbled papers	5,000	6,000
e.	Heavy paste compositions	8,000	10,000

2. Paintings

0–15	1,000 francs per point
20–60	750 francs per point
larger	500 francs per point

Should any provison of the present agreement fail to be executed by either partner, it shall be declared null and void if, within fifteen days after notification by registered letter with return receipt containing a statement by the more diligent party of the infraction and requiring performance by the other party, said other party shall not have conformed to the terms of the agreement. Competence is assigned to the chief judge of the Civil Court of the Seine to determine whether the conditions for nullification have been met.

Done at Paris in two copies on this date of _____ .

Read and approved   Read and approved
[signature of the dealer]   [signature of the artist]

5. Contract between a French Painter and an American Dealer

Contract, as of _____ , 196–, between H. Galleries, party of the first part, and Mr. F. L., party of the second part.

Know all men that

In view of the mutual commitments and agreements embodied in the present contract, which are to be observed and executed by the parties hereto, the following has been decided:

1. The party of the first part is in the business of, among other things, buying, showing, and selling paintings, and the party of the second part is an artist whose work is to produce, show, and sell his own paintings.

2. By the terms of the present agreement, the party of the second part engages the party of the first part as his sole representative in the United States for the exposition and sale of his paintings in the United States. Furthermore, the party of the second part agrees that he shall accredit no other representative in the United States for said purpose during the period of the present contract. Said party of the second part also agrees that he shall accredit no other party in the United States for this purpose and that he shall sell no paintings in the United States through any other agent during the period of the present contract.

3. The party of the first part shall act as agent and sole representative for the party of the second part for the exposition and sale of the paintings of the party of the second part in the United States; furthermore, the party of the first part agrees to offer the paintings of the party of the second part for sale in the United States and to show said paintings as well as to promote their sale in the United States in every possible way. Dates and locations of said shows shall be decided at the sole discretion of the party of the first part. The party of the second part currently resides at _____ (France), where he is currently producing paintings. However, the present contract is not limited to paintings produced abroad but applies to all paintings done by the party of the second part.

4. If an artist under contract with H. Galleries sells to a European gallery or dealer, it is understood and agreed that these paintings shall not be offered for sale in the United States by any intermediary whatsoever.

5. The duration of the present contract shall be for three years ending _____ . Either party may, however, at its option end said contract upon expiration of the first year by sending written notice of said decision at least 90 days prior to the date of termination. Delivery of said notice may be made either personally or by registered or certified letter sent to the address that each party shall give for this purpose.

Until further notice, said address is as follows:

Party of the first part. _____

Party of the second part. _____

In witness whereof the parties have affixed their signatures this day of _____ , 1964.

6. Contract between a Painter under Thirty Years of Age and Four Collectors

Between Mr. h. J., a painter residing at _____ and a support group composed of

Mr. _____ residing at _____

Mr. _____ residing at _____

Mr. _____ residing at _____

Mr. _____ residing at _____

the following has been agreed:

1. Each member of the group shall pay Mr. H. J. the sum of 500 new francs per month, beginning _____ 1961.

2. The contract is to run for a period of two years ending _____ 1963.

3. Mr. H. J. agrees to furnish each member of the group a gouache of 50 × 65 or 56 × 76, to be chosen with priority from his recent or earlier work.

The selection will be made by each member of the group at the time the monthly stipend is paid.

4. The members of the group agree to do all within their power to promote the work of Mr. H. J. and defend it in the best interests of all concerned.

The present contract has been prepared in four copies. Read and approved

xxx

Notes

Introduction

1. On the origins of easel painting, see Pierre Francastel, *Histoire de la peinture française, la peinture de chevalet du XIVe au XXe siècle,* vol. 1 (Paris: Elsevier, 1955), pp. 3–6.

2. Maurice Halbwachs, *Esquisse d'une psychologie des classes sociales* (Paris: Librairie Marcel Rivière, 1955), pp. 53–54.

3. Interviews are identified by code number (D100–D175 for dealers, C1–C90 for collectors, and P200–P320 for painters). Initials used to identify excerpts from interviews with critics and appraisers have no relation to the actual initials of the persons interviewed.

4. Raymond Aron, Introduction to Max Weber, *Le savant et le politique* (Paris: Plon, 1959), p. 35.

Chapter 1

1. André Chastel, *Art et humanisme à Florence au temps de Laurent le Magnifique: Etudes sur la Renaissance et l'humanisme platonicien* (Paris: Presses Universitaires de France, 1959), p. 288.

2. Originally, the Salon (first held in 1667) was limited to members of the Royal Academy from the rector down to the youngest students, some forty painters in all. In 1748 an admissions jury was established, and only works by officers of the Academy were exempt from examination. After the Revolution the Salons were opened to painters who were not members of the Academy. At the Salon of 1806, 704 works were exhibited; 573 of them were paintings done by 293 artists. By midcentury the number of works accepted was about 2,000.

3. Harrison C. White and Cynthia A. White, *Canvases and Careers: Institutional Change in the French Painting World* (New York: John Wiley and Sons, 1965).

4. Pierre Marcel, "Les peintres et le public en France au XVIIIe siè-cle," *Mélanges Beraux* (Paris: E. de Boccard, 1924), pp. 205–213.

5. Francis Haskell, *Patrons and Painters: A Study in the Relations between Italian Art and Society in the Age of Baroque* (Oxford: Oxford University Press, 1963).

6. Boussod, Valadon, & Co., successors to Goupil, a dealer in engravings, did business at 9, rue Chaptal, and at two branch offices, one located at 19, boulevard Montmartre (of which Théo Van Gogh became manager in 1879), the other at 2, place de l'Opéra. I am indebted to Jean Diéterle, present owner of the gallery, who permitted me to examine the accounts of Boussod, Valadon.

7. In the early 1870s, an important painting by a well-known artist would have sold for between 10,000 and 20,000 francs (roughly $5,000 to $10,000 in today's currency). Prices are sometimes given in old francs, sometimes new. To distinguish, new francs are indicated by the use of a capital F: Francs, abbreviated F. See appendix 1 for conversion of old to new francs.

8. Lionello Venturi, *Les archives de l'impressionisme,* vol. 1 (Paris and New York: Durand-Ruel, 1939), p. 115.

9. The impressionist group held eight shows: 1874, 1876, 1877, 1879, 1880, 1881, 1882, and 1886. The number and identity of the participants varied.

10. Impressionist sales were held on 24 March 1875 and 28 May 1877.

11. In 1881 the government relinquished control of the Salon, and the Society of French Artists took charge. In 1884, in a climate similar to that which gave rise to the Salon des Refusés of 1863, the Society of Independent Artists was founded; this group staged an annual salon without jury or prizes. In 1890 a schism in the Salon of French Artists gave rise to the National Society of Fine Arts, and in 1903 younger artists associated with the Nationale organized the first Autumn Salon.

12. See Maurice Rheims, *La vie étrange des objets* (Paris: Plon, 1959), pp. 317, 320.

13. The Durand-Ruel stationery shop opened its doors on the rue Saint-Jacques in Paris in 1803. In the second generation a line of artists' supplies was added to the stock. Jean-Marie Fortuné Durand-Ruel moved the shop first to the rue des Petits-Champs, where it remained until 1855, and then to 1, rue de la Paix. In 1867 Paul Durand-Ruel rented space at 16, rue Laffitte (adjoining 11, rue Le Peletier). In 1924, the present gallery was built at 37, avenue de Friedland.

14. Led by Edouard Manet, this group of impressionist painters frequently gathered in the evening at the Cafe Guerbois in Batignolles.

15. F. F. (Fénéon): "Les grands collectionneurs, M. Paul Durand-Ruel," *Bulletin de la vie artistique,* 15 April 1920, cited by John Rewald,

The History of Impressionism (New York: Museum of Modern Art, 1946).

16. Venturi, *Les archives,* vol. 1, p. 14.

17. Rewald, *The History,* p. 225.

18. Venturi, *Les archives,* vol. 1, p. 52.

19. His private collection, which he was obliged to sell in 1894, included six Manets, six Monets, four Pissarros, three Renoirs, three Sisleys, three Cézannes, and eight Dégas.

20. These early collectors were soon accused of speculative manipulations. In July 1887 Pissarro wrote his son: "The art lover today looks upon the painting in exactly the same way as a share of stock. It's disgusting to belong to a guild that has fallen so low!" Camille Pissarro, *Lettres à son fils Lucien* (Paris: Albin Michel, 1950), p. 158.

21. Vincent Van Gogh, *Lettres à son frère Théo* (Paris: Gallimard, 1956), p. 271.

22. The word is Max Ernst's.

23. André Level, *Souvenirs d'un collectionneur* (Paris: Alain C. Mazod, 1959), pp. 32–33.

24. Ambroise Vollard, *Souvenirs d'un marchand de tableaux* (Paris: Club des Librairies de France, 1957), p. 227.

25. Antonina Vallentin, *Picasso* (Paris: Albin Michel, 1957), p. 235.

26. Gyula Helász Brassai, *Conversations avec Picasso* (Paris: Gallimard, 1964), p. 27.

27. William Makepeace Thackeray, *Book of Snobs* (London, 1869), p. 70.

28. Rheims, *La vie étrange des objets,* p. 346.

29. Level, *Souvenirs,* pp. 71–72.

30. Ibid., p. 76.

31. Dimensions of paintings are given in centimeters.

32. D.-H. Kanhweiler, *Mes galeries et mes peintres,* "Interviews with Francis Crémieux" (Paris: Gallimard, 1961), pp. 163–164.

33. Gerald Reitlinger, *The Economics of Taste* (London: Barrie and Rockliff, 1961), p. 209.

34. The following list of shows at the Charpentier Gallery (est. 1941, 76, rue du Faubourg Saint-Honoré) offers some idea of the public's taste:

1942: A century of watercolor; La Patellière; Pompon; French Landscape from Corot to the present; Van Dongen; Flowers and fruits.

1943: Watercolors by Constantin Guys; Paris scenes and figures; French gardens; Emile Bernard; Autumn; Van Dongen.

1944: Family life; Romantic and contemporary watercolors; Marine painting; Paris.

1945: Watercolors; Freshwater landscapes; French landscapes.

35. See Rose Valland, *Le front de l'art* (Paris: Plon, 1961).

36. Ibid., p. 76.

37. Kahnweiler, *Mes galeries,* pp. 186–187. Compare Kahnweiler's remarks with those of a broker I interviewed: "During the war I never had direct contact with the Germans, but things often reached them through several intermediaries."

38. The manifesto was published in the *Moniteur des arts* on 17 October 1884. See Pierre Angrand, *Naissance des artistes indépendants, 1884* (Paris: Nouvelles Editions Debresse, 1965).

39. Archives nationales, F 21/40. My italics.

Chapter 2

1. Etienne Gilson, *Peinture et réalité* (Paris: Vrin, 1958), p. 15.

2. Pierre Bourdieu, *Un art moyen: essai sur les usages sociaux de la photographie* (Paris: Les Editions de Minuit, 1965), pp. 134–135.

3. Bernard Dorival applies the word *contemporary* exclusively to artists born 1900 or later. Contemporary painters are the successors of what he calls the "celebrated . . . classics of modern painting." See Dorival, ed., *Peintres contemporains* (Paris: Lucien Mazenod, 1964), p. 8.

4. Henri Focillon, *La peinture aux XIXe et XXe siècles* (Paris: Librairie Renouard, 1928), p. 91.

5. Braun Gallery, show of "Young Painters in the French Tradition," 1941.

6. André Chastel, "Dix ans d'art français," *Médecine de France,* 1959, no. 100.

7. Jean Paulhan, "Les nouvelles images," *Jardin des arts* (November 1963): 4.

8. Focillon, *La peinture,* p. 302.

9. See Roger Caillois's comments on this subject, in particular his *Méduse et Cie* (Paris: Gallimard, 1960).

10. Robert Klein, "Peinture et phénoménologie," *Critique* 191(April 1963).

11. Jean Grenier, *Essais sur la peinture contemporaine*·(Paris: Gallimard, 1959), p. 194.

12. The "point" is a traditional way of indicating a painting's size. See Appendix 2: Designation and Dimensions of Canvases.

Chapter 3

1. See Appendix 3: Map of Paris art galleries.

2. Compare the definition of *le mercier,* or seller of jewelry and art objects, in the *Grande Encyclopédie.*

3. D.-H. Kahnweiler, interview, 15 January 1958.

4. M. Guicheteau, "Essai sur l'esthétique spontanée du marchand de tableaux," *Revue d'esthétique* 5(1952):53.

5. Pierre Cabanne, *Le roman des grands collectionneurs* (Paris: Plon, 1961), p. 253.

6. Ibid., p. 265.

7. Jean Clay, "L'épopée des Wildenstein," *Réalités* 158(March 1959): 77.

8. Ibid., pp. 77–78.

9. Ibid., p. 78.

10. Cabanne, *Le roman,* p. 264.

11. André Chastel, "La 'Salle' Jacquemart-André. Monsieur G. W. et l'Institut de France," *Le Monde,* 29 July 1961.

12. Cabanne, *Le roman,* p. 262.

13. Kahnweiler, *Mes galeries.*

14. Ibid., pp. 135–136, 109.

15. Vollard, *Souvenirs,* p. 250.

16. Kahnweiler, *Mes galeries,* pp. 11–12.

17. Ibid., p. 15.

18. Ibid., p. 38.

19. Ibid., pp. 31–32.

20. Ibid., p. 38.

21. Ibid., pp. 32–33.

22. Ibid., p. 158.

23. Kahnweiler, Interview 15 Jan. 1958.

24. Ibid.

25. Kahnweiler, *Mes galeries,* p. 47.

26. Ibid., p. 102.

27. Ibid., p. 104.

28. Ibid., p. 103.

29. Kahnweiler, Interview 15 Jan. 1958.

30. Kahnweiler, *Mes galeries,* pp. 29–30.

31. Ibid., pp. 40, 107.

32. Ibid., p. 57.

33. Kahnweiler, Interviews 15 Jan. 1958 and 7 July 1959.

34. Kahnweiler, *Mes galeries,* p. 47.

35. Ibid., pp. 110–111.

36. Kahnweiler, Interview 15 Jan. 1958.

37. Kahnweiler, *Mes galeries,* pp. 49–50.

38. Ibid., p. 102.

39. Kahnweiler, Interview 15 Jan. 1958.

40. Kahnweiler, *Mes galeries,* p. 111.

41. As reported by Cabanne, *Le roman,* p. 269.

42. Kahnweiler, *Mes galeries,* p. 111.

43. Joseph Schumpeter, *Capitalism, Socialism, and Democracy* (New York: Harper & Row, 1951), p. 132.

44. Kahnweiler, *Mes galeries,* p. 136.

45. Vollard, *Souvenirs,* p. 47.

46. Kahnweiler, *Mes galeries,* p. 156.

47. "Once too many paintings have been sold, this becomes financially impossible. And in any case it's dangerous. If collectors are sure of getting high prices, they'll keep putting paintings up for sale." [D131]

48. Joseph Schumpeter, *Théorie de l'évolution économique,* trans. J. Anstett (Paris: Dalloz, 1935), p. 359. [Here retranslated from the French.—Trans.]

49. Jacques Berque, *Structures sociales du Haut-Atlas* (Paris: Presses Universitaires de France, 1955), pp. 271, 276, 279.

50. Pierre Loeb, *Voyages à travers la peinture* (Paris: Bordas, 1946), p. 35.

51. Gilson, *Peinture et réalité,* p. 23.

52. E. Teriade, "Entretiens avec Henry Kahnweiler," *Cahiers d'art,* 1927, no. 2.

53. Gabriel Brunet, review of *Souvenirs d'un marchand de tableaux,* by Ambroise Vollard, *Mercure de France,* 1 December 1937.

54. Vollard, *Souvenirs,* appendix, p. 251.

Chapter 4

1. Sainte-Beuve, cited by Pierre Moreau, *La critique littéraire en France* (Paris: Armand Colin, 1960), p. 8.

2. "Criticism follows the productions of the mind as shadow follows substance." Entry for 13 January 1857, *Journal d'Eugène Delacroix,* vol. 3 (Paris: Plon, 1950), p. 14.

3. Pierre de Boisdeffre, foreward to show catalogue of Roger Montané, Bernier Gallery, 16 May–10 June 1958.

4. Georges Besson, preface to show entitled "Troisième groupe Boissière," Boissière Gallery, March 1964.

5. Roger Dulac, preface to catalogue for Toffoli, "Thirty-five gouaches recounting his travels throughout the world," at the Roger Dulac Gallery.

6. Guy Dornand, preface to show of Maurice Chapuis, Gallery des Orfèvres, 5–23 December 1961.

7. Emile Kaufmann, preface to show of Lemeunier, Gallery du Colisée, 20 November–3 December 1962.

8. Jean Goldman, preface to show of Henri Larrière, Gallery Simone Badinier, 3–26 October 1963.

9. J. P., preface to show of J. Bréant, Gallery Espace, 4–19 May 1962.

10. Marcel Aymé, preface to show of Roger Bertin, C. Pacquement Prize, Vendome Gallery, 22 March–9 April 1960.

11. Maximilien Gauthier, preface to show by A. Fougeron, recent works, Montmorency Gallery, 26 April–15 May 1960.

12. René Barotte, preface to show of J. Gachet, Critics' Prize, 1959, Presbourg Gallery, 12 May–12 June 1960.

13. Marcel Pagnol, preface to show by Pierre Ambrogiani, Paul Ambroise Gallery, November–December 1959.

14. Florent Fels, preface to show of René Morere, Vendome Gallery, 25 November–10 December 1959.

15. Claude Roger-Marx, preface to show of Bernard Ganter, Gallery Espace.

16. René Barotte, preface to show of J. Laillard, Vendome Gallery, 3–9 November 1960.

17. Juliette Darle, preface to show by the Group of Nine, Vendome Gallery, 29 January–16 February 1964.

18. Preface by Freddy Noë to the show of Charles de Castelbajac, Gallery Rond-Point-Elysées, 13 November–1 December 1963.

19. Compare Gilson, *Peinture et realité,* pp. 238–299.

20. Pierre Restany, "Monochrome et Vitalisme," preface to show of Yves Klein, Left Bank Gallery, 11 October–13 November 1960.

21. Julien Cracq, *La libération à l'estomac* (Paris: José Corti, 1950), p. 11.

22. Marcel Proust, *A la recherche du temps perdu:* vol. 3, *La prisonnière* (Paris: Gallimard, 1956), pp. 254–256.

23. Herbert Read, "Le dilemme du critique," *L'oeil* 72 (December 1960).

Chapter 5

1. Daniel Cordier, "Huit ans d'agitation," catalog for show at Cordier Gallery, 8, rue de Duras, Paris, June–July 1964.

2. Roger Caillois, *Les jeux et les hommes* (Paris: Gallimard, 1958), p. 61.

3. Compare Werner Sombart, *Le bourgeois. Contribution à l'histoire morale et intellectuelle de l'homme économique moderne* (Paris: Payot, 1926).

4. Rivalry among collectors is evident at public auctions: two Greek shipowners bid up the price of a second-rate Gauguin from the collection

of Margaret Thompson Biddle to more than 100 million francs (Charpentier Gallery, Maitre Maurice Rheims, 14 June 1957). In a fierce bidding war like this one, the value of the painting to each bidder is determined by how badly the other wants it.

5. Marcel Mauss, *Sociologie et anthropologie* (Paris: Presses Universitaires de France, 1950), pp. 152–153.

6. On Duveen, see N.-S. Behrmann, La chasse aux chefs-d'oeuvre (Paris: Hatchette, 1953).

7. *Les grandes collections privées*, pp. 192–197.

8. L'hôtel de Chanaleilles devient la plus somptueusse demeure de Paris," *Connaissance des arts* 105 (November 1960).

9. "The Pleasures of Figurative Art" was the title of a show at the Recio Gallery, 25, rue La Boétie.

10. The speaker is a housewife married to an industrial executive. Collecting is her hobby, and she buys works of painters under fifty years of age. The most common subjects in her collections are scenes of rural life and fishing ports.

11. A second sale was held at the Hotel Drouot on 30 April 1958, also under the direction of Maurice Rheims. It included paintings by Andreu, Jean Béraud, C. Blanchard, Chochon, Dagnan-Bouveret, Victor Dargaud, Darrel, Goubie, Haas, Monticelli, Rosselli, Serans, and others.

12. Douglas Cooper, ed., *Les grandes collections privées* (Paris: Plon, 1963), pp. 116–125.

13. Ibid.

14. Introduction by Kenneth Clark to Cooper, ed., *Les grandes collections*, p. 18.

15. Claude Lévi-Strauss has this to say: "There is no doubt that the passion I felt for Cubism in my adolescence was not based solely on my honest, straightforward reaction to the paintings themselves. It was also an opportunity for me to declare my independence from my elders." Georges Charbonnier, *Entretiens avec Lévi-Strauss* (Paris: Plon-Juillard, 1961), p. 133.

16. Catalogue of Henie-Onstad collection, 1960–1962, Kirstes Boktyrkkeri, Oslo. The artists included in the collection are: Karel Appel, Willi Baumeister, Jean Bazaine, André Beaudin, Roger Bissière, Pierre Bonnard, Georges Braque, Jean Dubuffet, Raoul Dufy, Max Ernst, Maurice Estéve, Sam Francis, Juan Gris, Hans Hartung, Paul Klee, Fernand Léger, Alberto Magnelli, Alfred Manessier, Henri Matisse, Joan Miro, Jean Le Moal, Edvard Munch, Endre Nemes, Pablo Picasso, Serge Poliakoff, Jean-Paul Riopelle, Georges Rouault, Gustave Singier, Marie-Hélène Vieira da Silva, Pierre Soulages, Nicolas de Staël, Rufino Tamayo, Jacques Villon, and Jakob Weidemann.

17. *Itinéraire d'un jeune collectionneur 1948–1958.* Kléber Gallery, 24, avenue Kléber, October 1959. Included in the catalogue were Bettencourt, Bissiére, Dubuffet, Fautrier, Georges, Götz, Hantai, Hartung, Karskaya, Loubchansky, Manessier, Mathieu, Matta, Michaux, Poliakoff, Sonderborg, Vieira da Silva, and Viseux.

18. The speaker is a professional man.

19. As Proust says of the jargon of the Guermantes in *A la recherche du temps perdu:* vol. 2, *Le côté de Guermantes* (Paris: Gallimard, 1956), p. 818.

20. Proust, *Le côté de Guermantes,* p. 470.

21. Arthur Koestler, *L'ombre du dinosaure* (Paris: Calmann-Lévy, 1956).

22. Pierre Bourdieu and Abdelmayek Sayad, *Le déracinement* (Paris: Les Editions de Minuit, 1964), p. 88.

23. Sombart, *Le bourgeois,* p. 210.

24. Johann Huizinga, *Homo ludens, essai sur la fonction sociale du jeu* (Paris: Gallimard, 1951), p. 92.

25. See E. Goblot, *Le barrière et le niveau. Etude sociologique sur la bourgeoisie franÇaise moderne* (Paris: Alcan, 1925).

26. Cooper, ed., *Les grandes collections privées,* pp. 170–173, 178.

27. Ibid.

28. "Taste is arbitrary in a number of things, such as jewelry, carriages, and things not belonging to the fine arts; in such cases it should be called fancy rather than taste. It is fancy rather than taste that produces new fashions." Voltaire, art. "Taste" in *La grande encylopédie,* vol. 7, p. 761.

29. Pierre-Henri Roché, "Adieu brave petite collection," *L'oeil,* 1951, no. 51.

30. Guillaume Apollinaire learned about Negro artifacts from Vlaminck, Picasso, and Derain. They are mentioned in one of his poems:

Tu marches vers Auteuil, tu veux aller chez toi à pied
Dormir parmi les fétiches d'Océan et de Guinée
Ils sont des Christs d'une autre foi et d'une autre croyance
Ce sont les christs inférieurs des obscures espérances.
[You are walking toward Auteuil, you want to return home on foot
and sleep among your idols from Guinea and the Islands.
They are the Christs of another faith and creed, the inferior christs of
obscure hopes.

Alcools (Paris: Gallimard, 1920), p. 15.

Chapter 6

1. Daniel Cordier, "Le peintre et son public," *Arguments,* 1960, no. 19. See also Raymonde Moulin, "La peinture soviétique contemporaine," *Revue d'esthétique* 12 (July–September 1960).
2. Renée B., introduction to the Degottex show at the International Gallery of Contemporary Art, 1960.
3. François Mathey, introduction to Dodeigne show, Jeanne Bucher Gallery, March–April 1964.
4. Georges Mathieu, interviewed by Jeanine Warnod, *Le Figaro,* 4–5 November 1962.
5. Documenta I, 1955; II, 1959; III, 1964.
6. Read, "Le dilemme du critique."
7. Huizinga, *Homo Ludens.*
8. Philippe Vergnaud, *Les contrats conclus entre peintres et marchands de tableaux* (Bordeaux: Rousseau Frères, 1958). Vergnaud's analysis is largely theoretical, however, and therefore tends to minimize the practical importance of power relations.
9. See appendices 1 and 4 for sample contracts.
10. See appendix 2.
11. The tax depends on the nature of the gallery and the type of business it does.
12. One dealer made available the following price schedule for one of his artists, a nonfigurative painter not yet thirty-five years old. Advances ranged from 100,000 to 150,000 francs per month.

1 point	13,000 francs
2 points	14,500 francs
3 points	16,000 francs
4 points	17,500 francs
5 points	19,000 francs
6 points	22,000 francs
8 points	25,000 francs
10 points	27,000 francs
12 points	30,000 francs
15 points	35,000 francs
20 points	40,000 francs
25 points	50,000 francs
30 points	60,000 francs
40 points	70,000 francs
50 points	80,000 francs
60 points	90,000 francs

80 points   100,000 francs
100 points   110,000 francs
120 points   120,000 francs
(Interview, 21 May 1959)

13. Attributed to Daniel Cordier, *France Observateur*, 11 June 1964, p. 16.

14. Kahnweiler, *Mes galeries*, p. 107.

15. Article 1165 of the Civil Code.

16. Karl Marx, *Theories of Surplus Value*, vol. 1 (Moscow: Progress Publishers, 1963), p. 401.

17. Letter cited by Maurice Rheims, *La Vie étrange des objets*, p. 237.

18. See appendix 3.

19. See Francis Haskell, *Patrons and Painters: A Study in the Relations between Italian Art and Society in the Age of Baroque* (Oxford: The University Press, 1963), especially part 1, chapter 1.

20. "I know well that the shrewd artists, I mean the really energetic shrewd artists, make their fortune, but if they don't move as swiftly as the clouds they suffer the great misfortune of feeling inferior and degraded. All that is a matter of temperament. . . . Yes, you will say, but the problem is how to earn money. It's a question of commercial flair, which is inherent in the individual. You have to know how to ingratiate yourself, how to put yourself forward in a quiet way, holding all the reins in your hand and guiding the whole business the way a good coach driver guides his coach." Camille Pissarro, *Lettres à son fils Lucien*, letter of 31 October 1883, p. 64, and letter of 8 May 1892, pp. 282–283.

21. Joan Miro, "Une histoire de respiration," *Le nouvel observateur*, no. 27 (20 May 1965).

Chapter 7

1. Paintings can of course deteriorate, and they are subject to forgery. As material objects, works of art are perishable.

2. Art works lack three of the economic properties of gold: a fixed [or relatively stable] parity with currency; liquidity, thanks to low transaction costs; and fungibility, which means that a gram of gold of a certain purity is worth the same as any other gram of the same purity.

3. In England and the United States, a distinction is made between the "auction price" and the "market price."

4. See appendix 1: Table of deflator coefficients.

5. Gilson, *Peinture et réalité*, pp. 288–289.

6. "The difficulty of attainment which determines value is not always

the same kind of difficulty. It sometimes consists in an absolute limitation of the supply. There are things of which it is physically impossible to increase the quantity beyond certain narrow limits. Such are those wines which can be grown only in peculiar circumstances of soil, climate, and exposure. Such also are ancient sculptures; pictures by the old masters; rare books or coins, or other articles of antiquarian curiosity." John Stuart Mill, *Principles of Political Economy,* vol. 1, book 3, chap. 2 [pp. 546–547 of the 1904 edition published by Appleton & Co., New York, and based on the 5th London Edition]. See also David Ricardo, *Principles of Political Economy and Taxation,* chap. 1 and especially section 1, paragraph 4.

7. John Maynard Keynes, *Essays in Persuasion. Economic Possibilities For Our Grandchildren,* p. 365.

8. Gaë Fain, *Les placements* (Paris: Presses Universitaires de France, 1966), pp. 49–50.

9. Jacques Thuillier, "Le Dossier Caravage par André Berne-Joffroy," *L'oeil,* November 1959, no. 59.

10. For example, *The Portrait of a Young Girl* (47–43, circa 1660) was bought by the American collectors Mr. and Mrs. Charles B. Wrightsman of Palm Beach and Houston for $350,000 in 1955. In 1816 it had been sold in Rotterdam for 3 florins (about $1.80). In less than 150 years the value of the painting increased 190,000-fold.

11. This figure is taken from François Duret-Robert, "Les tableaux sont-ils des valeurs boursières?" *Direction,* May 1963, no. 95.

12. On the changing tastes of American buyers, see René Brimo, *L'évolution du goût aux Etats-Unis d'après l'histoire des collections* (Paris: James Fortune, 1938).

13. See André Chastel, "Le problème du Caravage," *Critique,* November 1956, no. 114, and André Berne-Joffroy, *Le dossier Caravage, Psychologie des attributions et psychologie de l'art* (Paris: Les Editions de Minuit, 1959). The latter traces the first signs of the Caravaggio revival to the early part of the twentieth century and stresses the importance of contemporary aesthetic concerns in shaping our view of the past: "If it is correct to say that the triumph first of Courbet and then of Manet preceded the revival of Caravaggio, the reason has to do with a general law according to which the evolution of art history follows that of art itself. Thus, as Lionello Venturi has pointed out, it was Michelangelo who enabled Vasari to admire Giotto and Poussin who enabled Bellori to revere Raphael. Who revived the completely unknown Vermeer? Thoré, a fervent admirer of Rousseau and Corot, and later the first admirer of Monet and Renoir. And would the Arezzo frescoes [of Piero della Francesca—trans.] have been placed on the pinnacle before Cézanne and Seurat?" [pp. 11–12]

14. Charles Sterling, *La nature morte* (Paris: Tisné, 1959). See also Michel Faré, *La nature morte en France* (Paris: Cailler, 1963).

Chapter 8

1. To open its show of "Masterpieces of the Ecole de Paris" in 1946, the Charpentier Gallery sent invitations to 5,000 couples. The number of invitations normally sent out by various progressive Left Bank art dealers follows.

D106: 1,000–1,500 to France and abroad
D129: 1,000 to France, 700 abroad
D156: 1,500–1,800 to France and abroad
D104: 3,500–4,000 to France and abroad
D164: 5,500 to France and abroad

2. A group of speculators can sell a number of paintings back and forth among themselves. Their problem is to know when to call a halt to the "tennis match," and to determine how many paintings they wish to hold at that point.

3. John Maynard Keynes, *The General Theory of Employment, Interest, and Money* (London: Macmillan, 1936; New York: Macmillan, 1974), pp. 155–156.

4. Schumpeter, *Capitalism, Socialism, and Democracy*, p. 84.

5. Piero Sraffa, "The Laws of Return under Competitive Conditions," *Economic Journal*, 1926, pp. 535–550; E. H. Chamberlin, *The Theory of Monopolistic Competition* (Cambridge, Mass.: Harvard University Press, 1927); Joan Robinson, *Economics of Imperfect Competition* (London, 1933).

6. Figure taken from Reitlinger, p. 237.

7. Reitlinger, p. 237.

8. Ibid.

9. Quoted in "Moscou, capitale de l'art," *France Observateur,* 11 June 1964.

10. Van Gogh, *Lettres*, p. 407.

11. Marcel Duchamp, whom André Breton called "the most intelligent man of the first half of the twentieth century" and who gave up painting more than forty years ago, has a clear vision of the problems. Consider this exchange:

Q. It is unprecedented that man who has enjoyed international success should give up his work. How do you explain it?
A. I never worked as a craftsman in paint turning out so many paintings a year at so much per painting. Generally speaking, a painter works out a formula, which he changes once every ten years or so if they have the energy. But you can't expect a man to come up with a new idea every ten years. . . . I didn't

want to copy my own work. I therefore stopped painting professionally. But also I'm not that much of an artist. There are other ways to live.

Q. You refuse to repeat yourself, but would you allow others to make thousands of copies of your work, as Vasarely does?

A. No. I have no problem with limited editions of, say, eight copies as for my "ready-mades" in the Schwartz exposition being held right now in Milan. It's scarcity that authenticates a work of art. [Interview in *L'Express,* 23 July 1964.]

12. In less than seven years' time Lawrence Rubin, Illeana Sonnabend, David Anderson and Jacques Mayer, and Alexandre Iolas opened galleries on the Left Bank.

Chapter 9

1. International auction sales are far more prevalent now than in the past, and French dealers no longer dominate the world art market. Hence the figure for the final period reflect foreign sales.

2. E. von Böhm-Bawerk, *Histoire critique des théories de l'intérêt du capital* (Paris: Giard, 1903), p. 99.

Select Bibliography of Works Published Since 1967

Works on which I relied heavily are indicated in the notes. The complete bibliography may be consulted in the original French edition. Here I have included those books and articles published since 1967 most relevant to the subject of this work.

Adler, Judith. *Artists in Offices*. New Brunswick, N.J.: Transaction, Inc., 1978.

Albrecht, Milton C., James H. Barnett, and Mason Griff, eds. *The Sociology of Art and Literature*. New York: Praeger, 1970.

Alloway, Laurence. *Network: Art and the Complex Present*. Ann Arbor, Mich.: UMI Research Press, 1984.

Balfe, Judith H., and Margaret J. Wyszomirski, eds. *Art, Ideology and Politics*. New York: Praeger Publishers, 1985.

Baumol, William J. "Unnatural Value of Art Investment as Floating Crap Game." Paper prepared for the International Conference on Cultural Economics, Avignon, 12–14 May 1986.

Becker, Howard S. *Art Worlds*. Berkeley: University of California Press, 1982.

Becker, Howard S. "Distributing Modern Art." In *Sociologie de l'Art*, Proceedings of the International Colliquium of the French Sociology Society (Marseille 13–14 June 1985). Paris: La Documentation Française, 1986.

———. *Sociological Work*. Chicago: Aldine, 1970.

Bell, Daniel. *The Cultural Contradictions of Capitalism.* New York: Basic Books, 1976.

Blaug, Mark, ed. *The Economics of the Arts.* London: Martin Robertson and Co., 1976.

Boudon, Raymond. "L'Intellectuel et ses publics: les singularités françaises." In *Français, qui êtes-vous?,* dir. J. D. Reynauld et Y. Grafmeyer. Paris: La Documentation Française, 1981.

Bourdieu, Pierre. *La Distinction: critique sociale du judgement.* Paris: Les Editions de Minuit, 1979.

Bourdieu, Pierre. "Le Marché des biens symboliques." *L'Année Sociologique* 22(1971).

Bourdieu, Pierre. "La Production de la croyance: contribution à une économie des biens symboliques." *Actes de la Recherche en Sciences Sociales* 13 (February 1977): 3–43

Bourricaud, François. *Le Bricolage idéologique: essai sur les intellectuels et les passions démocratiques.* Paris: Presses Universitaires de France, 1980.

Bystryn, Marcia. "Art Galleries as Gatekeepers: The Case of the Abstract Expressionists." *Social Research* 45 (Summer 1978): 390–408.

Centre Georges Pompidou, Musée national d'art moderne. *Daniel-Henry Kahnweiler, marchand, éditeur, écrivain.* 22 November 1984–28 January 1985.

Chatelain, Jean. *Oeuvres d'art et objets de collection en droit français.* Paris: Berger-Levrault, 1982.

Clair, Jean. *Considérations sur l'état des beaux-arts: critique de la modernité.* Paris: Gallimard, 1983.

Crane, Diana. *Avant-Garde Art and Social Change: the New York Art World, 1940–1985.* Chicago: University of Chicago Press, 1987.

———. "Reward Systems in Art, Science, and Religion." In Richard A. Peterson, ed. *The Production of Culture.* Beverly Hills, Calif.: Sage Publications, 1976.

Danto, Arthur C. "The Artworld." *Journal of Philosophy* 61 (1964): 571–584.

De Coppet, Laura, and Alan Jones, eds. *The Art Dealers.* New York: Clarkson N. Potter, 1984.

Dickie, George. *Aesthetics: An Introduction.* New York: Pegasus, 1971.

———. *Art and the Aesthetic: An Institutional Analysis.* Ithaca: Cornell University Press, 1975.

Freidson, Eliot. "Les Professions artistiques comme défi à l'analyse sociologique." *Revue Française de Sociologie.* Special issue. "Sociologie de l'art et de la littérature" (July–September 1986).

Frey, Bruno S., and Werner W. Pommerehne "International Trade in Art: Attitudes and Behavior." Paper prepared for the International Conference on Cultural Economics, Avignon, 12–14 May 1986.

Gans, Herbert. *Popular Culture and High Culture*. New York: Basic Books, 1974.

Gombrich, E. H. *Ideals and Idols: Essays on Values in History and Art*. Oxford: Phaidon, 1979.

Grana, César. *Bohemian versus Bourgeois*. New York: Basic Books, 1964.

————. *Fact and Symbol: Essays in the Sociology of Art and Literature*. New York: Oxford University Press, 1971.

Haskell, Francis. *Rediscoveries in Art*. London: Phaidon, 1976.

Hendon, William Scott, James L. Shanahan, and Alice J. Mac Donald, eds. *Economic Policy for the Arts*. Cambridge, Mass.: Abt Books, 1980.

Hirsch, Paul M. "Processing Fads and Fashions: An organization-Set Analysis of Cultural Industry Systems." *American Journal of Sociology* 77 (1972): 639–659.

Hirschman, Albert. *Shifting Involvements: Private Interest and Public Action*. Princeton, N.J.: Princeton University Press, 1982.

Kadushin, Charles. "Networks and Circles in the Production of Culture." *American Behavioral Scientist* 19 (July–August 1976): 769–784.

Kamerman, Jack B., and Rosanne Martorella, eds. *Performers and Performances: the Social Organization of Artistic Work*. New York: Praeger, 1983.

Keen, Geraldine. *The Sale of Works of Art: A Study Based on the Times-Sotheby Index*. London: Nelson, 1971.

Klein, Robert. *La Forme et l'intelligible: écrits sur la renaissance et l'art moderne*. Paris: Gallimard, 1970.

Levine, Edward M. "Chicago's Art World." *Urban Life and Culture* 1 (1972): 292–322.

McCain, Roger A. "Market for Works of Art and Markets for Lemons." In William Scott Hendon, James L. Shanahan, and Alice J. Mac Donald, eds., *Economic Policy for the Arts*, pp. 122–135. Cambridge, Mass.: Abt Books, 1980.

McCall, Michael M. "Art Without a Market: Creating Artistic Value in a Provincial Art World." *Symbolic Interaction* 1 (Fall 1977): 32–43.

Melot, Michel et al. *L'Estampe: histoire d'un art*. Paris: Skira, 1981.

Menger, Pierre-Michel. *Le Paradoxe du musicien: le compositeur, le mélomane et l'Etat dans la société contemporaine*. Paris: Flammarion, 1983.

Mercillon, Henri, and Pierre Gregory. "Le Marché parisien de l'art. Les ventes publiques: bilan comparatif." *Commentaire* 10 (1980): 309–315.

Mercillon, Henri. "Les Musées: institutions à but non lucratif dans l'économie marchande." *Revue d'Economie Politique* 4 (1977): 630–641.

Montias, John M. *Artists and Artisans in Delft: A Socio-Economic Study of the Seventeenth Century.* Princeton, N.J.: Princeton University Press, 1982.

Moulin, Raymonde. "Les Bourgeois amis des arts: les expositions des beaux-arts en province, 1885–87." *Revue Française de Sociologie* 17 (1976).

———. "Champ artistique et société industrielle capitaliste." In *Science et conscience de la société, Mélanges en l'honneur de Raymond Aron.* Vol. 2, pp. 181–204. Paris: Calmann-Levy, 1971.

———. "La Genèse de la rareté artistique." *Revue d'Ethnologie Française* 8 (1978): 241–258.

———. "Le Marché de l'art." *Encyclopaedia Universalis,* 1985.

———. "Le Marché et le musée: la constitution des valeurs artistiques contemporaines." *Revue Française de Sociologie* 3 (1986).

Moulin, Raymonde, ed. *Sociologie de l'Art* Proceedings of the International Colloquium of the French Sociology Society (Marseilles, 13–14 June 1985). Paris: La Documentation Française, 1986.

Peterson, Richard A. *The Production of Culture.* Beverly Hills, Calif.: Sage Publications, 1976.

Pomian, Krzysztof. "Entre l'invisible et le visible: la collection." In *Encyclopedia Einaudi,* vol. 3, Milan, 1978. French translation In *Libre* (1978): 3–55.

Robinson, John P., ed. *Social Science and the Arts.* University Press of America, 1985.

Schneider, F., and Werner W. Pommerehne. "Analysing the Markets of Works of Contemporary Fine Arts: An Exploratory Study." *Journal of Cultural Economics* 7 (1983): 41–69.

Scitovsky, Tibor. *The Joyless Economy: An Inquiry into Human Satisfaction and Consumer Dissatisfaction.* London and New York: Oxford University Press, 1978.

Seaman, B. "An Assessment of Recent Applications of Economic Theory to the Arts." *Journal of Cultural Economics* 5 (June 1981): 36–48.

Simpson, Charles R. *Soho: The Artist in the City.* Chicago: University of Chicago Press, 1981.

Singer, Leslie P. "Microeconomics of the Art Market." *Journal of Cultural Economics* 2 (June 1978): 21–46.

———. "Rivalry and Externalities in Secondary Art Markets." *Journal of Cultural Economics* 5 (December 1981): 39–57.

Stein, John Picard. "The Monetary Appreciation of Paintings." *Journal of Political Economy* 85 (October 1977).

Webb, L. R. "Price Formation in the Art Market." *Economic Papers* 35(September 1970): 8–19.

White, Harrison, and Cynthia White. *Canvasses and Careers.* New York: John Wiley, 1965.

Wolff, Janet. *The Social Production of Art*. New York: St. Martin's Press, 1981.
Zolberg, Vera L. "Changing Patterns of Patronage in the Arts." In Jack B. Kamerman and Rosanne Martorella, eds., *Performers and Performances: The Social Organization of Artistic Work*, pp. 251–268. New York: Praeger, 1983.
———. "Conflicting Visions in American Art Museums." *Theory and Society* 10 (1981): 103–125.

Index

abstract art, 160–162; classification of, 28–29. *See also* progressive painting

Academy (Royal Academy of Painting and Sculpture), 10–12, 109–110, 204n7; Salon, 11–13, 23, 203n2

aesthetic value: innovation and, 51; junk painting and, 141; moral judgments and, 70–71, 90; price and, 141, 157, 170; success and, 15–16

America: competition by, 170–171, 216n12; emigration to, 22

art: classification of, 25–29; as commodity, 3, 136, 179, 213n2; as cultural good, 145

art, relation to: collectors of, 80–82; dealers of, 59, 63–65; painters of, 125–126, 131

art dealers. *See* dealers

artists. *See* painters

art market: la Belle Epoque and, 16–17; contemporary, 153–171, 177–178; Great Depression and, 19–20; impressionist period and, 12–16; international, 33–34, 44, 157–158, 171, 216n1; junk painting and, 139–143; Old Masters and, 143–151, 177; Parisian and provincial, 32–34; pre-impressionist, 9–12; structure of, 137–138, 178; World War I and,

17–19; World War II and, 20–24. *See also* supply and demand

Autumn Salon, 32, 91, 204n11

avant-garde. *See* progressive painting

Barbizon School, 13, 19

Batignolles group, 13, 204n14

Bearskin Sale, 16

Belle Epoque, la, 16–17

Bellier, Alphonse, 18

Berenson, Bernard, 43

Bernheim-Jeune & Co.: sample contracts of, 190–199

Biddle, Margaret Thompson, 91

Boudin, Eugène, 174–176

bourgeoisie, 86–91, 101; impressionism and, 12, 16, 17

Boussod, Valadon & Co., 12, 204n6

Braun Gallery, 22

brokers, 38–40. *See also* dealers

Brunet, Gabriel, 65

Buffet, Bernard, 164–165

buyers. *See* collectors

Camus, Albert, 73

canvases: designation and dimensions of, 183

Clark, Kenneth, 93

classic painting: classification of, 26–27. *See also* traditionalist painting

collectors, 4, 79–106; bourgeois, 12,